PEARL S. BUCK

Recent Titles in
Contributions to the Study of World Literature

Reluctant Expatriate: The Life of Harold Frederic
Robert M. Myers

The Decline of the Goddess: Nature, Culture, and
Women in Thomas Hardy's Fiction
Shirley A. Stave

Postcolonial Discourse and Changing Cultural Contexts
Gita Rajan and Radhika Mohanram, editors

Prometheus and Faust: The Promethean Revolt in Drama
from Classical Antiquity to Goethe
Timothy Richard Wutrich

English Postcoloniality: Literatures from Around the World
Radhika Mohanram and Gita Rajan, editors

The Vonnegut Chronicles
Peter Reed and Marc Leeds, editors

Satirical Apocalypse: An Anatomy of Melville's *The Confidence-Man*
Jonathan A. Cook

Twenty-Four Ways of Looking at Mary McCarthy: The Writer and Her Work
Eve Stwertka and Margo Viscusi, editors

Orienting Masculinity, Orienting Nation: W. Somerset Maugham's
Exotic Fiction
Philip Holden

A Matter of Faith: The Fiction of Brian Moore
Robert Sullivan

Samuel Johnson and the Essay
Robert D. Spector

Fighting Evil: Unsung Heroes in the Novels of Graham Greene
Haim Gordon

PEARL S. BUCK

A Cultural Bridge Across the Pacific

KANG LIAO

Contributions to the Study of World Literature,
Number 77

GREENWOOD PRESS
Westport, Connecticut • London

Library of Congress Cataloging-in-Publication Data

Liao, Kang.
    Pearl S. Buck : a cultural bridge across the Pacific / Kang Liao.
      p. cm.—(Contributions to the study of world literature,
  ISSN 0738-9345 ; no. 77)
    Includes bibliographical references and index.
    ISBN 0-313-30146-8 (alk. paper)
    1. Buck, Pearl S. (Pearl Sydenstricker), 1892-1973—Political and
social views. 2. Women and literature—United States—History—20th
century. 3. United States—Relations—China. 4. China—Relations—
United States. 5. Peasantry in literature. 6. China—In
literature. 7. East and West. I. Title. II. Series.
PS3503.U198Z6984 1997
813'.52—dc20   96-25016

British Library Cataloguing in Publication Data available.

Library of Congress Catalog Card Number: 96-25016
ISBN: 0-313-30146-8
ISSN: 0738-9345

First published in 1997

Greenwood Press, 88 Post Road West, Westport, CT 06881
An imprint of Greenwood Publishing Group, Inc.

Printed in the United States of America

The paper used in this book complies with the
Permanent Paper Standard issued by the National
Information Standards Organization (Z39.48-1984).

10 9 8 7 6 5 4 3 2 1

Dedicated to my father Dong-hsian Liao and my mentor Gaston Caperton, governor of the state of West Virginia from 1989 to 1996.

CONTENTS

PREFACE

Pearl Buck was the first American woman writer to win the Nobel Prize for literature. However, she has been largely neglected by American critics since 1940. She was severely criticized in China during the 1930s and 1960s. Was she overestimated at first? Did she misrepresent China? What are the main values of her literary works? Are they still valuable today?

This book applies the reception theory to analyzing the reasons for the early success of her novels and the ensuing neglect of her works by the critics, historicizes the significance of her unique function in changing the American image of the Chinese people, uses the multicultural approach to evaluate some of her books, and discusses her pioneering role in writing about the Chinese peasants.

This book indicates that the social, historical, and cultural values of Pearl Buck's literary works exceed their aesthetic value. The portrayal of the Chinese people in her novels of the 1930s considerably improved the image of the Chinese people in the American mind. This improvement helped to repeal the Chinese Exclusion Act and to obtain the American people's support for China's war of resistance against the Japanese invasion. She evaluated the Christian missions in China by illustrating the noble and heroic efforts of some individual missionaries but demonstrated the follies and impossibilities of the whole movement through two biographies. She also suggested what China really needed, how China could be helped, and what the West could learn from China in her novels of the late 1940s.

The cultural value of her works can be better appreciated in this age of multiculturalism than her age of Eurocentralism. For this reason, along with her apolitical description of Chinese peasant life, Pearl Buck is undergoing a revival and exerting a greater influence in China. Nevertheless, the lack of modernism and the introduction of superfluous romances in some of her realistic novels reduce their artistry, and because of her strong sense of mission to promote understanding between the East and West, some of her novels suffer from didacticism and some characters are stereotyped.

This book does not attempt to give a comprehensive evaluation of Pearl Buck's literary works. Instead, it emphasizes only their cultural and cognitive values. Some questions are answered, some are discussed, and many are raised suggesting that more research work needs to be conducted in the rediscovery of this extraordinary American woman, whose role in the cultural exchange between the East and West is more than just historical.

ACKNOWLEDGMENTS

This book is a relatively solitary undertaking of studying a relatively solitary American writer. All the more, therefore, I appreciate the help, advice, and encouragement so kindly and generously offered to me by a few friends, professors, and family members. Without them, I could not have completed my studies.

First of all, I must give my thanks to Governor Gaston Caperton, who not only has supported me in studying Pearl S. Buck at West Virginia University but also has been encouraging me to study English and the Western culture ever since we met at Beijing Normal University in the autumn of 1979.

I am also grateful to Professor R.W.B. Lewis of Yale University, who first gave me a hand to make it possible for me to be a visiting scholar and to do research work in this country. He has continuously given me advice and encouragement to study Pearl S. Buck, among other American writers.

I am in debt to Professor Avery Gaskins, the director of my dissertation committee, and to Professor Wesley Bagby, Professor William French, Professor Frank Scafella, and Professor Hayden Ward, all members of the committee, who have gone out of their way to direct my studies of a subject unpopular in the academic world. I thank them for giving me confidence when I desperately needed it and for offering me valuable advice on how to improve my dissertation. I should also mention Professor Rudolph Almasy, Professor Patrick Conner, Professor Elaine Ginsberg, and Professor Arthur Buck, whose advice and assistance helped me keep working on my dissertation from which this book is converted.

Among many professors in Beijing Normal University, I want to thank Professor Nengjee Shih as a representative teacher, from whom I learned more English than from any other professors. I also want to thank Professor Hsingju Yuan, who alone expressed regret but understanding of the decision I made under the stern circumstances of 1989, for this book is one of the fruits of that decision.

My special thanks are due to Wei Zhang and Yanping Liu, who took care of my son Ruofan Liao in China for more than five years so that I could go on with my studies in this country without being crushed by worries for my son, who, more than anyone else, kept my hope alive.

I feel especially obliged to Rui Jiang, who came to me with love and care in the most difficult time of my life. No words can fully express my gratitude to her, who helped me in every possible way to continue and complete this book.

Finally and most important, I am deeply grateful to my father Dong-hsian Liao, who, besides all the love and duties a father shows to and performs for his son, cultivated my desire for learning and helped me, if not forced me, to develop the habit of studying science at the time when studying anything other than Mao's works was a crime. Without my father's extraordinary effort to train me and to teach me, I would have remained a worker in a small factory.

1

A PARADOXICAL ENIGMA

Pearl Buck was a paradoxical enigma: she was a serious writer, and she was a popular novelist; she was a phenomenal prizewinner in literature, but she was largely neglected by academic critics; she was a liberal thinker far ahead of her time and yet a defender of certain conventions and traditional values; she was a humanitarian in word and in deed; she was registered on McCarthy's list of Red Sympathizers in 1950s, and she was banned in Mao's China for nearly thirty years. What was she?

Pearl Buck was a serious writer mainly in the sense that most of her books have serious subject matter and they are meant to teach readers as well as to entertain them. One of the consistent themes of her books is the conflict and confluence between the East and West. Her first novel *East Wind: West Wind* [1930] deals with the differences between Chinese traditions and American traditions and their effects on each other. We find the same theme in many of her other books set in China. *The Exile* [1936] and *Fighting Angel* [1936], the biographies of her parents, illustrate the heroic endeavors but the tragic failures of the American missionaries. Her novels *Pavilion of Women* [1946] and *Kinfolk* [1949] demonstrate how a noble missionary influences a rich Chinese lady and describing appropriate ways for the Americans to give help that China desperately needs. Her historic novel *Imperial Woman* [1956] shows how the last Empress of China, the most stubborn and headstrong Chinese monarch could also change with time and accept Western ways. *Peony* [1948] describes the natural assimilation of the Jews in Kaifen, China, a unique phenomenon in the world. Her autobiography *My Several Worlds* [1954] tells her own stories as an outsider in the conflict between East and West, and portrays herself as a product of the confluence of the Eastern and Western cultures. Three of her novels set in other Asian countries deal with the same serious theme. *The Hidden Flower* [1952] reveals the heartbreaking tragedy of the cultural conflict when an American officer marries a Japanese girl. It also examines the effects of state anti-miscegenation laws that "were enforced in almost half of the fifty American states" (P. Doyle 1980, 150). *Come, My Beloved* [1953] demonstrates the difficulty for even the most devoted American missionary: to pass the final test of one's belief in racial equality and the final acceptance of cultural differences---the marriage between his daughter and his best Indian assistant. *The Living Reed* [1963] illustrates the willingness of the Korean people to learn from the West yet it also illustrates their disappointment caused by the mistakes and failures of American foreign policy toward East Asia.

Other themes of Pearl Buck's novels are less consistent but more abreast of current issues. *The Good Earth* [1931] deals with a farmer's hard struggle against hardships in nature and weaknesses in human nature, a timely theme during the Great Depression. *Dragon Seed* [1942] describes the Chinese resistance to Japanese aggression and the disappointment caused by the America's appeasement of and trade with Japan, also a timely theme after the bombing of Pearl Harbor. *Command the Morning* [1959] discusses the moral questions and social consequences of the Manhattan Project and the use of the atom bombs. It was published when China and the Soviet Union were competing with the United States in the production of nuclear weapons. *Letter from Peking* [1957] was published when hundreds of thousands of Chinese intellectuals were being persecuted in the anti-Rightist movement. The novel unfolds a tragic story of a Chinese American who is devoted to China but cannot be trusted by the Chinese government.

As a woman writer, Pearl Buck generally dealt with women's problems in almost all of her books and particularly in some. *The Mother* [1934] describes a woman's needs and sufferings in a man's society and portrays a universal image of woman. *This Proud Heart* [1938] depicts the dichotomy of a talented woman artist who has to choose between family life and a career. *Portrait of a Marriage* [1945] illustrates the problems of a woman who has married beneath herself intellectually. As an American writer, Pearl Buck dealt with typical American themes. *The Angry Wife* [1947] probes into the marriage of a white man and a black woman and their struggles and joys. *The Townsman* [1945] challenges the myth of the cowboy and shows it was the ordinary men who established villages and towns of the old west. *Other Gods* [1940] demonstrates Americans' hero worship and the role that the media plays in making gods.

Moreover, Pearl Buck proves to be a serious writer in scores of her books and essays on issues of World War II---foreign affairs, the history and culture of China, mass education, sexual equality, racial discrimination, child welfare, religion, politics, art and literature. This serious subject matter distinguishes her from most other writers of best-sellers, who entertain readers with romantic tales, horror stories, thrilling adventures, or conspiracies. Whether one agrees or disagrees with Pearl Buck, one always sees the message clearly, sometimes too clearly, in her writing. She was by no means only an entertainer. She was, after all, the daughter of missionaries, who had a strong sense of mission---the mission to help other people. Where her father had failed to fulfill through the cross she succeeded by the pen.

Besides the thematic seriousness of her writings, we may see Pearl Buck's serious attitude toward art most clearly in her decision to use a pseudonym, John Sedges, to publish five of her novels---*The Townsman, The Angry Wife, The Long Love, Bright Procession,* and *Voices in the House*---at the time when her works were most popular. She wanted to know if people read her because of her fame or because of her art. She wanted to prove that she was not only a writer about China but that she could also write successful novels about American subjects. Later in the preface of *American Triptych*, a collected edition of three of the novels, she declared that she was giving up her nom de plume in order to be free to write on either American or Chinese themes and let readers evaluate her works without prejudice. Of the five novels, the first one, *The Townsman*, was an instant success. It is so realistic that the reviewer for the *Kansas City Star* said, as Theodore F. Harris recorded,"This book must have been written by one who has spent a lifetime in Kansas." Harris also told us that no one guessed who the real author of this novel was, and only Francis Hackett came close to the truth by saying, "This novel is written in the finest English tradition from George Eliot to Pearl Buck" (Harris 1969, 296).

Unlike most serious writers whom only well-educated people read, Pearl Buck is very popular in the United States and is, according to Hayes Jacobs, "the most widely translated author in the history of American literature" (40), and, according to Beverly Rizzon, only "Mark Twain comes near her in translations and she has doubled him" (170). Pearl Buck is certainly better known than William Faulkner by general readers. One hundred college students were asked to name one novel by the two writers respectively, sixty-seven came up with *The Good Earth*, but only fourteen came up with *Light in August, The Sound and Fury*, or *As I Lay Dying*. She is also better known than Ernest Hemingway, for only twenty-three of the same one hundred students could come up with *A Farewell to Arms, For Whom the Bell Tolls,* or *The Old Man and the Sea*. Moreover, *The Good Earth* was the best-seller of 1931, and it remained on the top of best-seller list for twenty-one months, "a record made up to that time by no other book since *Quo Vadis*" (Day 310). According to Alice P. Hackett and James H. Burke, Pearl Buck's *Sons* was the best-seller of 1932, *Dragon Seed* was the best-seller of 1942, and *Pavilion of Women* was the best-seller of 1946. "Her name recurs," as Paul A. Doyle said in the preface of his 1965 edition of *Pearl S. Buck*, "constantly on school reading lists. Not only does the sale of her books reach considerable proportions, but the borrowing of her writings from public libraries is frequent and exceptionally steady." Her books are also very popular abroad. "In 1970 a UNESCO survey reported that Pearl Buck's work had been translated into 145 different languages and dialects. According to this survey, Buck was more frequently translated than any other American writer" (Conn 2). Many of her "writings were translated into every important language in the world" (P. Doyle 1980, 81). By 1973, she had "one hundred publishers in ninety countries" (Rizzon 387). Today, twenty-three of her books are still in print, and I have not counted different editions of the same books listed in *Books in Print*: *1994-95*. No wonder Samuel I. Bellman categorized Pearl Buck as a popular American woman writer in the modern age along with Constance Rourke, Marjorie Kinnan Rawlings, and Margaret Mitchell (353-78).

The difference between Pearl Buck and the other American popular writers is that she has been not only a popular writer but also a phenomenal prizewinner in literature. In 1932, she was awarded the Pulitzer Prize for her second novel, *The Good Earth*. In 1935, she was honored with the Howells Medal for the most distinguished work of American fiction published during the period from 1930 to 1935. In 1938, she won the Nobel Prize in literature for "rich and genuine epic description of Chinese peasant life and masterpieces of biography." There was, of course, some dissatisfaction about choosing Pearl Buck to be the winner of the highest literary prize, but the critics "for the most part, found justification for the award in her books' popularity, their accessibility, and the idealism inherent in their themes, particularly as those themes applied to China" (D. P. Smith 460). In fact, most reviews of Pearl Buck's books had been favorable, and her impact was so great in the early 1930s that when J. Donald Adams reviewed *The Mother* in the *New York Times* on 14 January 1934, he even compared her work with Leo Tolstoy's.

Such high fame, however, did not last long. After her extraordinary success in the 1930s, she has been largely neglected by literary critics and commentators. A woman of such magnitude and energy somehow "slip[ped] away from our national consciousness" (Conn 3). According to Doyle's preface to his 1965 edition of *Pearl S. Buck*, "only a handful of significant essays and review articles have appeared since then [1930s], and no full-length critical study has been published" until the publication of his book in 1965. His book was revised and published again in 1980, but it had been the only book-length criticism on Pearl Buck's works until 1994 when *The Several Worlds of Pearl S. Buck: Essays Presented at a Centennial Symposium, Randolph-Macon Woman's College, March 26-28, 1992* was published. Rarely has she been studied on the college level, and not a single American student has written a doctoral dissertation on her or her works. The few reviews she received were not very favorable after her last big seller, *The Townsman*, published under her pseudonym John Sedges. Even the comments of her once favorite reviewers were much less enthusiastic, as evidenced by J. Donald Adams's unfavorable remark on Pearl Buck in the *New York Times* article, "Speaking of Books," on 22 September 1963. The disdain that fell upon her books came as suddenly as the adulation that they had first received.

Despite the adulation and disdain, one thing remains true: Pearl Buck was a liberal thinker and was often far ahead of her time. If Willa Cather was the writer who created the first strong American woman in literature, Pearl Buck was the writer who created the first strong ordinary Chinese woman in literature. Although we Chinese had the story of Hua Mulan who disguised herself as a man and served in the army instead of her father for many years and the story of Liang Hongyu who beat the drum and directed her husband's army to win a major battle---these were legendary women warriors. We never had a realistic portrayal of strong and ordinary Chinese woman in literature until the appearance of O-lan in *The Good Earth*, although we never lacked such women in life. O-lan is also the first good and ugly Chinese woman character ever created in a novel. She wins the reader's heart not by feminine beauty and virtues but by the admirable qualities that we used to find only in men: hardiness, industry, courage, and endurance. The film adapted from the novel catches this spirit and rightly ends with Wang Lung sighing, "O-lan, you are the earth!"

Other strong women created by Pearl Buck include: Jade (Katharine Hepburn's role in the movie) in *Dragon Seed*, who has the desire to learn book knowledge like Yentl and the will to fight the invaders like Joan of Arc; Madame Wu in *Pavilion of Women*, who is intelligent and administers a big family with love and wisdom. In Pearl Buck's novels set in the United States, we also find strong women such as Susan Gaylord in *This Proud Heart*, a versatile woman and gifted sculptress torn between family life and career who finally chooses the latter and Jane Earl in *Command the Morning*, a first-class scientist and a firm pacifist involved in the Manhattan Project. These strong women show the reader convincingly that women can perform and have performed physically and especially intellectually as well as men do. Although Pearl Buck was not a militant feminist and refused to admit that she was a feminist, her feminist ideas were clearly manifested in two essays on the themes of "America's Medieval Women" and "America's Gunpowder Women" published as early as 1938 and 1939, long before the feminist movement loomed large in this country. These two essays aroused much discussion about women's role in the modern world, and they should be regarded as important early feminist documents.

Not only was Pearl Buck the first writer who portrayed strong Chinese women, she was also the first writer who described Chinese peasants and farmers. The novel as a literary genre appeared much earlier in Chinese than it did in English,[1] but Chinese writers had never depicted peasants, the representative of the majority Chinese people, before she did in *The Good Earth*. In classic novels, Chinese writers portrayed bandits and officers in *Outlaws of the Marsh*, warlords and kings in *The Three Kingdoms*, aristocrats and gentlemen in *The Dream of the Red Chamber*, a rich merchant and his family in *The Golden Plum*, scholars and bluestockings in *The Garden of the Mirror*. Of course, servants and farmers appear in these novels here and there, but they are marginal figures. The New Culture movement of China that started in the late 1910s advocated using the Chinese vernacular in literature and writing about ordinary people. Yet, no one wrote a novel about peasants who worked the fields before Pearl Buck had done so. Proper peasants or farmers had never been in the center of a novel until *The Good Earth* in 1931 and *The Mother* in 1934, whose protagonist, unlike Wang Lung who becomes a rich farmer in the second half of the novel, remains an ordinary peasant to the end. If Frank O'Connor would subscribe to Turgenev's view that the writers of the similar themes "all came out from under Gogol's 'Overcoat'" (Wohlgelernter 128), which is the first appearance in fiction of the "little man," the novelists who wrote about the Chinese peasants should acknowledge the same kind of debt to Pearl Buck.

Pearl Buck was also one of the strong advocators of coeducation in the United States. In her book *Of Men and Women* [1941], she discussed the necessity and importance of a common education for both men and women. She believed that boys and girls should be taught the ssme subjects and contended that such coeducational training would remove the conventional antagonism between the two sexes and produce a deeper and closer mutural understanding. Thus, American women, she maintained, would achieve a greater measure of equality, contribute more to the nation, and have better relationships with men. The book attacks the notion of two biologically ordained gender-specific spheres and the separation of the two sexes. The author pleaded for the reuniting of men and women: "The home needs man, and the world outside needs woman" (184). The book, suggested John d'Entremont, "anticipated Betty Friedan's classic *The Feminine Mystique*" (51).

Although Pearl Buck was a liberal thinker ahead of her time in so many obvious ways, she also appeared to be an out-of-date believer in the basic goodness of humanity and seemed insensitive to the pain and anxiety of modern man. The first half of this century saw two world wars and fundamental changes in human beliefs, philosophies, and ways of life. World War I in particular smashed the beautiful dreams of most intellectuals and idealists. The totalitarian countries that emerged after the defeat of Nazi Germany and militant Japan again disillusioned many people who had devoted themselves to noble causes. Bleak pessimism, subjective studies of anguish, and searing indictments of humanity dominated the literary field in the West for most of this century. Our Age of Anxiety is haunted by Nietzsche's words: "God is dead" and is attuned to a Samuel Beckett mood of spiritual plague. Pearl Buck, however, "was *deliberately* out of step" (P. Doyle 1980, 152) with such bleak and pessimistic tendencies. Although she had been close to death during the Boxer Rebellion in 1900 and was almost killed by Chinese Nationalist soldiers in 1927, and even though she had seen more poverty, peril, misery, and disappointment than most Western writers had heard of and had experienced personal blows including having a retarded daughter to look after with borrowed money and to support all her life, Pearl Buck never lost her optimistic and affirmative point of view. She never lost her faith in progress but always tried to put forward her idealistic temperament and the hopeful aspects of human beings. Her positive attitude toward life and society is most clearly manifested in *American Argument* [1949], which criticizes contemporary novelists who "write books of futility and despite" and asserts that in their work "there is no vision, even though this is the most exciting age in human history, when the people of the whole world for the first time move with a common impulse toward a better life" (201). Such an attitude reminds readers of Henry W. Longfellow's didactic poem "A Psalm of Life." Unlike Longfellow a century before, Pearl Buck was not appreciated by contemporary critics for her optimism, and like Longfellow, whose reputation sagged in the mid-twentieth century, she also lost prestige in serious literary circles partly because of her seemingly naive outlook on life.

Moreover, in some of Pearl Buck's works we find sympathy for rather than criticism of some traditional conventions in the East, which even the Chinese are trying to abolish. The arranged marriage, she showed us, was not often loveless or miserable. It could be cooperative, constructive, stable, and enduring. Love could grow mature in such unromantic arrangements as in the marriage of Lao Er and Jade in *Dragon Seed*, of James Liang and Yumei in *Kinfolk*, of the eldest son and his wife in *The Mother*. Even concubinage was not completely evil under her pen. In *Pavilion of Women*, she demonstrated why the mistress of a big house finds her husband a concubine. In the novel, concubinage was shown as a reasonable convention, which provided poor women with a way of life much better than prostitution and gave rich men an outlet of lust somewhat better than adultery, wife-rape, or visiting the brothel. Although she did not praise the institution, the fact that she illustrated its raison d'etre is enough to make people think that she was reactionary, favoring outmoded social institutions. In some of her works, she clearly expressed her preference of human servants over mechanical devices such as the appliances in a typical American kitchen. She said in *My Several Worlds*, "I confess that sometimes I find myself nostalgic for a house where the servants are humans and not machines, the while I know and hate the poverty that makes human labor cheap. And yet the servants in our Chinese home enjoyed their life, and they respected themselves and their work and us" (56). Such preference makes her sound like a Chinese aristocrat rather than an American humanitarian.

Nevertheless, no one can deny that Pearl Buck was a true humanitarian in word and in deed. During her lifetime she "received more than three hundred humanitarian awards" (D. P. Smith 462). Her humanitarianism is seen in most of her works, in the way that she dealt with racial, sexual, religious, cultural, and political issues. In particular, she published three novels---*The Patriot* [1939], *Dragon Seed*, and *The Promise* [1943]---to expose the terrible ferocity committed by the Japanese invaders in China, to reveal to the world China's heroic resistance against Japan, to demonstrate the importance of a free China, and to arouse America's support for the Chinese who had been fighting the Japanese alone for years. For the same purposes, she gave numerous speeches and published many articles throughout the eight years of China's resistance including: "Western Weapons in the Hands of the Reckless East" in 1937; "Arms for China's Democracy," "Mind of the Militarist," and "Japan Loses the War" in 1938; "Soldier of Japan" and "Free China Gets to Work" in 1939; "Women and War" in 1940; "Warning to Free Nations," "New Patriotism," "No Union without China," "People in Pain," and "Freedom for All" in 1941; "What We Are

Fighting for in the Orient," "Total Victory," and "Freedom, East and West" in 1942; "Post War China and the United States" and "China Front and the Future of Asia" in 1943; "Our Last Chance in China" and "Darkest Hour in China's History" in 1944; and "Tell the People" in 1945. In spite of all her strong support for China in its war against Japan, as David D. Buck put it, "she took the rather daring stand in 1943 of testifying against relocation and imprisonment of West Coast Japanese immigrants" (37). And she also took the firm stand against the use of atom bombs on Japan as shown in her article "Bomb, Did We Have to Drop It?" and in her novel *Command the Morning*.

Furthermore, Pearl Buck's humanitarianism is seen in her concern about one of the aftermaths of World War II, namely, the illegitimate children whom the American soldiers had fathered and abandoned in Asian countries. She published "Let Them Have Reality" in 1949, "Children Waiting" in 1955, "Welcome House" in 1958, "Child from Nowhere" in 1962, *Welcome Child* in 1963, *Children for Adoption* in 1964, and "Children America Forgot" in 1967 to draw the public attention to the welfare of such children, who had been discriminated against and found themselves ostracized in their native countries, particularly in Japan and Korea. Not only did she write about this problem, but she also acted. In 1949, she founded Welcome House, which at first was concerned with children of mixed blood born in the United States, and later developed into an agency to bring Asian American children from overseas for adoption. Welcome House has helped more than five thousand orphans and unwanted children find foster homes, making it possible that these children could develop into healthy American citizens (Conn 3).

However, since American laws were not amenable to any large-scale adoption from Asian countries, many children could not be taken into the United States of America. So in 1964, she established the Pearl S. Buck Foundation, which is a nonprofit agency dedicated to caring for children of half-American parentage who are forced to remain overseas. As the pamphlet of the foundation, *The New Children-Amerasians*, says, the purposes of the foundation are "1) to educate the American public to the existence and needs of the Amerasian children and the American responsibility to them; 2) to educate the Amerasian children so that they will, when adults, be responsible, productive human beings---a credit to both sides of their ancestry; 3) to build a climate of social acceptance for these children in the countries of their birth." This foundation has assisted "about twenty-five thousand children" and "about six thousand children in Asia are being assisted by the foundation" (Sum 75). This foundation gets its funds from the donation of average American citizens as well as from the royalties of several of Pearl Buck's books.

That Pearl Buck's humanitarian words are in keeping with her deeds is not only manifested in these two organizations, which united as one on 1 October 1991, but it is also seen in her personal life and in some small incidents, which are, nevertheless, decisive to the persons involved. She advocated racial equality as many other writers did, and moreover, she practiced it. Among the nine children whom she personally adopted, there are Caucasian as well as African and Asian Americans. Instead of claiming credit for herself, she summarized her gains from her giving love in the article "I Am the Better Person for Having My Two Black Children." Her only biological child was a mentally handicapped daughter, from whom, she told us in *The Child Who Never Grew,* she had also learned to be patient, to respect every human mind, to understand that "all people are equal in their humanity and that all have the same human right." In a word, "[her] child taught [her] humanity" (52). In this book she described the handicaps and the ordeals she had gone through to cope with the situation. The book and other writings she published on the problem have helped many parents deal with similar difficulties at home and have called considerable public attention to the welfare of mentally handicapped children. All the profits of the book are given to The Training School at Vineland, New Jersey, which is a famous institute for treating and taking care of people with mental handicaps and has done valuable research into the causes of this illness.

One example of the many incidents that illustrated her humanitarianism was the closing of Ellis Island in New York harbor as an Immigration Center by the U. S. government in 1954 and the use of the Federal House of Detention in Manhattan and in Westchester County Jail to hold new immigrants. These immigrants were guilty of no crimes but were suffering at the hands of true criminals and were mistreated for months until their papers were processed. When some friends and relatives of these inmates contacted Pearl Buck, she published a letter in the *New York Times* on 16 November 1954 to protest this practice that mocked the words carved on the Statue of Liberty. Because of her effort, America's conscience was moved, the Immigration and Naturalization Service ceased the practice on 10 December 1954, and the detained aliens were removed from the prisons. The *New York Times* published an editorial on 11 December to applaud the government's improvement and to thank Pearl Buck for having first drawn public attention to the problem (P. Doyle 134).

However, this humanitarian was suspected of being a Communist and was registered "on the list of Red Sympathizers devised by Senator Joseph McCarthy in the 1950s" (La Farge 88-89). Pearl Buck's FBI file "reaches nearly three hundred pages, of which a little over two-thirds has been declassified" (Conn 2). Indeed, she had been showing a profound love for China even when it became the enemy of the United States during the Korean war from 1950 to 1953. She had been giving strong sympathy to the poor Chinese peasants and their revolutions when the proletarian dictatorship was becoming an increasing threat to the Western democracy. She criticized American foreign policy toward China before and during World War II. She praised the guerilla warfare against the Japanese invaders conducted by Mao's small forces rather than Generalissimo Chiang Kai-shek's [Jiang Jieshi's] regular armies. She had close contact with some Americans who had different insight into the problem of China from the U. S. government including Edgar Snow and John Service, who were persecuted by the McCarthyites, and she shared with them the view that the Roosevelt

Administration should support the Chinese Communist as well as the Chinese Nationalist in their fight against the Japanese and arm Mao in China as the United States had armed Tito in Yugoslavia. She and her second husband Richard Walsh founded the East and West Association and published the magazine *A sia* to promote understanding between Asian and American peoples. She was also friends with the Chinese writer Lao Sher and the actress Wang Ying, who visited the United States in the late 1940s and early 1950s and chose to return to China when the Communist Party assumed power. They became red China's favorite and most celebrated writer and artist.

Despite all that she had done for China, Pearl Buck was disliked by the Chinese governments, Nationalist and Communist alike. In *Sons, A House Divided* [1937], among other writings and speeches, she exposed some evils of China under the warlords, criticized the corruption of the Nationalist government, and condemned its cruelty in dealing with the patriotic and revolutionary youths. Although most of her representation of China was true and the Chinese translations of her novels were not banned by Chiang's Nationalist government, that government did express its dissatisfaction with her for being too candid by withdrawing its officials from the Nobel Prize presentation in Stockholm in 1938 as she recalled in *My Several Worlds* (342). In *The Patriot, The Promise,* and *Kinfolk* she presented a searing picture of Chiang as an opportunist. She detailed his defective leadership and his government's apathy toward the sufferings of the poor people. However, the Chinese Communist government did not like her any better for the realistic depiction of its opponent. After all, she was not writing for or against any of the political parties but simply holding a mirror to the reality of China.

In the above mentioned books, she also exposed the communist guerilla fighters' cruel treatment of the Japanese prisoners of war and expressed her disapproval of the radical and violent methods of the Communists in their attempt to improve the society. In *Letter from Peking*, she told a tragic story of Gerald MacLeod, a patriotic Chinese American man who chooses to stay in and to work for China even when it is taken by the Communists. Through his experiences, she showed how the government distrusts the most valuable people of the country, its intellectuals, how cruelly the party forces them to reform, how closely the ruler controls their communication with the West, and how ruthlessly a good person is killed when he refuses to obey. This novel was published in 1957 when the Chinese Communist Party was conducting the so-called anti-Rightist movement, a persecution of the intellectuals. She was not trying to declare her political inclination through this book, for her trouble with the McCarthyites was over by then. What she said about "the artist's sense of order that leads [her] to undertake such a cause as displaced children" applies to this case, too. "It's just that a writer must be involved in the mainstream of life in order to write, and I cannot endure disorder in any form. When I become involved and find a situation that is not right, then I must try to do something to change it" (Harris 1969, 190). Of course, she could not change anything in

China this time, but from then on her books were banned in China until 1982 when Mao's radical ideology gave way to Deng's moderatism.[2] Similarly, in 1969 when the Cultural Revolution was at its height, she published *The Three Daughters of Madame Liang* to describe how a good restaurant business is depressed once the Communists take it over and how the new intellectuals as well as the old revolutionists were suspected and persecuted by the state.

It was primarily because of these two books and the movie *Satan Never Sleeps*[3] that she was denied a visa for visiting China after its door had been opened by President Nixon. For months all her letters to the Chinese VIPs went unanswered as she told us in *China Past and Present*, and finally she received a letter from a Second Secretary of China's embassy in Canada saying, as she recorded in the same book, "In view of the fact that for a long time you have in your works taken an attitude of distortion, smear and vilification towards the people of new China and their leaders, I am authorized to inform you that we can not accept your request for a visit to China" (171). She was heartbroken and greatly distressed by the letter, which abrogated her last wish and chance to visit the land she loved so much as her second homeland, to visit the tombs of her parents and four brothers and sisters who had died in China, and to visit with her friends who had survived many political movements. Her heartbreak is fully expressed in the thirty-four-page monologue with which she closed *China Past and Present*. She was in such a deep despair that although she said that she had conquered it, she was actually never able to come back to herself and to writing her last novel *The Red Earth*. She stopped at chapter one and died less than ten months later. Ironically, while she was regarded as pro-Communist by a few and considered pro-Chinese by many in the United States, her name was almost unknown to young readers in China for more than two decades.[4] Not until 1982, six years after the Cultural Revolution, did the Chinese people begin to rediscover this American woman who helped the West understand China through literature, received the highest honor for it, and yet paid the ultimate price for being misunderstood. By now many of her major works have been translated into Chinese. Entries on Pearl Buck appear in Chinese literary dictionaries and encyclopedias of foreign literature. Conferences commemorating her and evaluating her works have been held in Zhenjiang, her Chinese home town, and at Nanjing University, where she taught English in China. Scholars including Xipei Yao and Haiping Liu have written articles about her. A collection of critical essays in English, *Pearl Buck in Perspective: Voices from China,* is being edited.

This book is an attempt to further this rediscovery, not so much to clarify the enigma---although it is my wish that that would be a by-product of the book ---as to discuss the cultural contributions of her works: how they help to demythologize China and Chinese people in the American mind; how they evaluate the missionary movement in China; how they enhance the American people's understanding of the Chinese culture; what are the immediate impact and far-reaching influence of the better understanding between the two nations;

what is the importance of her genuine portrayal of the Chinese peasants and farmers to Chinese readers. I shall historicize some of her works and use a multicultural approach in my evaluation of both the historical and enduring value of her works in this nuclear world where we need more tolerance and better understanding if we are to survive as a human species, and in this post-cold war world where ideological conflicts are giving way to racial and cultural conflicts.

I believe that literature is not just belles lettres. The cognitive value of literature is as important as its aesthetic value. Without the former, literature is only a language game or play on words. Without the latter literature is boring and loses its basic properties. The masterpieces of literature are always the harmonious combination of reflecting or revealing the truth of life and providing or stimulating aesthetic pleasure. The final function of great literature is still education, which is not necessarily a moral lesson as found in the end of a fable but is often imperceptible and yet irresistible, existing within the entertainment. Such education is not forced upon us like a compulsory course in a college; it is so subtle and yet so forceful that it exerts a lasting influence upon our character, judgment of right and wrong, way of thinking, sense of beauty, or outlook on life, without our being aware of it. The greater a piece of literature is, the more harmoniously it combines the two values and the better education it gives. However, the two values of a certain piece of literature are not always obvious owing to its historical and cultural factors or the reader's education and level of knowledge. Therefore, one of the major tasks of literary criticism is, by whatever theory, to discuss either the cognitive or aesthetic value, or both, of a piece of literature, so as to help the reader to enjoy the literature more and learn more from it, and to give the author an appropriate evaluation.

I shall, in this book, lay particular emphasis on the discussion and evaluation of the cognitive value of Pearl Buck's literary works, not only because this is the main strength of her works, but also because little has been said about her contributions to the understanding between different cultures, which is now particularly important in our age of multiculturalism. Although our age has seen enormous advances and improvements in communication and transportation, literature is still a vital means for people and different nations to understand each other. It was, of course, much more so fifty years ago when the telephone was a luxury even to Americans, and travelers had to take a ship, not a plane, to cross the Pacific Ocean. People needed and still need to read novels in order to learn about each other and to understand our differences on the basis that we are all the same human species. Of course, we can also learn by studying history, philosophy, sociology, anthropology, and so on, but definitely the majority of people learn by other means such as visiting each other, watching their different ways of living on television, or reading literature. Indeed, if one wants to know how other peoples live, what different gods they worship and how they worship them, what different customs and manners they have, and how they toil, rejoice, despair, and hope, if one wants this kind of knowledge, what means can be cheaper, more convenient, and more rewarding than reading novels?

Pearl Buck's novels are unequaled as far as learning about China and particularly the Chinese peasants and farmers in the first half of this century is concerned, and they will remain so because her contemporaries have all died without producing nearly as important works. Moreover, her works are not only valuable for English readers and the readers of many other languages in learning about China, but they are also valuable for us Chinese in learning about ourselves and particularly about the majority of the Chinese people, the peasants and farmers, of whom we had little truthful and realistic representation in literature until after the Cultural Revolution ended in 1976. Her historic contributions have been well acknowledged in terms of honors and medals in the West, but the historic significance of her works has been little discussed even in her own country. The acknowledgment of her contributions and discussions of her works are rare in her adopted country owing to China's nationalism and the information blockade during the cold war. It is indeed high time that she be properly studied from the viewpoint of China. I shall discuss the function of her works in changing the image of the Chinese people in the American mind. I shall historicize the importance of the change: how the change helped to bring about the Americans' support to China's War of Resistance against Japan, and how the change helped to repeal the sixty-one-year-old Chinese Exclusion Act.

Furthermore, the cognitive value of her works is not only an important historic contribution to America's understanding of and support to the Chinese at the momentous time of the Japanese invasion and occupation of China, but it is also an important reference in today's multicultural studies. One of the major developments in the cultural exchange between the East and the West was the missionary movement. The American missionaries had been active in China for more than a century before they all left for good in 1949. Generations of endeavors and millions of dollars had been spent there. What did they achieve? Why did they fail eventually? What lessons can we learn from their achievement and failure? What did Chinese people really need from America? What could Americans learn from China? Not many scholars have discussed these questions.

Pearl Buck, being a daughter of missionary parents and having lived in China for the first half of her life, felt deeply the conflicts between the Christian culture and the Chinese culture. She indirectly answered the above questions by illustrating the lives, efforts, and effects of missionaries in the biographies of her parents, *The Exile* and *Fighting Angel,* and in some novels including *Dragon Seed, Pavilion of Women,* and *Kinfolk.* She also saw the cultural confluence between the minority nationalities, such as Jews, and the majority nationality of China. She wrote a novel *Peony* that vividly demonstrates the Jews' assimilation in China, a unique phenomenon, for we know that Jews have not assimilated anywhere else except in America. Her answers and the way she suggested the answers to the above questions, as I shall discuss, are very valuable to scholars as well as to general readers, for we are now still encountering the same problems of cultural conflicts and confluences that she dealt with then. For some of these issues she had answers. For some she had suggestions. For some she was also seeking the answers. I shall demonstrate how she embraces in her books all that is humane and beautiful including the traditional Chinese customs, virtues, and modern American ways, how her works illustrate the strong as well as the weak points of the Chinese and American cultures, and how she criticizes Western cultural imperialism in her concealed artistic method. All this is rarely discussed in the reviews and criticism of her works, but this is one of the most important values of her works, and it coincides with the historical and philosophical wisdom of some scholars including Bertrand Russell, John Fairbank, and Edward Said. I shall discuss Pearl Buck's function as one of the few lamps that shed light from her age of Eurocentralism upon our age of multiculturalism.

The final contribution of Pearl Buck's books is that they are a historic mirror that reflects the reality of China's rural life more truthfully than the works of contemporary Chinese writers, who were often guided by political theories such as Mao's "philosophy of strife." The most famous of the so-called proletarian literature includes Zhou Leepo's novel *The Storm* and Ding Ling's novel *The Sun Shines upon the Sanggan River* in which the Chinese peasants and farmers are portrayed as nothing but class enemies to each other. On the one side are the "poor and lower-middle" peasants; on the other are the rich farmers and landlords. Nothing exists between these two sides but class struggles, which result in violent revolutions, beatings, killings, and new oppressors over the oppressed. Such novels nurtured and encouraged hatred and jealousy, and killed love and sympathy. Having illustrated, or rather, created the methodology of the class struggle, such novels became the manual for the revolutionists to follow in the Land Reform. The result was to have accelerated the catastrophe so that numerous rich farmers and landlords not only lost their properties but also their lives or their human dignity. Even their children had to pay for their so-called crimes, most of which were just being more industrious and getting a little richer than others, nothing like the crimes committed by the father and uncle of Charles Darney as described by Charles Dickens in *A Tale of Two Cities*. Such novels had been the mainstream of China's literature from 1942 to 1976, and they had exerted tremendously negative influence upon us Chinese readers. We became constantly alert to the "counterattack" of the class enemy, although it did not exist in reality. We became merciless to the counter-revolutionaries if they were caught in their activities, such as stealing apples in a state orchard or corn in a commune field. We were ceaselessly looking for reactionaries to fight and making revolutions one after another: the Land Reform, the Cooperative Transformation of Agriculture, the People's Commune, the Great Leap Forward, the Four Clean-ups. When we finally woke up from the nightmare of the Cultural Revolution, the greatest cultural disaster in China's four thousand-year history, we asked, among many other questions: What was the real situation in the rural areas when the land belonged to individuals rather than to the state? How did the peasants and farmers work and become rich then? What was the customary relationship between the laborers and the landlord? How did the farmers feel about the land they owned? What did they need and desire? How did Confucianism function among the illiterate peasants and farmers? Now that the traditional values have been largely destroyed, and communist ethics have proved inapplicable, what can replace them? Should we have wholesale westernization in China? How can we keep our national identity? What should we inherit from our tradition? To my surprise, Pearl Buck dealt with most of these questions in her works. Although she did not answer them all, her works, as I shall discuss, shed light on these questions.

For the reasons mentioned above, I believe it is necessary and important to conduct more serious studies of Pearl Buck, who had been the singularly significant spokeswoman for China in American literature in the years from 1931 to 1973. The studies will be timely, if not overdue, because China is waking up. Its economy has been developing rapidly in recent years. China has been playing an increasingly important role in the world market and international affairs. The West is having more and more contact with China in politics, the military, trade, science, technology, sports, and culture. The studies of China will therefore inevitably become more and more significant. To study Pearl Buck will help to gain information about China and the part of China that is hardly retrievable anywhere else. To study Pearl Buck will also help in understanding part of America's intercourse with China in the past. These studies will shed some light on today's interaction between the two countries, especially in the cultural respect. These studies will also shed light on the recognition of Western culture and Americans themselves in contrast and comparison with the Chinese culture and Chinese people. Pearl Buck was, after all, a woman of letters, and therefore, no matter how much emphasis I lay on the cognitive value of her works, it is still indispensable to discuss their aesthetic value, on which many elitists have frowned, but some, including Paul A. Doyle and Samuel I. Bellman, have been expecting more serious discussions.[5] I shall argue that two of her fiction pieces, *The Good Earth* and *The Mother*, and two of her nonfiction, *The Exile* and *Fighting Angel*, combine cognitive value and aesthetic value so harmoniously that they will endure the test of time and prove to be classical works that deserve to be added to the multicultural canon of literature.

NOTES

1. One of the first influential Chinese novels *Shui Hu Chuan* (100 chapters) was written at the very beginning of the 15th century. A shorter edition of this classic work (seventy chapters) was translated into English for the first time by Pearl Buck and was published under the title *All Men Are Brothers* in 1933. The complete edition of the novel was translated into English by Sidney Shapiro and published under the title *Outlaws of the Marsh* in 1988.

2. In 1982, an anthology of foreign short stories entitled *Life and Love* was published by Gui Zhou People's Press. This anthology includes three stories by Pearl Buck and uses her story *Life and Love* as the title, signaling quietly the beginning of a revival of this American woman writer.

3. She wrote the first script of the movie. The final product presents an ugly picture of the Communist leaders and tells a not very believable story of their persecuting the Catholic missionaries and oppressing the people in 1949.

4. Haiping Liu believed that perhaps 99 percent of the educated Chinese under the age of forty-five would not have known who Pearl Buck was in the 1970s and would probably have confused her Chinese name Sai Zhenzhu with Sai Jinhua, the name of a famous courtesan in the late Qing Dynasty (58).

5. See the end of Bellman's essay, chapter 13 of *American Women Writers* edited by Maurice Duke et al (378).

2

A NEGLECTED LAUREATE

Before I begin my discussions, it is helpful to summarize what the representative critics and reviewers have said about Pearl Buck's works and to see where she stands in American literature, so that I can argue about different judgments, refer to the existing criticism, and avoid unnecessary repetition of opinions and evaluations. I shall also offer some reasons for her phenomenal success and, more important, for her present low status in American literature.

Although Pearl Buck had been publishing on average a book a year in her lengthy writing career from 1930 to 1973, the responses of most critics and reviewers to her works made her career appear like a meteor, burning brightest in 1938. No sooner had she received the Nobel Prize for literature that year than her brilliance began to dim in the eyes of the critical beholders. While it is arguable as to whether or not all her post-Nobel Prize books are inferior to her pre-Nobel Prize books, it is understandable that the phenomenal success of her early works, especially her second novel *The Good Earth*, set the high standard against which all her later works were measured. When they fell short of the expectation, no matter how little, she was naturally thought to be on the decline. Thus, the critics who had been encouraging before the prize became harsh after it.

Pearl Buck's first published book *East Wind: West Wind*, in Isidore Schneider's words, is an "ordinary, quite mechanical novel, full of plot and sentiment, but empty of any lifelikeness in its characters or significance in its thesis---the clash between modern and traditional China" (1930, 24). However, the emerging writer received much encouragement for her maiden work. In his review, Nathaniel Peffer evaluated the cognitive value of her book saying that "she tells more of contemporary China than a year of newspaper headlines or a shelf of volumes by political minded experts, and tells it entertainingly" (1930, 6). Approving her attitude toward China and a different culture, the reviewer for the *New York Times* commented, "Only one, who like the author, has lived all her life in China, yet being American still holds to Western concepts of romantic love, marriage and the scope of filial duty---only a lover of China, but no convert to her code of family and clan supremacy over the individual, could have written this beautiful novel" (8). As for the style of her book, Edwin Seaver said these encouraging words: "Mrs. Buck has written with a fine simplicity and delicacy and charm. One would say *East Wind: West Wind* was an exquisite book, did not the word, in this connection, so often connote preciosity" (10m).

Such compliments, we must bear in mind, were given to a new writer, whose book they compared, at most, with the best of Lafcadio Hearn. After Pearl Buck became a Nobel laureate, the critics would compare her not only with the best of her own work, but also with the masterpieces of other laureates. Commenting on the first novel that she published after the award, Hassoldt Davis said, "In *The Patriot* she has returned to the Orient to present a fictional biography which not only is compelling by its timeliness but is probably the best of her books since *The Good Earth*. It is none the less not comparable; though her craft is surer now. *The Patriot* lacks the wide cultural dimensions of the earlier book" (269). Thus the later novel, good as it is, was eclipsed, as George Dangerfield judged the writer of *The Patriot* in the *Saturday Review of Literature*: "Certainly a story of this kind should tell us whether or not that rich vein, first revealed in *The Good Earth*, is really running thin. The answer is not a reassuring one" (5). In discussing the style of *Dragon Seed*, Paul Doyle compared it favorably with Hemingway's style.[1] Then he decided, "In the sustained excellence of its style *Dragon Seed* comes close to *The Good Earth*; its prose does not, however, possess as much poetry and color as Buck's most famous novel" (P. Doyle 1980, 109).

This kind of comparison haunted Pearl Buck for the rest of her life. Her novel *Pavilion of Women*, in Mary McGrory's words, "is a searching, adult study of women written with high seriousness and sympathy, which should find a multitude of women readers" (6). J. J. Espey also predicted in *Weekly Book Review* that the novel would "be hailed as a moving and profound love story by the many thousand readers it is certain to have" (1946, 6). Indeed, the novel proved to be successful and was on the *Book-of-the-Month* Club list, but in comparison with *The Good Earth*, it lost its brilliance. As Margaret Williamson put it: "One puts down *Pavilion of Women* with a small sigh that it is hardly Mrs. Buck at her supreme best" (1946, 14). Commenting on the characterizations of this novel, the reviewer for *Kirkus* also compared it with Pearl Buck's highest achievement: "The figures never take on the emotional values that made her *Good Earth* so poignantly moving" (553).

Thus, *The Good Earth* set the standard for its author. Even in praising Pearl Buck's novel of 1949, Feike Feikema would mention its inferiority to what she had already accomplished: "While *Kinfolk* is not as juicy or as colorful in detail, not so poetic in style as *The Good Earth*, it has something else---the full play of a mature and warm mind that has brooded long and thoroughly on Good and

Evil" (8X). *Imperial Woman,* in Pearl Buck's own opinion, is her best novel set in China.[2] Rodney Gilbert, in discussing its artistic quality, also gave it "a very high rating" (1). Inevitably, the novel was compared with Pearl Buck's zenith. After confirming the function of making the past intelligible, Jane Voiles maintained, "But her imagination supplies no connecting link with the present so that the sense of communication experienced abundantly in *The Good Earth* doesn't come through in this novel" (1956, 18). Preston Schoyer, too, made the comparison in discussing the style of *Imperial Woman*: "Eminently suitable in its simple, rolling solemnity to the peasant life she describes so well in her masterpiece, *The Good Earth,* that style seems less felicitous in application to the exotic worldliness, the complex subtleties, the urbane sophistication, and the exquisitely mannered nonsense of imperial Peking" (12). *Letter from Peking,* in the words of the *Kirkus* reviewer, is a "minor production in the distinguished list of Mrs. Buck's writings" (336), but it could not escape the comparison, either. Fanny Butcher said, "That this novel is not another *Good Earth* is undeniable, but it makes no pretense of being so. It is written in depth---probing one woman's emotion---not in cosmic scope" (1957, 1). Similarly, *The Three Daughters of Madame Liang* was in the shadow. Having said some nice words about its useful insights into the temperament of modern-day Chinese, the reviewer for *Christian Science Monitor* concluded, "How they [the daughters] decide and how their decisions affect them make a mildly entertaining story that would please a casual reader whose expectations had not been pitched too high by memories of *The Good Earth*" (11).

Only when Pearl Buck was publishing novels under a pseudonym John Sedges was she free temporarily from her trademark of Chinese themes and the shadow of *The Good Earth.* Of the five John Sedges novels *The Townsman* is the most successful, and she rightfully regarded it as her best American novel (Cevasco 1981, 19). Commending this Kansan pioneer story, the reviewer for *Commonwealth* said, "Only rarely does a novel on immigration have the quality or the sensitiveness of *Giants in the Earth.* Yet despite its well-worn theme *The Townsman* manages to compel and hold attention. John Sedges tells the simple story of an English family well and there are several elements which set off this volume from most of its contemporaries" (193). One of the elements is the background description. The reviewers then were comparing it with the way of other writers rather than with Pearl Buck's way as W. S. Lynch put it: "Mr. Sedges writes with restrained fullness that fits the mood of his theme admirably. He handles his detail of background excellently, never letting the sodhouse, the calicoes, the furniture become obtrusive, in the Sears-Roebuck-catalogue way that many writers seem to think is necessary to provide a convincing setting" (30). No one imagined the novel could be written by a non-Kansan, let alone by someone who lived most of her life in China. What F. H. Bullock said was a typical opinion at the time:

The Townsman is a sturdy book, almost massive in its comprehensiveness. Yet it never loses its way in generalities. The name of the author, John Sedges, is a pseudonym chosen because the novel grew out of the author's own family background and experience. This accounts in part for the rich authenticity of detail in the story, and for its overall plot. But to the writer himself is due grateful recognition of a creative power at work that gives outstanding interest to *The Townsman* as a novel which incidentally is the true story of a town and a man. (1945, 6)

However, after the identity of John Sedges had been revealed, *The Townsman* was inevitably compared with *The Good Earth*. Discussing the weaknesses of the former, Paul Doyle mentioned its occasional sentimentalism and contended, "It blows over the story from time to time. This factor, together with sporadic moralizing, gives the work a softness it could better do without. How these features would have blurred *The Good Earth* if they had been allowed to enter that excellent book!" (1980, 116).

Exactly how excellent is *The Good Earth*? Upon its publication in 1931, it received, in Dody W. Thompson's phrase, "critical hosannas" (85), and most reviewers did rate it far above the other novels of its kind. Nathaniel Peffer gave it the following commendation:

This is China as it has never before been portrayed in fiction, the China that Chinese live in and as Chinese live. By comparison *The Bitter Tea of General Yen* is the artifice of a clever and imaginative undergraduate, sparkling, entertaining and untrue, a synthetic romanticization of the "Oriental" as an escape from our own daily lives. *The Good Earth* is, however, much more than China. One need never have lived in China or know anything about the Chinese to understand it or respond to its appeal. (1931, 1)

H. C. Harwood commended the novel even more highly: "Never have I read such a book as *The Good Earth* wherein without effort or anger an alien civilization is quietly presented. It is so easy to be funny about China and so easy to be funny about the collisions of alien cultures. Mrs. Buck turns away from all that and explains Wang Lung" (722). The reviewer for *New Statesman and Nation* preffered this judgment:

I can recall no novel that frees the ordinary, flesh-and-blood, everyday Chinaman so satisfyingly from those screens and veils and mirrors of artistic and poetic convention which nearly always make him, to the Western reader's eye, a flat and unsubstantial figure of a pale colored ballet. ... Mrs. Buck does not compel one's interest by any particular dexterity in prose or inventiveness, but simply by the clarity and honesty of her narrative. ... *The Good Earth* is not a book to be passed over. (430)

Florence Ayscough, who had lived in China for many years, confirmed the outstanding authenticity of *The Good Earth*: "At last we read, in the pages of a novel, of the real people of China. They seem to spring from their roots, to develop and mature even as their own rice springs from a jade green seed bed and comes to its golden harvest" (676). Having discussed the merits of the novel and the factors of its success, Carl Van Doren concluded, "*The Good Earth* for the first time made the Chinese seem as familiar neighbors. Pearl Buck had added to American fiction one of its large provinces" (353).

Many critics juxtaposed Pearl Buck's novel with the masterpieces of the world. Mentioning that Mr. Phelps was the first to call *The Good Earth* a masterpiece, Malcolm Cowley contended in "Wang Lung's Children," a book review of *The Patriot*, "If we define a masterpiece as a novel that is living, complete, sustained, but still somewhat limited in its scope as compared with the greatest works of fiction---if we define it as *Wuthering Heights* rather than *War and Peace*---then Mr. Phelps has found exactly the word for *The Good Earth*" (1939, 24). Will Rogers said that *The Good Earth* was "not only the greatest book about a people ever written, but the best book of our generation" (qte. in Day 311). Discussing naturalism, Oscar Cargill compares the similarities and differences between *The Good Earth* and Zola's *La Terre* saying that the Wang family is "as typical of contemporary China, we judge, as was the Rougon-Macquart family of France of 1848-1870" (148). Paul Doyle made the same comparison and further pointed out that the "principal difference between Zola's Naturalism and the Naturalistic aspects in *The Good Earth* resides in the authors' attitudes toward free will. ... Zola's characters are caught in a deterministic world, shaped by heredity and environment. In *The Good Earth*, on the other hand, free will exerts considerable influence" (1980, 39). Commenting on such a positive attitude toward life, Van Wyck Brooks linked *The Good Earth* with the works of Balzac, Molière, and Dickens, regarding her novel as "a universal book of our own time, which conveys, in characters with whom words have their full weight, a sense of the basic integrities on which societies are built" (187). Talking about the promulgation of her ideas, James Gray maintained that Pearl Buck "occupies a position a little like that of George Eliot in relation to the circle of intellectuals she dominates" (29). Discussing its style, Paul Doyle concluded, "In its economy and in its laconic but vital lyricism, the descriptive passages in *The Good Earth* often remind us of Ernest Hemingway's writing. The style bears no dross; only descriptive details necessary to convey the scene or to reinforce the mood are recorded" (1980, 33).

Almost every critic who talked about the style of *The Good Earth* noticed its biblical quality and commended its appropriateness. Discussing biblical style as a feature of the modern saga, Alexander Cowie mentioned Ruth Suckow, Willa Cather, Ellen Glasgow, and Pearl Buck, calling the latter's *The Good Earth* "perhaps the most popular of all the saga stories." He observed that in the writings of such style "the Aristotelian conception ... beginning, middle, and end was often discarded as old hat. The aim of the new writers was to establish that sense of the continuous present which T. S. Eliot conveys in 'Burnt Norton' ... The aim was to get at the texture of experience, not to interpret life in its totality" (751). Joseph W. Beach maintained that the style well suits the content: "The biblical simplicity of her style corresponds to the grave matter-of-factness of her chronicle. Without censoriousness and without sentimentality, the

Occidental Christian delineates the manners and morals of the Chinese peasant, following through the whole cycle of life from boyhood to old age, from indigence to wealth, keeping always strictly within the limits of a provincial Chinese mentality" (233). Speaking of the Biblical style of the novel, Carl Van Doren exclaimed, "Fluent and flexible, it was simple in idiom and cadence, like a realistic pastoral of a humane saga. ... The style gives an agreeable music to the convincing history." This style, Van Doren asserted, "was actually close to the style of Chinese novels" (353). Paul Doyle also believed that it "is based on the manner of the old Chinese narrative sagas related and written down by story-tellers and on the mellifluous prose of the King James version of the Bible. ... Many similarities exist between the two forms, ranging from the use of parallelism to an old-fashioned, even archaic, form of expression" (1980, 33).

Most Chinese critics also responded positively to the translations of *The Good Earth*. Zhao Jiabi, an influential critic and publisher, began an article entitled "Mrs. Buck and Wang Lung" as follows:

Inspired by Marco Polo's travelogue and encouraged by the recent gains of Western aggressions, many people have written books about China. On the covers of these books is usually drawn a "Chinaman" grotesquely attired, flanked by some lopsided, incomplete and unintelligible Chinese calligraphy. None of these, of course, can be considered works of literature. The one book that has changed the whole situation is Mrs. Buck's *The Good Earth*. The reason it has won praises the world over, including in China, is that it shows part of their soul. Except for its medium of writing, everything else, such as the subject matter, the characterization, the milieu and the mood, is Chinese. The book, on the whole, is very authentic, and one can hardly believe it was written by a foreign hand. (qtd. in H. Liu 60)

Discussing *The Good Earth*, Haiping Liu also recorded that Hu Zhongchi, a Chinese critic, even exulted, "Pearl Buck's body was no doubt born of her American parents, but it was China that endowed her with spirit and soul" (58). Another critic, Zhuang Xinzai, discussing the important role literature played in creating and upholding a nation's reputation, called Pearl Buck "a friend of the Chinese nation" (qtd. in H. Liu 59).

The Good Earth, however, was by no means free from attacks. The earliest appeared in the *New Republic* on 1 July 1931 written by Younghill Kang, an enthusiastic Asian American who found Pearl Buck's "picture of excessive child bearing" completely "out of proportion." He claimed that her characters spoke with too much "frankness, a thing abhorrent to the traditional Oriental." He asserted that no man in China would have a love affair with his bondmaid and no woman, not even a slave girl, would have premarital sex. He believed if a father did such a disgraceful thing, his son would probably commit suicide. He insisted that Pearl Buck's emphasis on "romantic love" in *The Good Earth* reduced Confucian society "to a laughable pandemonium" (185). A more vehement attack came from Kang-hu Kiang, professor of Chinese Studies at McGill University in Montreal. He published an essay in the *New York Times* on 15 January 1933 accusing Pearl Buck of making errors of fact and distorting certain aspects of Chinese life. He declared that non-Chinese novelists could not possibly write accurately of life in China. He maintained that peasants and the low-class people about whom she wrote were too few in China to represent the majority of Chinese people or the mainstream of Chinese culture. He also inferred that modern China had no bandits any more. Partly for reasons of this kind---not glorifying modern China through literature---and partly for Pearl Buck's honest answers to the inevitable questions of newspaper reporters about China and Chiang Kai-shek, the Nationalist government of China was displeased with Pearl Buck to the extent that its officials even withdrew their presence from her Nobel Prize presentation.

The most severe attack, ironically, was launched by Professor Lifu Wu, one of the first Chinese translators of *The Good Earth*. He prefaced his translation with a critical essay accusing Pearl Buck of distorting China as a country governed by "human instincts, where robbery plays a crucial role in the changes of a man's life," and filled with "frequent droughts and famines, the ignorance of the peasants, male greed and miserliness, female humbleness and humilities, the threat of soldiers, robbers, and communists, and innumerous other disasters" (1). He criticized her for refusing to see and depict the reality of China, whose class structure and the underlying economic relations were not the same as represented in the novel. It was the collaboration between such feudal forces as warlords and foreign imperialists, Professor Wu asserted, that posed the main obstacle to China's agricultural development (20). He also attacked her attitude of white supremacy as shown in the story when Wang Lung hears that foreigners pay rickshaw boys twice as much as Chinese would. "There have been many instances that Chinese rickshaw boys were beaten by foreign soldiers," Wu declared. "Why does the author not think of writing about those in her novel?" (25).

Good or bad, *The Good Earth*, however, was not the only book for which the Nobel Prize was awarded to Pearl Buck. In his speech at the presentation in Stockholm, the permanent secretary of the Swedish Academy, Per Hallstrom, particularly mentioned another novel, *The Mother*, saying the nameless mother "is the most finished of Pearl Buck's Chinese female figures, and the book was one of her best" (7). Indeed, when *The Mother* was published in 1934, it received no less favorable reviews than *The Good Earth* had done previously. Comparing it with *The Good Earth*, Fanny Butcher remarked, "It is written in the same biblical style as *The Good Earth*. It has the same tragic overtones, the same calm melody. It has not the cosmic power that was in the pages of *The Good Earth*, but it has the same deep and rich and rooted reality" (1934, 15). Comparing it with *East Wind: West Wind, The Good Earth*, and *Sons*, G.R.B. Richards lauded *The Mother* as follows:

Simple in theme, it moves along as quietly as a lowland stream, with a restrained emotionalism that the more complex novels lack. Spiritual change, as deeply harmonious as it is tranquil, characterizes the book which, despite its lesser theme, in many ways surpasses its predecessors. It is more finely done. The simplicity of the peasant mind stands out in bolder relief and the conflicts of opposing natures is less dramatic and more real. Poetic but not sentimental, distinguished by sympathetic understanding and appreciation of unseen struggle, it is essentially artistic, essentially commonplace, essentially and universally human in its conception and in its execution. (1934, 1)

Also discussing the execution of the simple theme in *The Mother*, Mary Ross maintained, "Such a theme in the hands of a lesser writer might have the blurriness of a composite photograph or slur into platitudes and sentimentality. Mrs. Buck's telling has the authentic simplicity of strength and sureness, the power of an understanding that is whole and deep" (1934, 3). Emphasizing such simplicity, strength, and understanding, J. D. Adams concluded, "*The Mother* has an architectural unity and a driving simplicity and strength to a degree more marked than in any of Mrs. Buck's previous work. That simplicity and strength have almost an elemental quality. And not only that; it has been Mrs. Buck's achievement that she has rendered the life of a people deeply alien from ourselves in terms of universal human values, and those values are in this book appreciably intensified" (1934, 1). Talking about the effect of *The Mother* on the reader, Isidor Schneider said, "It is so direct in its appeal to the emotions that it draws tears to the eyes. And it has a certain quality common to some of the world's finest books and peculiarly satisfying in whatever book it appears, of presenting its characters safe, in the integrity of their destinies, from envy, scorn and censure" (1934, 136). Herschel Brickell also commended it: "The more I look back upon *The Mother*, the greater is my admiration for it. It is far enough off the beaten path to make a quick judgment a little difficult, although I was never in any doubt of my own very genuine pleasure in reading it" (1934, 7).

In his Nobel presentation speech, Per Hallstrom included Pearl Buck's biographies of her parents saying that "in character descriptions and the story-teller's art she is at her best in ... *The Exile* (1936) and *Fighting Angel* (1936). These should be called classics in the fullest sense of the word; they will endure, for they are full of life" (8). In *My Several World*, Pearl Buck recalls that Selma Lagerlof, the first Swedish Nobel Prize winner for literature, told her, "the two biographies of my parents had decided her vote for the Nobel award for me that year" (348). Indeed, these two books received very favorable reviews in the United States, too. Mary Ross said, "Restrained, temperate, the book of a novelist who not only loves life but looks at it clear-eyed, *The Exile* is a story of fact as exciting and as moving as any of the fiction in which Pearl Buck has showed life as Carie helped her to see it" (1936, 3). Discussing the manner of this book, E. L. Van Alen concluded, "The biography is no carefully tabulated and documented affair concerning a life-history which was never front-page news anyway. Rather, the author has written an impressionistic sketch within the loose confines of a cinematic narrative. The result is as loving and almost as objective a study as Daphne Du Maurier's contemporary portrait of her actor father, Gerald. Viewed as such, if less artistic, it is as absorbing as any of her novels" (370). Katherine Woods rated the biography even higher: "Clear, incandescent, gripping in its interest, written in a style of beauty and unerring rightness, this 'Portrait of an American Mother' is an epic of our country. It is one of the noblest epics of our day" (1936, 1). To answer the question as how to reconcile the matter and the manner of *The Exile*, Mark Van Doren said, "I am not sure that it can be done, or could at any rate be done in another case. In Mrs. Buck's case I am disposed to agree with the general judgment that she had better be taken as we find her" (1936, 195). Paul Doyle regarded *The Exile* as "an amazingly and genuinely frank and complete picture of a missionary wife," despite its occasional sentimentalism and diffusion. He concluded that "the portrait drawn of Caroline Sydenstricker remains imprinted in one's memory; and the character analysis is rendered with persuasive depth. The reader not only sees the principal external events of her life, but, more importantly, is taken into her mind and being and brought to a convincing understanding of her aspirations, her temptations, her spiritual turmoil, her sorrows, and her frustrations" (1980, 71). As for Pearl Buck's biography of her father, Paul Doyle considered it "an even better one." Compared with *The Exile*, he said, "*Fighting Angel* is much more taut and focused. ... less sympathetic and more objective; hence the portrait of Absalom Sydenstricker unfolds in a harsher, rougher fashion" (1980, 72). Discussing the style of the two biographies, Katherine Woods commented, "In the limpid flowing beauty of Pearl Buck's writing, in the unerring clarity and directness of every word and image and expression, she has done in *Fighting Angel* what she did in *The Exile*---has drawn a portrait with far more than mere personal vividness, touched problems as deep as all humanity. And her incandescent realism lights the very heart of our thought" (1936, 3). L. T. Nicholl thus reviewed *Fighting Angel*: "This is the work of maturity---hard-won maturity of heart. A good many layers of soil had to be lived away and written away before this rock could be laid bare" (3). Summarizing the difficulty and achievement of *Fighting Angel*, G. F. Finnie decided,

To attempt the biography of one's own father is to court disaster either by allowing sentiment to overcome reality or by offending the tender decencies of life by frankly presenting the truth as one sees it, irrespective of family obligations. If the author has erred in any direction, it is in the realism of this unique book. ... Needless to say, the book is a piece of high literary craftsmanship. It is good reading, and again attests the fact that Pearl Buck is among our foremost writers of today. (183)

The erring of the biography is but so slight that the reviewers all emphasized the objectiveness of the book, as Kenneth S. Latourette put it: "This is an amazing book. That is not because of its syle, for it possesses the literary charm which is unfailingly associated with the name of Pearl Buck. Nor is it because of its setting. ... It is amazing, rather, because of its objectivity and its understanding of its central figure" (1936, 10). The reviewer for the *Springfield Republican* confirmed the above view: "The book is written in Mrs. Buck's beautiful prose, with delicacy of feeling and a true sense of seeing things as they are. She draws an understanding portrait of her father, showing him at his best, but not neglecting those austere characteristics that made him the unusual man he was" (7e). It was for these four books, rather than for *The Good Earth* alone,[3] that the Nobel Prize was given to Pearl Buck, as the Nobel Committee citation that accompanies the award reads: "For rich and generous epic description of Chinese peasant life and masterpieces of biography."[4] Nevertheless, it was undeniable that it was not just artistry that won her the prize.

Pearl Buck's first novel had appeared only eight years before. She had published only ten books, one of which was the translation of a classical Chinese novel, and the prize is not for translations, no matter how good they may be. Even though four of her books were well written, two were best-sellers, and one was a phenomenal success, she was by no means the best American writer. Theodore Dreiser was at the time the most acclaimed novelist in the United States, which she also acknowledged.[5] William Faulkner had published *Sartoris, The Sound and the Fury, As I Lay Dying, Sanctuary, Light in August,* and *The Unvanquished.* Ernest Hemingway had published *In Our Time, The Sun Also Rises, Men without Women, A Farewell to Arms, Death in the Afternoon,* and *To Have and Have Not.* Robert Frost had published the bulk of his best-known poems. Carl Sandburg, Van Wyck Brooks, Sherwood Anderson, Upton Sinclair, F. Scott Fitzgerald, and John Dos Passos were also flourishing. If the award had to go to an American woman, then Willa Cather or Ellen Glasgow should be a better candidate as many commentators suggested in the major newspapers in 1938. How on earth did the Swedish Academy decide to award Pearl Buck the prize?

The award given to her had much to do with Nobel's will and some historic factors at the time. The Nobel Prize for Literature was established in 1901; according to Alfred Nobel's will, one of the five annual awards for "those who, during the preceding year, shall have conferred the greatest benefit on mankind" was to go to "the person who shall have produced in the field of literature the most outstanding work of an idealistic tendency" (Opfell viii). As for how greatly a literary work benefits mankind, there is simply no objective method to measure it. Dody W. Thompson said, "By the broadest definition it can be said that any masterpiece should benefit mankind; but as humanitarianism is usually much easier to recognize than genius, whose manifestations are apt to be thorny and ahead of time, the committee, being human and often conservative, has tended to honor obvious morality before high art" (97). An idealistic tendency is also hard to judge and like the works of Emile Zola, Thomas Hardy, August Strindberg, and Maxim Gorky, Theodore Dreiser's novels demonstrate "crudely cynical naturalism, immorality, and lack of religious and ethical substance" in the judgment of some of the members as reported by Esmark (Riggan 16).

Thus, Dreiser fell short of "idealism" in its surface meaning. An earlier example was Leo Tolstoy who was not awarded the prize because he "turned to writing educational and religious tracts and preaching a kind of fundamental anarchism that was the very antithesis of Nobel's prescribed 'idealism' and 'benefit to mankind'" (Riggan 15). Pearl Buck's fiction and biographies, the Swedish Academy decided, had the idealistic essence: "a heart-felt appreciation for the dignity and the worth of people. Most impressive was the theme that virtue is gained from the cycle in which people, like the food they eat, are born of, gain sustenance from, and return to the earth. A corollary vision is that natural hardships need not separate man from nature. Droughts, wars, plagues, and floods are endured through an abiding faith in the land and its bounty" (D. P. Smith 459). Particularly, Pearl Buck's portrayals of women as individuals uniquely capable of enduring both natural difficulties and cultural prejudices demonstrate "that hardship is not defeat, that sorrow is not surrender, that the temporary ugliness of the world is not the permanent eradication of beauty" (D. P. Smith 459). Thus, her works met the requirements of "benefit on mankind" and had an "idealistic tendency." Oscar Cargill gave this argument for her award: "To reflective Americans outside the [literary] fraternity, to the 'barbs' at least, the prize seemed well given as a reminder that pure aestheticism is not everything in letters. If the standard of her work was not so uniformly high as that of a few other craftsmen, what she wrote had universal appeal and a comprehensibility not too frequently matched" (154).

Moreover, the political situation in both Asia and Europe helped Pearl Buck to win the prize in 1938. The Nobel Prizes, especially those for peace and literature, had always been politically determined. In 1937, Japan started to invade the inland of China and seized Peking, Tientsin, Shanghai, Nanking, and Hangchow. China's capital was forced to remove from Nanking to Hankow, and later to Chungking. The Nationalists led by Chiang Kai-shek were united with the Communists led by Mao Tse-tung (Mao Zedong) in the common effort of resisting the Japanese aggression. Some historians regarded this year, rather than 1939 when Germany invaded Poland, as the beginning of World War II. At one of the fierce battles, the Japanese planes even sank the U.S. gunboat "Panay" in Chinese waters. A year earlier, Italy had withdrawn from the League of Nations and joined the Anti-Comintern Pact signed by Germany and Japan. In that same year, Japan ignored the condemnation of the world and also withdrew from the League of Nations. It further invaded China, took Tsingtao, Canton, and Hankow, and installed a puppet government in Nanking. Under such adverse circumstances, to award Pearl Buck the Nobel Prize would certainly direct the attention of the West to the suffering land and fighting people on the other side of the globe. In Europe, the international situation was also uneasy. Hitler appointed himself War Minister, and German troops marched into Austria. Sudeten Germans in Czechoslovakia demanded autonomy, and Germany had general mobilization. Then, the Munich conference took place, Germany occupied Sudetenland, and Slovakia and Ruthenia were granted autonomy.

Although peace was temporarily maintained by sacrificing the sovereignty of Czechoslovakia, the conflicts were by no means resolved. Pogroms began in Germany. The anti-Jewish legislation was enacted in Italy. The extensive coordinations of the Axis were clearly seen. President Roosevelt's appeal to Hitler and Mussolini to settle European problems amicably received no positive responses. The United States and Germany recalled their ambassadors. In such pending danger of war, to award Pearl Buck the Nobel Prize would send a message to the Axis that the peace lovers and freedom fighters were united on the same front.

Literature is unlike natural sciences. A scientific discovery is definite, and the advance of a material kind can be proved. Literary beauty and greatness are more in the eyes of the beholders and less easy to be judged unanimously. The taste of literary appreciation varies in space and changes with time much more than the evaluation of scientific achievements. Very often, contemporary readers are more likely to grasp and comprehend the zeitgeist reflected in literary works. The farther away we are from them, the harder it is for us to do them justice. Only through the interplay between the readers and the literary works can we acquire their full richness and be affected by their charm and power, which, like everything else, will inevitably diminish as time passes. Some writers were lucky to have caught the mood of their time and to have provided the preferable local flavor. The sufferings and struggles of the ordinary peasants in *The Good Earth* certainly struck a sympathetic chord among Americans as well as Europeans during the Great Depression. Pearl Buck also "enjoyed a certain kinship with Selma Lagerlof, Grazia Deledda, and Sigrid Undset" (Opfell 109). These three female Nobel laureates, her predecessors, had written family and peasant sagas, too. Such reasons, along with Pearl Buck's vivid portrayals of women characters, especially in *The Mother,* brought her to the literary forefront in Scandinavia. Robert Spiller recorded in his *Literary History of the United States* that her books were "particularly liked in Sweden. Ten of her books appeared there between 1932 and 1940, more than were translated from any other American author during the years covered by the *Index Translationum*." In Denmark she "was the most popular American author from 1932 to 1939." Not until 1940 did Hemingway and Steinbeck begin to surpass her (Spiller 1383-84). Therefore, even though Pearl Buck might not be the best American candidate for the prize in 1938, she won it not without sufficient reasons, some of which were indeed not artistic or aesthetic.

Her good fortune proved to be a mixed blessing. She was fully aware of her "unworthiness," kept a modest low profile, and said to the *New York Times* reporter of the article, "Pearl Buck Wins Nobel Literature Prize" on 11 November 1938, "Theodore Dreiser merits the honor ... I feel diffident in accepting the award" (1). She also spoke humbly of herself in the reception speech, as recorded in *My Several Worlds*: "I accept, for myself, with the conviction of having received far beyond what I have been able to return through my books. I can only hope that the many books which I have yet to write will be in some measure a worthier acknowledgment than I can make tonight." And more important, she said, she accepted the award for her country, especially for American women, who needed to be recognized, and she accepted the award also for the people of China, her foster country, which was fighting for its freedom (344-45). Despite all this, the highest prize given to a woman writer who had only eight years' history of publication generated a certain amount of resentment among the white male dominated American academics in 1939. "It was claimed," as Paul Doyle summarized, "that she was too youthful, that she had written too few important books to be considered of major stature, and that no woman writer deserved the award. She was even charged with not being an American writer since her subject matter and even her places of residence were almost completely Chinese" (1980, 82). Robert Frost complained about Pearl Buck's winning the prize, as Warren Sherk recorded: "If she can get it, anybody can." Dr. Sherk also recorded William Faulkner's discontent with the Swedes' selection: "I don't want it. I'd rather be in the company of Sherwood Anderson and Theodore Dreiser than S. Lewis and Mrs. Chinahand Buck" (106). Yet, Faulkner would not hesitate to accept in 1949 when he was selected to receive the same prize.

As D. P. Smith put it, "As much as the Nobel Prize honored her, it also branded her as a writer almost exclusively identified with China---a limiting characterization from which she spent the remainder of her career trying to escape" (462). The critics, however, thought her American novels were no match for her Chinese novels. Reviewing *Other Gods*, Clifton Fadiman stated, "I am not one of those who think that Mrs. Buck can write effectively only about China. Still there is no doubt that her American novels do not as yet measure up to even the least successful of her memorable Chinese stories" (1940, 76). About *Portrait of a Marriage*, the reviewer for *New Yorker* said, "Mrs. Buck rings all the possible changes on talent, marriage, and love with her customary assurance and simplicity, but the generalities that served her so well in China are occasionally out of key in the rolling hills of Pennsylvania" (130). Discussing *Letter from Peking*, which is primarily set in the United States, the reviewer for the *Times Literary Supplement* said, "Perhaps she herself is happier, as a story-teller, with pure Chinese than with Chinese-American themes" (582). Of her American novels, only *The Townsman* was unanimously acclaimed as a success; the theme is original, the details are authentic, the story is excellently told, and "the real merit of the book," J. T. Flanagan maintained, "is the characterization of Johnathan Goodliffe. He is not a sensational figure; he is plodding rather than brilliant, but in his quiet firm way he dominates both the community and the novel" (1). All the good reviews had been given before the true identity of John Sedges was known.

A general opinion of Pearl Buck was that her post-Nobel Prize books, like most other winners' post-Nobel books, are conspicuously poorer in quality. Paul Doyle said that "after this decade [1930s] she never again reached the same level of achievement" (1980, 82). He further asserted, "After 1939 she became more facile at constructing her plots, handling dialogue, and in the technical aspects of her craft; but no subsequent significant growth in the artistic features of novel writing occurred in Pearl Buck's work." What was even more pitiful than this, Doyle continued, was that "she broke away from objectivity; didacticism became a dominant feature and the quality of her work declined" (1980, 149). This criticism was representative of the few reviews her novels received after the Nobel Prize. The reviewer for *Catholic World* had this to say about *The Patriot*: "There are several scenes, vivid and appealing, which make one regret that Miss Buck lingered over extraneous matters when the potential drama lay in the clash of ideologies that made the Japanese invasion inevitable" (375). George Dangerfield said that the novel had another fault: "It lacks---or at any rate seems to lack---the necessary passion. The characters are not substantial enough" (5). Similarly, the plot of *Kinfolk*, as H. R. Forbes reviewed it, "is too contrived to be convincing; character development is superficial" (1949, 546). Jane Voiles commented that at times "the story becomes hopelessly didactic" (1949, 14). About her novel *Other Gods*, the reviewer of *Christian Science Monitor* decided: "If Mrs. Buck wished to point out the dangers of hero worship and, indirectly, of dictatorship, which seems to have been the case, one applauds her attempt. The trouble is one does not find it possible to believe in her legend. It does not seem to have any remote bearing upon the truth" (18). Acknowledging *Other Gods* as an absorbing and tremendous story, Katherine Woods said, "On the other hand, the denouement of the story is real enough, though it may seem satiric to some readers and sentimental to others and is indeed perhaps both" (1940, 1). Although *Dragon Seed* received some favorable reviews, it was criticized as a war propaganda novel. Its sequel, *The Promise*, was highly praised by Struthers Burt for its "vivid description of Burma, and the Burmese fighting, and especially the Burmese jungle." Yet, it also suffered from didacticism, as Burt continued: "It is only in her role as conscious propagandist that I have reservations about Mrs. Buck. She is too acrid, too quick tempered, too absolute, too fierce. Her blacks are too black, her whites too white. She raises her spiritual voice" (6). On another book, *God's Men*, Jane Voiles commented, "A part of the novel is moving because it is written with passion, the rest is in her customary didactic vein" (1951, 18). F. H. Bullock made a similar comment on the novel: "If *God's Men* lacks some of the rich and living warmth with which Mrs. Buck has endowed her previous novels, it is because in it she seems more concerned here with ideas than with people---but the ideas are vital" (1951, 3). *Command the Morning* has the same problem, Paul Doyle criticized: "The didacticism is too heavy, and the propaganda pulls the story away from artistic balance" (1980, 127).

Another common criticism of her post-Nobel Prize works was the unnecessary romances inserted in many of her novels as a Hollywood recipe. The love between Lao San and Mayli in *Dragon Seed* was criticized by the reviewer for *New Republic* as "one ludicrous romance" (214). Paul Doyle also considered it as "the chief factor in the failure of *Dragon Seed* to achieve artistic success. The Mayli incident is a disastrous attempt to insert romantic materials into a context of realism" (1980, 108). Even Hollywood cut it out when they adapted the best-seller into a movie. In *The Promise*, the sequel, "the two lovers," as C. B. Palmer commented, "seem an unnecessary device to create suspense, if that was the purpose" (6). Pearl Buck's *Pavilion of Women*, the *New Yorker* reviewer said, "is vivid and extremely interesting. When, however, she is telling the story of the aging wife and her sublimated passion for a dead foreign priest, she loses her grip on reality, even Oriental reality, and becomes a mite dull" (122). Similarly, the reviewer of *Times Literary Supplement* found "fascinating detail and convincing formality" in *Imperial Woman*, but thought it "was perhaps a pity to introduce the theme of a lover whom royalty must abjure for duty's sake, and to concentrate on the romantic youth of Tsu Hsi (Ci Xi) rather than on her tyrannical old age; both these emphases are less successful than the exciting story which history offers" (325). In *Kinfolk,* Paul Doyle found "Dr. Liang himself is much attracted to a beautiful Chinese 'modern' woman, and their relationship constitutes a Hollywood motif out of keeping with the scenes in China" (1980, 124).

However, a closer look at the book reviews reveals that critics did not find all of Pearl Buck's post-Nobel Prize books poorer than all her pre-Nobel Prize books; they found a few exceptions. *The Patriot*, published in 1939, was regarded superior to some of her earlier novels. Hassoldt Davis made the following comment: "It would be unfortunate if Pearl Buck's new novel, coming in the wake of the Nobel Prize award to her, were no more successful than the novels of the American scene which she has written in the last several years. In *The Patriot* she has returned to the Orient to present a fictional biography which not only is compelling by its timeliness but is probably the best of her books since *The Good Earth*" (269). Clifton Fadiman also asserted, "One is glad to note that Mrs. Buck has abandoned entirely that pseudo-Biblical style which made some of her books rather difficult going. She possesses, as always, the unlearnable gift of the story-teller, a gift admirable and effective even in this novel, in which the story line and the character development are both so simple that the reader can almost prophesy them for himself" (1939, 74). Forrest Reid found the novel a success, next only to *The Good Earth* and *The Mother.* He commented, "*The Patriot* ... struck me as a sincere and honest piece of work, a little heavy now and then, but well written, and completely free from that blend of melodrama and sensationalism which colors most novels of the East" (684). The reviewer for *Times Literary Supplement* also found Pearl Buck "at her sympathetic best in this story of Chinese nationalism in the making" (201).

On the other hand, critics agreed that some of her American novels after the Nobel Prize were better than *This Proud Heart,* her first novel set in the United States and published in 1938. The *Christian Science Monitor* reviewer made this comment on *This Proud Heart*: "It is all swift and a little frenzied---this development of a genius. ... No, Mrs. Buck cannot safely stoop to the ordinary American novel" (16). J. K. Merton criticized, "The story is skillfully told, so skillfully that one forgets its frequent lack of reality" (556). In comparison, Olga Owens thought *Other Gods*, published two years later, was "the best of her American" novels (1). F. H. Bullock even claimed that "by the critical standards which Somerset Maugham so frequently enunciates it rates A plus; from the first word to the last it entertains!" (4). Another post-Nobel Prize novel, *The Townsman*, was found by most commentators, as mentioned before, to be realistic and convincing.

Besides, critics concurred that Susan Gaylord, the heroine of *This Proud Heart*, did not quite come to life. Having praised the comprehensiveness and dramatic power of the novel in dealing with the feminist theme, Florence Milner regretted, "If one would offer any criticism, it is that too great strain both physically and spiritually has been put upon Susan, more than any one woman could expect to endure, although Susan did" (1). Merton also said in the review cited above that "most of the characters---including Susan herself---are never completely disengaged from the marble." Having conceded the generous and moving moments of the novel, Mark Van Doren remarked,"Susan is not to be believed; or if she is, then creation is a more trifling thing than we ever thought it, and glibness is eloquence" (187). Margaret Wallace expressed the similar opinion: "Few readers will be convinced, on putting this book aside, that Susan's qualities of stubbornness, egotism and naivete are the sole and necessary attributes of greatness" (6). However, critics including J. T. Flanagan and W. S. Lynch considered Jonathan Goodliffe, the hero of *The Townsman*, a well-portrayed character. Paul Doyle assured that he "is well depicted. His motives and feelings make sense; his life, his ideas, and his influence on the life of Median possess the genuine feel of truth" (1980, 115). Burt Holm, the hero of *Other Gods*, was also found to be vivid and lifelike. As Katherine Woods put it: "In the national hero of her novel Pearl Buck has drawn a masterly and original portrait of a creature of impulse and immediacy, a man who cannot grow up---not even when he becomes a god" (1940, 1). If one notices in *This Proud Heart*, as Paul Doyle did: "the lack of poetic beauty, the lack of exquisite descriptions, and the pedestrian nature of writing" (1980, 80), one cannot fail to notice such beauty and magnificence in *Other Gods*, as the reviewer for the *Springfield Republican* did: "When Mrs. Buck is writing about the actual mountain climbing she holds one by the vividness with which she makes the scene stand out, by the beauty of her style and thoughts" (7e). Paul Doyle also acknowledged that *Other Gods* demonstrates "what might be called Buck's American style has improved. It is more mature, more elaborate, and more pliable than that of *This Proud Heart*" (1980, 101).

Moreover, in most critics' opinion, Pearl Buck's autobiography, *My Several Worlds*, compares very well with her Nobel Prize biographies, *The Exile* and *Fighting Angel*. The *New Yorker* reviewer considered *My Several Worlds* as a "rambling, discursive, and thoroughly delightful autobiography, which may well be one of the best books Mrs. Buck has written" (186). The *Kirkus* reviewer also found it "[n]ot only Pearl Buck's most important book, but, on many counts, her best book" (603). Margaret Parton assured, "Those who have read all her books may feel that *My Several Worlds* is her finest achievement. Those who have not can take it as the rich autumnal flowering of a varied and sensitive mind whose roots are in the common soil of all humanity" (17). Edgar Snow said, "It is an absorbing narrative told with warmth and humor and insight, often as moving as her best novels, with the easy grace and integrity notable in her biographies of her missionary parents. Written in modesty and humility, the book faithfully mirrors the mind and heart and strength of a truly admirable and distinguished American" (426). E. D. Canham made the following evaluation of the autobiography: "If any book can build a bridge of understanding between Asia and America in these urgent times, this is it. For Pearl Buck shows us with her incomparable vividness and accuracy the growth of modern China, its deeply grounded mistrust for the West, but the opportunity the United States has to escape from present misunderstandings back into the old friendship" (5). Thus, when the reviews and criticism of Pearl Buck's autobiography, *My Several Worlds*, and novels including *The Patriot, Other Gods,* and *The Townsman* are examined and compared with those of her Nobel Prize biographies and novels other than *The Good Earth, The Mother,* it is not true to say, even according to the critical receptions, that she went downhill consistently after the award.

Why, then, does Pearl Buck have such a low position in American literature now? Why is she seldom studied on the college level? Why is she not even included in *The Heath Anthology of American Literature,* which does include a few stories on Chinese American themes? To say simply she was a woman would not answer the questions completely, for women writers including Emily Dickinson, Edith Wharton, Gertrude Stein, Willa Cather, and Ellen Glasgow are often studied in American universities. To blame the resentment on her Nobel Prize would not be quite fair either, for such an easy assumption could never be fully proved, and certainly not every critic resented her. The reasons for her present low status, I believe, lie in the fact that she did not develop with the contemporary literary movement; her style was too straightforward and informative; she wrote too much; she wrote mainly about China, which was a minor Other; few scholars had the authority to judge her novels, and those who had were affected by their nationalism or communist ideology; besides, she was not Chinese, and so she slipped away from the traditional classification.

The mainstream of the 20th-century American literature began to change dramatically in theory and in form after World War I. The spiritual unrest and skepticism deeply rooted in some English Victorians including Matthew Arnold and Thomas Hardy prevailed over the optimistic idealism represented by the works of Charles Dickens and were transmitted into the United States by such writers as William James, George Santayana, Henry Adams, Hamlin Garland, and Theodore Dreiser. Dostoevski, Chekhov, and Turgenev rather than Tolstoy among the Russians, and Flaubert, Balzac, and Zola rather than Hugo among the French began to inspire modern American writers, who also esteemed their own Poe, Melville, and Twain more highly than Irving, Cooper, or Longfellow. Not only did romanticism become a mere genteel survival in the United States. Realism and even naturalism were also giving way to modernism. The transition signified a painful loss of the faith in God, ideals about social systems, the meaning of the universe, and confidence in human goodness, and it demonstrated modern man's anguish and despair at such loss. From romanticism to modernism literature has traveled not a circle, but a spiral, and as far as man's position is concerned, it is a spiral upside down. Man has not come back to the same spot but to the spot lower than where he started. It is true that both romanticism and modernism emphasize man, the individual, and self, but they regard man differently. Romanticism is a literary theory that tends to see man at the center of universe; it places the individual at the center of art; it makes one's unique feelings and particular attitudes the most valuable materials of literature; and it values one's experiences, no matter how fragmentary they may be, more than it values the unity of literary forms. The romanticists are interested in transcending the immediate to find the ideal, and their protagonists are always persons with uncommon ability, intellect, or sensibility. Even though they are not necessarily prince and princess, they are literally heroes and heroines or spiritual aristocrats.

Realism takes the first step down from such a high position of man in literature. It tries to be, in William Dean Howells's words, "nothing more and nothing less than the truthful treatment of material" (73). Man and everything else are equally represented realistically. This mimetic theory of art, however, does not advocate making a mere copy of life but an artistic copy of life. Since selection is a necessary part of art, which aspect of life to be selected is the key for realists. Generally speaking, they believe in pragmatism and democracy. So they are unusually interested in the effect of their work on the audience and society. They center their attention on the immediate, here and now, the specific action, and the verifiable consequences. Their democratic attitudes often make them value the individual, and characterization is still the center of the novel. Yet the protagonists are more often than not from bourgeois or middle class, neither uncommon nor very common.

Naturalism as a literary response to the revolution in thought that science has produced tends to emphasize either a biological or a socioeconomic determinism, and it strives to be as objective as possible in presenting materials, as amoral as possible in viewing the struggles of human beings among themselves or with nature. It neither condemns nor praises human beings for actions beyond their control, but it tries to test the hypotheses of the author about the nature and operation of the forces that work on human beings. They are, therefore, no more than other experimental objects studied by scientists. Thus naturalists try to examine the actual or superficial to find the scientific laws that control actions. Their protagonists are often ordinary people, if not proletarians.

Modernism, in many respects, is a reaction against realism and naturalism, as well as the scientific postulates on which they rest. It revels in a dense and often unordered actuality as opposed to the pragmatic, systematic, and scientific world of realism or naturalism. It again elevates the individual over the social, and it emphasizes the inward over the outward, but it is not a return to romanticism. It does not posit man at the center of the universe, nor does it study the relationship between man and the universe, but it practices the solipsism that the individual creates the world in the act of perceiving it. Such perception is not the same as the romanticist's meditation or the naturalist's rationality, both of which give man, at least the authors, much importance. Modernism prefers the unconscious or subconscious to the self-conscious. Thus man is seen and represented more like other animals---selfish, aimless, impulsive, and instinctive. The modernist's protagonist is always an anti-hero or anti-heroine, isolated or alienated, weak, sick, idiotic, or maniac. What man is most proud of, our civilization, is also rejected by modernists. They reject not only history but also the society that has fabricated the historical records. They reject traditional values as well as the rhetoric by which such values have been sanctioned and communicated. Therefore, Europe, the most advanced continent of the world, was depicted as a wasteland, where the sun rose and set caring not about the human sufferings. America, the most developed part of the new world, was revealed as fair without and foul within. Tragedies were performed on this side of paradise, satires were aimed at the standardized mediocrity of the small towns and villages, and repudiations were made of the meaningless mechanism of capitalistic America by looking backward to the past. The naturalistic and modernistic novels of social protest and satire by Dreiser, Sinclair Lewis, Dos Passos, Fitzgerald, Hemingway, and Faulkner manifested the breakup of formerly sustaining values. Every Victorian political, moral, and aesthetic code was being examined and criticized.

Pearl Buck did not join this mainstream. Her novels are basically realistic with some romantic tinge except for *The Good Earth* and *The Mother*, which are naturalistic to some extent. She was always hopeful, as she said at the end of her autobiography, *My Several Worlds*: "In spite of dismaying contradictions in individuals in our national scene, I feel the controlling spirit of our people, generous, decent and sane. In this mood of faith and hope my work goes on. A ream of fresh paper lies on my desk waiting for the next book, I am a writer and I take up my pen to write" (407). She had reasons to be so hopeful: China's progress, her phenomenal success, the achievements of the New Deal, and the victory of World War II. She never experienced the disillusionment shared by her peer American intellectuals during and after World War I. She did not see the national extravagances, corruptions, and social decadence of the Jazz Age. Nor had she lived through the notorious scandals of the Harding administration, the era of violence, terror, and moral delinquency with organized crime thriving on the violation of the unpopular prohibition laws and the venality of officials. What she learned about the West was her parents' "shining memories of America," which, in Dody W. Thompson's words, "were passed intact, enshrined and polished like a fly in amber, to their children in a strange land" (89). She grew up in China and was raised by her Presbyterian missionary parents, who were so devoted to the work that they chose to live among the Chinese rather than in the foreign compound. Her education was partly Christian, mainly given by her mother, and partly Confucian, taught by Mr. Kung, her Chinese tutor. Both of the cultures believe in human goodness and hold it true that progress is possible through the improvement of human nature rather than the improvement of social systems. Her education was more concerned with morality and the propriety of human behavior than with natural and social sciences. Her living in China did not give her any sense of the Western superiority and confidence in the material prosperity, which were hard not to acquire for the Westerners who lived with the benefits of science, technology, imperial exploitation, and capitalistic production. Thus, when World War I and America's domestic corruption and irresponsibility broke the faith and ideals of many intellectuals like Faulkner and Hemingway, she was not touched in the same way.

Pearl Buck's mold, as Dody W. Thompson put it, "was irrevocably set a generation behind what would have been her normal one. If later she exchanged the rickshaw for jet planes, if the deep peace of her childhood gave way to revolution, and she both read and traveled widely, her deepest roots nevertheless were locked away in time, as she herself had been in space" (89). She herself clearly admitted in *My Several Worlds*, "I somehow got the notion of incredible perfection in America, and I grew up misinformed" (63). We find no belief crisis at all in her autobiography. Instead, she said that even in 1932 she did not understand the "American culture, compelled by scientific discovery and invention to move so rapidly from a pioneer stage to high industrialism, was violently shaken by the First World War" (270). It is true that she was in the United States attending Randolph-Macon Woman's College from 1910 to 1914, but as she said in *My Several Worlds*, "I had had no home during college and thus I had never become a part of the American scene" (271). She was not lost because she had never been led to the black forest. Her novels do not deal with the kind of spiritual agony found in most Western modernist literature. The problems that concerned her were different from those that concerned other American writers, and she almost always dealt with the problems optimistically. Therefore, her fiction is considered by modern critics "too simple for adults in our effete and complex age." Thompson continued, "Such work is then convincing only to the young, which is to say the unsophisticated of any age, who are credulous, and, like all primitive beings, more open to illusion than the worldly. Only a Candide can believe Pangloss, and events teach him not to" (108-109). The lack of modernism makes her fiction a preferable choice compared with the works of Dreiser, T. S. Eliot, O'Neill, or Faulkner for high school students whose youthful hope has not yet been eroded by experience, and they can easily share her optimistic idealism and the firm belief in human goodness and in the rational means to improve the world.

Living on the turbulent yellow land of China for the first half of her life, Pearl Buck, of course, also saw and experienced much hardship, misery and even near deaths, but they were of a different nature. They were primarily toil in the field, struggle in poverty, fights against natural disasters, escape from wars and riots, humiliation in sexual and racial discrimination, defense of state sovereignty and national identity. These were the problems that she tackled in her books. Obviously she regarded these problems as much more urgent and essential than spiritual agony. In *A House Divided*, she portrayed Sheng as a pathetic figure who imitated modern Western poets. Definitely she considered the problem of survival and recovery from wars much more important than belles lettres for China. When she described, in *Kinfolk*, the grand party of the Dialectic Society in Shanghai right after World War II, she mentioned that the rich American patroness was talking with the members about whether Robert Browning's work improved or deteriorated after his marriage to Elizabeth Barrett. Dr. James Liang, the protagonist of the novel, "longed to cry out at them, 'Do you really discuss such things---even here, even now?'" (56). In a sense, Pearl Buck was indeed more like a modern Chinese writer than a modern American one. She belonged to none of the three groups of her contemporary American writers: expatriates who were publishing little magazines in Europe; rebels against the village who were producing satires in Cambridge, New Haven, and Greenwich Village; or seekers of a tradition of order who were writing Agrarian poetry, criticism, and novels in the South. Her work has few concerns or characteristics in common with any of theirs. Nor did she develop her literary interest, attitude, and method along with these movements when she came back to the United States to settle down in 1934.

Pearl Buck's realism is Victorian and is affected by the Chinese storytelling tradition. She recalled in *My Several Worlds* that she had read the high Victorians and especially Dickens, whose novels she went through once a year for nine years in her youth. She said "he had his usual influence, and this is always to stir alive the young imagination and create wonder about human beings" (75). She was also immersed in the indigenous Chinese novel and storytelling. She dug up as many stories from her Chinese amah, friends, and neighbors as she could, read all the Chinese novels that she laid hands on, and benefited a great deal from her four years' efforts of translating one of the four classical Chinese novels, *Shui Hu Chuan*. When she became famous with the success of *The Good Earth*, she gave speeches in Shih Nai-an's words in the prelude of *Shui Hu Chuan*. In Stockholm she delivered her Nobel Prize lecture titled "The Chinese Novel." The Chinese novel she talked about embodies an idiom much older than the objective realism of the 19th-century Western literature. It is more like the folk-telling tradition, the Homeric tales, and Icelandic sagas. The literary traditions that she inherited favor fast-moving action, simplicity of style and vocabulary, and characterization by the character's own action and words rather than by the author's explanation. The point of view is always the omniscient third, which she constantly used in her fiction. She advocated these in her Nobel Prize lecture on the Chinese novel: "the story teller ... found that the style which they [the people] loved best was one which flowed along, clearly and simply, in the short words which they themselves used every day, with no other technique than occasional bits of description, only enough to give vividness to a place or a person, and never enough to delay the story. Nothing must delay the story" (qtd. in Harris 1969, 223). The result of such traditions is the horizontal novel about the external world.

However, modern literature in the West had been changing this traditional novel paradigm into "a more vertical and static one of depth exploration, in which the only actuality, as in *The Trial*, was apt to be subjective and the surface action so subordinated that vast novels, like *Ulysses*, could take place within the confines of one day even while encompassing a life" (Thompson 98-99). The author's imposition had become an essential part in the portrayal of characters as seen in all of Henry James. The modernist writers were more interested in the internal world, and they were experimenting with new methods including stream of consciousness to explore the inner growth of their characters, the spiritual nature of man, and the value of his society and institutions. The limited third or the first person point of view was often adopted to facilitate the studies of the internal world. French naturalism is mingled with primitivism in Faulkner's novels, with Freudian elements in Jeffers's poetry and O'Neill's plays, since primitivism, often supported by the premises of Freudian psychology, assumes that basic truths of human behavior are best observed where conditions are least inhibited by refinements or sophistication. These writers all went further into the psychological probing of the spiritual personality and moved toward intellectual depth or brilliance. High art parted ways with popular art. Serious novels, however great, were increasingly less likely to become best-sellers. Gone were the days of Defoe and Dickens, or Hawnthorne and Mark Twain when people who had a few extra shillings or dimes would go to get the masterpieces. Dime novels were gaining ground in American readership, but a novel that sold well often suggested mediocrity. The damage of commercialism to art and literature was looming larger and larger.

Pearl Buck was either unaware of these changes or deliberately went against the tide. In her Nobel Prize lecture she made this statement of her literary position:

And for the novelist the only element is human life as he finds it in himself or outside himself. The sole test of his work is whether or not his energy is producing more of that life. Are his creatures alive? That is the only question. And who can tell him? Who but those living human beings, the people? ... Like the Chinese novelists, I have been taught to want to write for these people. If they are reading their magazines by the million, then I want my stories there rather than in magazines read only by a few. For story belongs to the people. They are sounder judges of it than anyone else, for their senses are unspoiled and their emotions are free. No, a novelist must not think of pure literature as his goal. ... He is a story teller in a village tent and by his stories he entices people into his tent. He need not raise his voice when a scholar passes. But he must beat all his drums when a band of poor pilgrims pass. ... To them he must cry, "I, too, tell of gods!" And to farmers he must talk of their land, and to old men he must speak of peace, and to old women he must tell of their children and to young men and women he must speak of each other. He must be satisfied if the common people hear him gladly. (qtd. in Harris 1969, 237-38)

This statement clearly reflects the influence she received from China's New Culture Movement, which advocated, among other things, the use of the Chinese vernacular and opposed the use of classic Chinese. It was truly a great cultural revolution comparable with Martin Luther's translation of the Bible and William Wordsworth's breakaway from the neoclassic bondage put together. The living literature that Pearl Buck mentioned is primarily the folk songs, ballads, stories, and novels written in the Chinese vernacular including *Shui Hu Chuan*. The dead literature is primarily classic poems, Confucian doctrines, imperially sanctioned histories, Buddhist scriptures, philosophies, the discourses of and commentaries to these works, all written in Classical Chinese, which is comparable to Latin, if the Chinese vernacular is compared to the European vernaculars. Therefore, it was a kind of anachronism to apply the revolutionary position of China's New Culture Movement to modern Western literature, whose question was not whether to use the vernacular any more, but how to use it; whose question was not how to popularize any more, but how to be perfected artistically. Besides, to educate the masses was a matter of life or death for China especially in the first half of this century, and so the books were meant to be understood by as many people as possible, but in the United States what artists hated most was to lower the level of their works in order to sell more copies and to meet the needs of capitalist commercialization. No wonder her position was not accepted by modern American writers and critics.

It might be due to this position that Pearl Buck never tried to experiment with new novel forms. All her novels set in Asian countries have the omniscient third person point of view. Every one of them covers hundreds of, if not thousands of miles, and spans at least two, and often three generations. Story, as she emphasized, or rather, plot, always seems to be the priority in her novels, whereas very little exploration of the characters' psychology can be seen in any of them. The influence of her life in China and the New Culture Movement was so strong that her college majors, psychology and philosophy, do not emerge prominently in her literary creation, nor do her graduate studies of English literature at Cornell show much impact. It is not hard to imagine that neuroses were not a major problem in China when the majority of its people were struggling hard to feed themselves as the Americans did during the Great Depression, when China was fighting against imperialistic aggressions to maintain its ancient civilization, or when the Chinese were resisting the Japanese invasion to survive as an independent nation. It is not hard to imagine that Freudian psychoanalysis and its application in literature should be quite different in China, where the racial unconscious and the collective subconscious are not the same as those in the West. In China, for example, original sin is an unknown concept to most people. The Confucian, Taoist, Buddhist, and naturalistic attitudes toward sex and sexual taboos are all different from the Christian and somewhat different from each other. Moreover, the core of the Freudian psychology, I believe, is not sex, but guilt, often caused by unduly sexual desires. In China, or any other totalitarian country, it is often the guilt caused by political taboos and the wrongs in the political movements that lead to the victims' neuroses. Pearl Buck's American education probably could not help her very much in writing about Chinese themes.

Pearl Buck's style has as much to do with her purpose as with her Bible reading and the Chinese influence. As she said in *My Several Worlds*, she wrote to promote understanding between the East and West. So she often explained things in her novels, always tried to make everything oriental as clear as possible for the Western readers. No myths or mysteries, no fate or supernatural forces, no ambiguities or obscure allusions are found in her books, although all these elements are very rich in traditional Chinese literature and she, as a well read and learned scholar of the tradition, must have been fully aware of them. But like many Chinese writers of the New Culture Movement, she broke with the tradition, and moreover, it was her intention and mission to serve as a cultural expositor. Her style is, therefore, always straightforward, her novels always contain some unmistakable messages, and her message is always plain and simple. Truth is never hidden in her work, or in other words, her works lack sophistication and suggestive power and are often found by critics to be didactic. Modern literature, however, cherishes just the opposite: ambiguities, archetypes, allusiveness, conceits or the combination of intellect and images, defamiliarization, eccentricities, erudition, mystery, novelty and strangeness, obscurities and profundities. "A poem," as Archibald MacLeish said in *Ars Poetica*, "should not mean." In other words, literary language should not be so communicative as everyday language or indicative as a science language. Pearl Buck was out of tune with modern literature and was naturally not taken seriously by modern critics. Her identification with people and popular art kept her away from scholars and academics. Jason Lindsay meant to praise her when he stated, "It cannot be said of her (as it can be, for example, of William Faulkner) that her work is rich in contradictions. It is straight-forward, one-tracked, single-purposed. Pearl Buck is the least ambiguous of any major contemporary writer. Anybody on earth can read and understand Pearl Buck" (27-28). But these qualities are just the weaknesses that most critics found in her novels. Different standards result in different evaluations. Lindsay's criteria indicate that he was anything but modern. No wonder he complained, "Her efforts in behalf of communication have caused certain undiscerning critics to describe her as a simple writer" (28).

It is also undeniable that some of Pearl Buck's novels are mediocre by any standard. They are slipshod as a result of her over-prolificness. She turned out on average a book a year, and sometimes, two or even three books a year. In 1942, she wrote *Dragon Seed* and *China Gold*. In 1945, she published *China Flight, Portrait of a Marriage,* and *The Townsman*. In 1949, she published

Kinfolk, American Argument, and *The Long Love.* In 1952, she wrote *The Bright Procession* and *The Hidden Flower.* In 1953, she wrote *Voices in the House* and *Come, My Beloved.* And in addition, she produced many short stories and nonfiction pamphlets and essays throughout these years. It would take a great genius to make so many writings in so little time all high quality products. Some of her novels lack reality or imagination, and many characters are types. On *Portrait of a Marriage* L. S. Munn commented, "The novel is vitiated by the substitution of logy sentimentality for earthy reality, and all achieved is a pedestrian tome devoid of vigor and truth" (4d). On *The Hidden Flower* H. R. Forbes commented,"Though the descriptions of Japanese landscape and customs are interesting, the characters are not presented with enough force to arouse our sympathy" (1952, 894). All the John Sedges novels are, as Paul Doyle put it, "characterized by the good man as hero: the solid citizen, the loyal husband; the decent, upright individual" (1980, 117), such as Jonathan Goodliffe in *The Townsman,* Edward Haslatt in *The Long Love,* Stephen Worth in *The Bright Procession,* and William Asher in *Voices in the House.* Her weaker works like some of these have disappointed mature readers and reviewers. As a result, in Peter Conn's words, she "has been victimized by a kind of aesthetic Gresham's Law" (3).

Besides, China has been an unimportant Other to the United States and there was little contact between the two countries from 1949 to 1978. Consequently, Pearl Buck, who was primarily a writer about China, slipped away from the national attention of the Americans. If we look at the canon of American literature, we find among the non-American themes works about Europe, scenes set in Europe, conflicts with Europe, nearly everything related to Europe alone. The cultural root of American literature is basically in Europe. Almost no works of Asian, African, or Australian themes are regarded as masterpieces. Eurocentralism has dominated American academics until recent years. The critics just did not know where to place Pearl Buck. Actually, they did not know where to place any writers who wrote about neither American nor European themes. Moreover, China, a big country as it is, has been weak for the last 150 years or so. It has much less commercial, cultural, military, and political contact with the United States than Japan does. Lafcadio Hearn gets more academic attention than Pearl Buck (he has twenty-one items in *MLA Bibliography* in the last ten years while she has only twelve) not so much because he wrote better than she did, or he knew Japan, which is the subject of his writings, better than she knew China, as because Japan has been economically more powerful than China. The United States cannot afford to neglect Japan, including its culture, as much as it neglects China. If time used to help Pearl Buck succeed in the sense that Americans could easily identify with Chinese who were struggling with poverty and destitution just as they were during the Great Depression, and who had been fighting the same enemy that attacked Pearl Harbor in World War II, the more recent history, however, was adverse to her works. After 1949 when the United States "lost" China, so to speak, mainland China had no diplomatic relationship with the United States for nearly thirty years. Especially since the Korean War when the two country became enemies, they even had very little unofficial contact in all those years. Had China been more powerful, it would have been better studied as an enemy. During the Cold War, the Soviet Union was America's main concern, and so, the "China Hand" and her works were neglected along with China as a whole.

Even if Pearl Buck should be studied, who would be able to conduct the studies? It must be someone who knows both the Western and Chinese cultures very well, who understands both American and Chinese peoples, and who has a good command of both English and Chinese. Without the knowledge, one cannot discern the importance of her selection of certain customs such as Wang Lung's tolerance of his lazy and troublesome uncle living under the same roof, one cannot see the authenticity of certain details such as the mother's delay to buy medicine for her daughter's eyes in *The Mother*, and one cannot appreciate her speech presentation in English of the way Chinese people speak in their native language, which is always grammatically correct and has no short forms such as "There're" and "I'm gonna rock 'n roll." Qualified scholars are few in this country, and they work in the fields of anthropology, economics, geography, history, linguistics, philosophy, politics, and sociology rather than American literature. When Jason Lindsay expressed the indignation: "They [American critics] would like to erase her name from the list of American writers and give her to the Asians" (29), he did not consider the practical difficulties.

Those who are engaged in the comparative studies of Chinese and American literatures are too few to patronize Pearl Buck. Besides, the scholars who dominate the field, including Professor Chih-Tsing Hsia of Columbia University, grew up in China when it was oppressed by the Powers, when there was a park in Shanghai that forbade the admission of dogs and Chinese, and when the Nationalist government and the intellectuals were building up Chinese nationalism, which was clearly reflected in the critical responses to *The Good Earth* as mentioned earlier. Their nationalism was also seen in the request made by the Chinese youths studying in Columbia University that Pearl Buck should not publish the Chinese classical novel, *Shui Hu Chuan,* which she had just translated, because it contains cannibalism.[6] She politely declined their request, but they were not pleased and were afraid that Western readers would think the Chinese uncivilized. It is not surprising that scholars with such strong nationalism would later ignore her works, which often mirrored China objectively, good and bad alike. The withdrawal of the Nationalist officials from her Nobel Prize presentation represented the standpoint of these Chinese patriots who could not tolerate any criticism or unfavorable truth-revealing of their beloved country despite the kind intention. The withdrawal heralded a long-term neglect of her in China, Taiwan, and among the Chinese American scholars in the United States.

Not only were the Chinese scholars who followed their government dissatisfied with Pearl Buck, but so also were those who strongly criticized the government all the time. Lu Hsun (Lu Xun), China's greatest man of letters in this century, was undoubtedly the representative of such scholars. Whenever Pearl Buck mentioned Lu Hsun in writings or interviews, she expressed concerns and admiration for him. She introduced him and his works to the American readers through the magazine *Asia* that she and her husband Richard Walsh edited. Lu Hsun, however, was unfair when he mentioned her. In his letter to Yao Ker on 15 November 1933, he gave the following opinion, which became well known among Chinese scholars:

It is always better for Chinese to write about Chinese subject matters, as that is the only way to get close to the truth. It is no exception even with someone like Mrs. Buck, who was warmly welcomed in Shanghai, and who regards China as her own motherland. Her books, after all, reveal no more than the position of an American woman missionary who happens to have grown up in China. It is not surprising that she should praise such a book as *The House of Exile*, for what she knows about China is but superficial. Only when we Chinese begin to do it, can some truth be revealed.[7]

As we can see, Lu Hsun's dismissal of Pearl Buck was goaded by national pride, which was a natural reaction to the international oppression that China had experienced by then. Under such circumstances, a fair evaluation of her works by Chinese scholars would be hard to make, as E. M. Forster said at the end of *A Passage to India*, "No, not yet, ... No, not there." Years later, a Japanese Sinologist wrote to Lu Hsun challenging the views expressed by Hu Feng's critical essay on *The Good Earth*. Lu Hsun replied to him on 15 September 1936, "I will pass onto Hu Feng your letter about *The Good Earth*. The translation of Hu Zhongchih may not be very reliable. If that were the case, it would be unfair to the author of the original text" (qtd. in Yao 41). But there was no more said of her work either by Hu Feng or Lu Hsun. Haiping Liu regretted, not without good reason, "Unfortunately, the Japanese scholar's letter has been lost, and Lu Xun gave the matter no further thought. Had he done so, the great weight of his influence in China both before and since 1949 might have ensured Pearl Buck a very different reception" (63).

During the Cold War period of Sino-American hostility [1949-1973], Chinese criticism of Pearl Buck's books, as Haiping Liu analyzed, was the product of the ideological struggle and one-sided opinion under the influence of the Soviet model and the Chinese Communist Party. Negative critical articles include Gao Junqian's translation from Russian to Chinese, "Pearl Buck: An Old China Hand Gone Bankrupt," Xu Yuxin's "Pearl Buck: A Vanguard of U.S. Imperialist Cultural Aggression," Li Wenjun's "Pearl S. Buck: An Anatomy of the Reactionary American Writer," and Shi Mo's "The Curse of an Owl---A Critique of Pearl S. Buck's *Letter from Peking*." None of them discussed the artistic value of her books nor mentioned her work "on behalf of China's war of resistance against Japan, ... her help for such writers and artists as Lao Sher, Cao Yu, and Wang Yin, her part in publishing excerpts from Edgar Snow's pro-Communist *The Red Star over China* in *Asia* magazine, or her contributions through her numerous books toward correcting Westerners' distorted image of the Chinese" (H. Liu 65). These articles are politically partial and have done much injustice to her and her books.

Furthermore, Pearl Buck was, after all, an American, and so, when the representative works of Chinese-Americans were selected or anthologized, she was ineligible for consideration. For instance, *The Heath Anthology of American Literature* is now the most multicultural collection, and one of the editors is Professor Amy Ling, whose specialty is multi-ethnic literature in the United States and Chinamerican literature. She selected works on Chinese themes by Edith Maud Eaton [1865-1914], Maxine Hong Kingston [b. 1940], Amy Tan [b. 1952], Gish Jen [b. 1955], Cathy Song [b. 1955], and David Henry Hwang [b. 1957] among others. Pearl Buck would bridge the chronological gap between Eaton and Kingston nicely, but Pearl Buck was not anthologized, not because her works have less artistic value than theirs, but because she had no Chinese blood. In the traditional classification of literature by nationality and race she was again an outsider, as she was when living in China, when attending Randolph-Macon Woman's College, and when settling down in the United States. An excerpt of Younghill Kang's *East Goes West* is included in the anthology, and in the headnote, Elaine H. Kim mentioned that Kang once commented that "it was his great misfortune that Pearl Buck's Pulitzer Prize-winning novel about China, *The Good Earth*, was published in the same year as *The Great Roof*, eclipsing his own tale of Asia" (1949). If Kang could live to see Ling's selection, he would sigh, "Such is the fate of an outsider!"

NOTES

1. See page 109 of Paul Doyle's *Pearl S. Buck*. A passage is quoted from *Dragon Seed* to demonstrate that it is "not far from the tone and manner of *A Farewell to Arms.*"

2. It is really strange that she should judge so. See George A. Cevasco's essay "Pearl Buck's Best Books" in *Notes on Modern American Literature* Summer 1981: 5 (3), item 19.

3. Even among those who defended Pearl Buck, some assumed that the Swedish Academy was thinking of only *The Good Earth*, as Henry Seidel Canby put it in *Saturday Review of Literature* on 11 November 1938: "[The Nobel Committee] must be crowning one book, a masterpiece which richly deserves exalted recognition ... a unique book, and in all probability belongs among the permanent contributions to world literature of our times" (24).

4. See the *New York Times*. 24 December 1938: 13. The translations of the citation are often slightly different. The word "genuine" instead of "generous" appears in most of later quotations.

5. Pearl Buck's first response to the news that she had won the Nobel Prize was not to believe it, thinking it was a practical joke the reporters played on her. After a verifying phone call to Stockholm, she said the prize should have gone to Theodore Dreiser. See *New York Times*, 11 Nov. 1938: 1 or *My Several Worlds*, 77.

6. See *My Several Worlds*, p. 283.

7. This is quoted from Hsih-pei Yao's essay, "What Pearl Buck Said about Lu Xun," *Lu Xun Monthly* 6, 1990. The translation is mine. *The House of Exile* by Nora Waln was published by Little, Brown and Co. in 1933. Pearl Buck wrote a blurb for the novel.

3

A SINGLE-HANDED CRUSADER

The image of the Chinese people in the American mind had been anything but pleasant for almost a century before 1931. The earliest use of the derogatory term "Chinaman" was found in Ralph Waldo Emerson's *Letters and Social Aims* in 1854: "The disgust of California has not been able to drive nor kick the Chinaman back to the home" (*OED*). Later the insulting singular form "Chinee" arose in vulgar use also in the United States and was first used in the written form by Bret Harte in his comic ballad, "The Heathen Chinee" in 1871 (*OED*). The use of these terms reflected the general attitude of the American people toward the Chinese in the United States as well as the writers' attitudes. Americans' prejudice and hostility against the Chinese were even institutionalized in 1882 when the "Chinese Exclusion Act" was passed. Labor competition was the main reason why Americans disliked the Chinese. Cultural differences and the lack of communication and understanding between the two cultures caused the prejudice. Travelers' tales, popular fiction, and the words of some scholars and men of letters strengthened such dislike and prejudice and created the American image of the Chinese as mean, barbaric, and vicious. Pearl Buck played a singularly important role in promoting Americans' understanding of China and the Chinese. Her works considerably improved the image of the Chinese in the American mind. Consequently, the improvement helped to repeal the "Chinese Exclusion Act" in 1943, to arouse Americans' sympathy for the Chinese who were suffering from Japan's aggression, and to win America's support to China, which had been fighting the Japanese invaders alone for years.

To Americans, China was the ultimate Other. The first thing they learned about China was probably that it would be found at the other side of the globe if one could drill a hole through the earth. Things there seemed to be just opposite as when it is daytime here, it is night there. Their pens were soft but their pillows were hard. Their first names are their family names. The Chinese seemed to do everything the other way around. They shook their own hands when greeting others. It was always "Gentleman first" never "Lady first" among them. Chinese women bound their feet rather than their waists. Men had queues and women wore trousers. They purchased coffins while they were still alive. They wore white, not black, at a funeral. Sweets were served first and soup last at a formal dinner. The Chinese drank hot water rather than cold water. They wrote up and down the page from right to left. They respected the old much more than they admired the young. They worshiped many gods rather than one God and actually, they did not revere any god as much as they cared about the spirits of their dead ancestors.

Beyond these superficial observations were the travelers' tales and writings of the traders, diplomats, missionaries, and scholars, who at first exaggerated the Chinese civilization as Marco Polo had done and then went to the other extreme. If the dominant American attitudes toward the Chinese characterized the 18th century as the "Age of Respect" as Harold Isaacs decided (71), then the Opium War between China and Britain in 1840 marked the beginning of the "Age of Contempt," which, in my opinion, lasted till 1937 when China's War of Resistance against Japan began. Between these two ages was a transitional period filled with different opinions about the veiled country.

The earliest American contact with China was commercial, as the Chinese proverb says, "Men are lured by fame and profit to the places so far away that even wild geese cannot reach." It is not surprising that early American traders should exaggerate the riches of the mystic land, for they expected great wealth in the trade. If a country was rich, it was likely that its people were highly civilized and honorable. So we find in the comments of early traders friendly references to hong merchants, as recorded by L. W. Jenkins, for example, Bryant Tilden of Salem regarded Paunkeiqua "worthy of being considered a true 'Celestial' gentleman of the Chinese empire---or any country" (23). Paunkeiqua, whose real name was Wu Ping-chen, was made an honorary member of the Massachusetts Agricultural Society in 1819 (Jenkins 10). The early traders found a high average of fair dealing as William C. Hunter testified in his book, *The "Fan Kwae" at Canton before Treaty Days, 1825-1844*, that all Chinese whom he contacted were "honorable and reliable in all their dealings" (40). And historian Tyler Dennett contended that Hunter's book "embodies the prevailing spirit of the Americans toward the Chinese" (65).

John K. Fairbank observed in *The United States and China*, "American commercial interest in China has always had a large admixture of imagination and hope" (325). Once such hope and imagination were frustrated in the stern reality of an aged kingdom that had been conquered and governed by the Manchus with sword and spear for two centuries, that had not been able to develop its commerce abroad and industry at home, and that had been closed to the Western world and therefore ignorant of other civilizations until Englishmen came with opium and guns, the traders began to complain and report to their countrymen unfavorable things about the Celestial Empire and its people.

Erasmus Doolittle represented the traders' view of the harm China's political system did to the Chinese when he said, "Their government is admirably well adapted to make them hypocrites and knaves" (253). His remark might have identified one of the causes of dishonesty of some Chinese, but other traders emphasized the effects rather than the causes. Edmund Roberts had this to say about the subjects of the Celestial Empire: "The Chinese of the present day are grossly superstitious, ... most depraved and vicious: gambling is universal ... ; they use pernicious drugs, ... are gross gluttons" (152). W.S.W. Ruschenberger, a surgeon who went to China with Roberts, stated that China's excessive population made the Chinese "the most vile, the most cowardly and submissive of slaves" and had led to "baseness and extinction of every moral virtue" (431). Ebenezer Townsend mentioned some incredible swindles, from being sold wooden hams covered with fat and paint to rare birds and flowers with painted feathers and fake petals fixed to stems (93), stories that are so "utterly fantastic" that Stuart C. Miller commented, "One wonders how such ruses could have been very profitable considering the effort they must have required, and their frequency shakes one's faith in the reputation of these Yankee traders for shrewdness" (1969, 30). Nevertheless, the descriptions of these frauds were so widespread that they were even reported in the fourth edition of the *Encyclopaedia Britannica* (6: 36-37).   Many traders mentioned Chinese pusillanimity and even the Great Wall was reduced to "a labor of cowardice inviting attack because it displayed fear," as Doolittle declared (262).   On gambling, W. W. Wood asserted, "This vice prevails among people of every rank in society. Children play at gambling games. People game for purchases" (157-58). Talking about China's static state, Captain Edmund Fanning said, "The Chinese are a peculiar people in this respect and tenaciously adhere to old customs and forms" (22).   The Chinese were actually "hostile to all improvement," Ebenezer Townsend asserted, "If the world were like the Chinese, we should yet have worn fig-leaves" (5: 91).

Strange costumes and customs or habits of some Chinese people, of course, caught the traders' attention and evoked laughter. Erasmus Doolittle thus wrote their first impression:

The first impulse of an American, when he sees for the first time a Chinese, is to laugh at him. His dress, if judged by our standards, is ridiculous, and in a Mandarin, a stately gravity sets it off for a double derision. His trousers are a couple of meal bags ... , his shoes are huge machines, turned up at the toe, his cap is fantastic and his head is shaven except on the crown, whence there hangs down a tuft of hair as long as a spaniel's tail. (259-60)

It was only natural to describe strangers with some exaggeration to amuse the reader, but such amusement could be damaging when it was carried too far, such as the anonymous comic verse recorded by William Hunter:

Mingqua, his host, pressed on each dish
   With polished Chinese grace;

And much, Ming thought, he relished them,
  At every ugly face!

At last he swore he'd eat no more,
  'Twas written in his looks;
For, "Zounds!" said he, "the devil here
  Sends both the meats and the cooks!"

But, covers changed, he brightened up,
  And thought himself in luck
When close before him, what he saw
  Looked something like a duck!

Still cautious grown, but, to be sure,
  His brain he set to rack;
At length he turned to one behind
  And, pointing, cried: "Quack, Quack."

The Chinese gravely shook his head,
  Next made a reverend bow;
And then expressed what dish it was
  By uttering, "Bow-wow-wow!" (41-42)

Although Hunter himself denied that the Chinese ever ate "roast or boiled puppy" (41), who would remember the feeble denial better than the vivid verse? The damage was done as Stuart C. Miller pointed out, "Nothing was more firmly implanted in the American cognitive map of China than these culinary aberrations" (1969, 28).

The early diplomats' books on China were written mainly by Europeans including Aeneas Anderson, Sir George Staunton, Sir John Barrow, Andre Van Braam-Houckgeest, John M'Leod, Sir Henry Ellis, Sir John Davis, and George Timkowski, who claimed to have seen substantial parts of the interior of China. They were so influential in America that articles and books written on China throughout most of the 19th century never failed to cite or recommend them for authority (Miller 1969, 39). In the main, their views paralleled the critical themes and negative opinions of the traders with the exception of Anderson, who attempted to refute every popular charge against China. There were also two American diplomatic accounts written by Edmund Roberts and W.S.W. Ruschenberger, who were sent to Asia by President Jackson in 1832. Their harsh criticism of China was, as Miller said, "instrumental in shaking the confidence of the pro-Chinese editors of the influential *North American Review*" (1969, 54). Although Ruschenberger was well-educated, his criticism reveals partiality and ignorance as seen in this passage about the Chinese:

They are a people who destroy their own tender offsprings; a nation wherein the most infamous crimes are common; ... where the merchant cozens his fellow-citizen and the stranger; where a knowledge of the language is the remotest boundary of science; where a language and a literature, scarcely adequate to the common purpose of life, have remained for ages unimproved; where the guardians of morals are people without honor or probity; where justice is venal to an extent unexampled on the face of the earth; where the great legislator Confucius, so much revered, is unworthy of perusal, unless we excuse the poverty of his writings in consideration of the ignorance of the times in which he lived; where a chain of beings, from the emperor to the lowest vassal, live by preying upon one another. (431)

What upset many Americans even more was China's lack of religion, which they believed was the root of all those evils, for Roberts wrote this about the Chinese: "They are without God in the world, and estranged from the divine life, worshipping the works of their hands, to the disgrace of human reason" (79). This religious indignation distinguished Roberts from the European diplomats, who all "expressed great respect for China's religious toleration and religious indifference" (Miller 1969, 56).

To save the souls of the heathen Chinese, the American Board of Commissioners for Foreign Missions began to send missionaries to China, and their feedback made the gloomy American image of the Chinese even more so. Their first reports to friends and religious publications reflected a kind of shock and horror typical of the provincialists who just arrived in a broad new world, which they believed to be "Satan's empire." The following passage from "The Church and China" that appeared in *Methodist Quarterly Review, XXXII*, represents the religious prejudice and provincialism: "The monster stares us in the face and defies our power. Never before have we so ardently desired that eloquence that moves---the ability to utter those words that burn. It has startled our whole being to find ourselves fresh as we were from the land of Bibles and Sabbaths, and Christians, placed in the midst of these teeming multitudes who neither fear nor know the God whom we love and adore" (593). Some other reports were probably the hearsay that the missionaries preferred to believe or their own imagination out of the conviction of the absolute necessity to convert the helpless heathens. The Reverend Charles Gutzlaff in 1832 reported to *Chinese Repository*, an important missionary publication next only to the *Missionary Herald* at the time, "Girls scarcely twelve years old were given up to the beastly passions of men. Parents prostituted their daughters; husbands their wives; brothers their sisters---and this they did with a diabolic joy" (126). Later, the Reverend R. S. Maclay confirmed this observation that was opposite to most Westerners' descriptions of the Chinese "as exceptionally modest, almost prudish in their dislike for any public display of affection between the sexes" (Miller 1969, 63). He somehow saw licentiousness open and everywhere in China and wrote, "Its corrupting and debasing influences pervade all classes of society. ... Forms of this vice which in other lands sulk in dark places, or appear only in the midnight orgies of the bacchanalian revelers, in China blanch not at the light of noonday; ... this lust finds ready access to the precincts of the family, the forum, and the temple" (136-37).

This kind of subjective conjecture also extended to the issue of infanticide.

If the missionaries did not see the practice, they would cite another as an eyewitness, who actually had never claimed to be. For instance, the Reverend David Abeel wrote of Sir John Barrow: "Some of the scenes he witnessed while at Pekin [sic] were almost incredible. Before the carts go around in the mornings to pick up the bodies of infants thrown in the streets, ... dogs and swine are let loose upon them. The bodies of those found are carried to a common pit without the city walls, in which the living and the dead are thrown together" (134-35). Samuel Wells Williams calculated that up to 40 percent of the female infants were "murdered by their parents" (2: 260), and Abeel suggested that it ran as high as 70 percent (134). Both exceeded the previous estimations made by diplomats. Unlike most other Western reporters on the Chinese scene who blamed China's infanticide on poverty, the missionaries blamed it on paganism, and so, the practice seemed to be common and universal in China, as the Reverend Justice Doolittle argued, not just restricted to the lowest class under extreme circumstances (207).

The missionaries, especially when frustrated in their work, strongly attacked the Chinese language and culture as if they were Satan's instruments. The Reverend Doolittle felt the Chinese language was so perverse that it was impossible to conduct "evangelical truths" in it, and he even declared in exasperation, "*The invention of the Chinese language has been ascribed to the devil,* who endeavored by it to prevent the prevalence of Christianity in a country where he has so many zealous and able subjects" (2: 420). One article in the *Missionary Herald XXIX*, 1833, complained that in Chinese sin was equated with crime, and while "murder, arson and adultery" were considered crimes, "lying, deceit, fornication, gambling, drunkenness, pride and opium smoking" were not. The writer expressed indignant astonishment about the Chinese, who condemn leaving one's country while his parents are still alive but condone fornication "so long as both parties agree" (qtd. in Miller 1969, 70). One wonders if Angelo, the deputy in Shakespeare's *Measure for Measure*, would agree with this judgment. The missionary certainly thought the Chinese way of thinking strange, as the Reverend William Medhurst complained, "Their minds appear to have been cast in a different mould; and their thoughts arranged in a manner peculiar to themselves" (441).

Despite the obviously different appearance of the Chinese legendary animal "lung," it was translated into "dragon" because no better counterpart existed in the Western culture. Since the Chinese used "lung" as their royal symbol, this form of the devil depicted in the Apocalypse suggested to the missionaries an evil alliance with Satan. They declared in a text, *The People of China*, published by the American Sunday School Union, "Surely this great heathen monarch could not have adopted a more expressive device to indicate his allegiance to the 'Prince of the Power of the air' that worketh in the children of disobedience" (73). Of course, some missionaries said some nice things about China and the Chinese. When successful in converting sinners, they expressed their triumphant joy for the simple and primitive people, or otherwise, they conveyed their condescending sympathy for the wretched Celestial as Edmund Roberts had described, but on the whole, they painted the Chinese as the children of Satan, so that their mission appeared to be much needed and needing more support.

If some of the above comments on the Chinese expose prejudice, ignorance, partiality, subjectivity, Eurocentralism, or Christian superiority of the traders, diplomats, and missionaries, who were not in the rank of the most learned men in the United States at the time, then the passages below can demonstrate that even the best educated scholars at that time espoused the same kind of injustice and made statements that helped create the unfavorable American image of the Chinese. Emerson, as Professor Arthur Christy contended in *The Orient in American Transcendentalism*, was much influenced by Asian philosophies, which should include Confucius's ideas about social relationships, but the sage of Concord put the following 1824 entry in *The Journal & Miscellaneous Notebooks*:

The closer contemplation we condescend to bestow, the more disgustful is that booby nation. The Chinese Empire enjoys precisely a Mummy's reputation, that of having preserved to a hair for 3 or 4,000 years the ugliest features in the world. I have no gift to see a meaning in the venerable vegetation of this extraordinary (nation) people. They are tools for other nations to use. Even miserable Africa can say I have hewn the wood and drawn the water to promote the civilization of other lands. But China, reverend dullness! hoary idiot!, all she can say at the convocation of nations must be---"I made the tea." (2: 224)

Had Joseph Needham taken in such prejudice and misinformation expressed in this kind of generalization about China, he would never have compiled the seven volumes of *Science and Civilization in China.*

Samuel G. Goodrich, one of the most influential American geographers in the mid-19th century, wrote scores of geographies, histories, and gazetteers. In *A System of Universal Geography* he thus concluded about the Chinese: "Few nations, it is now agreed, have so little honor, of feeling, or so much duplicity and mendacity. Their affected gravity is as far from wisdom, as their ceremonies are from politeness" (905-906). Later, in *The Tales of Peter Parley about Asia*, he summarized, "The character of the Chinese is by no means an agreeable one. The men are servile, deceitful and utterly regardless of the truth. From the emperor to the beggar through every rank of society, through every grade of office, there is a system of cheating, and hypocrisy, practiced without remorse. ... No faith whatever, can in general, be reposed in the Chinese" (57-58).

By 1840, if there was still some doubt in the United States about the validity of China's evils and backwardness, if there were any lingering idealizations that the Jesuit missionaries made of the Celestial Empire in the 18th century, then the easy victory of the British in the Opium War with China convinced Americans as well as other Westerners that China was the "Sick Man of East Asia," sick in every sense of the word, although many Americans did not support the British. As the contempt for China developed, the unfavorable image of the Chinese in the American mind was proved and catalyzed, so to speak, by history. Then the Taiping Rebellion [1851-1864] started, and since it was led by Hung Hsiu-chuan (Hong Xiuquan), a converted Protestant Christian, it aroused widespread excitement and high expectations in the United States. However, Hung's outrageous pretensions, the blasphemous, fanatic, and superstitious behavior of the rebels and their barbaric killing of innocent people, as the newspapers reported to the West in 1854 (Miller 1969, 119), disappointed the enthusiastic Americans, and their disillusionment with the Taiping confirmed the existing unfavorable American image of the Chinese. Likewise, the Arrow Incident[1] in 1856, the ensuing Anglo-Chinese conflict until 1860, and the Tientsin Massacre in 1870 reported by the mass media all helped Americans to verify the image that the Chinese were heathen barbarians and, in the words of the *New York Times* on 8 October 1872, "incapable of civilization."

Not only did the mass media spread this notion about the Chinese, but scholars were also trying to provide proofs or give interpretations of the social phenomena in China. Edwin R. Meade in a paper read at the annual meeting of the Social Science Association of America offered such a piece of scientific evidence to support the conviction that the Chinese were incapable of civilization: "It is true that ethnologists declare that a brain capacity of less than 85 cubic inches is unfit for free government, which is considerably above that of the coolie as it is below the Caucasian" (17). With the coming of the Chinese immigrants to California in the gold rush, this kind of prejudice turned into hostility.

When the Taiping Rebellion made the poor Chinese peasants even poorer, the news that gold had been discovered at Sutter's Mill in California traveled to China. Soon many Chinese joined the fortune hunters from all over the world and made their way to San Francisco. The Chinese miners, concluded the congressional report prepared in March 1871 by Rossiter W. Raymond, the United States commissioner, enjoyed "universal reputation of conscientious fidelity," were "equal to those of any other race," and the Chinese labor would "come to be valued in this country not because of its cheapness, but because of its excellence" (Boutwell 6). The Chinese immigrants did not just work in gold mines, but as Franklin Tuthill informed us in *History of California*, they "brought in timber to build houses on land they reclaimed. They opened up the vineyards and rich farmlands. ... Many of them also pioneered in fishing businesses or worked in the wool and clothing industries." Besides, Tuthill continued, "They added dignity and discipline, order and wealth to a frontier land that when they came was not yet a state, not yet a community of law and order. They helped to link it with the rest of the continent and so make possible its great settlement. ... The cleanliness, politeness and good behavior of the Chinese was on everybody's mouth and what they contributed saved several counties from bankruptcy" (qtd. in Chen 117). As William Heintz acknowledged in the introduction to *The Chinese in California: A Brief Bibliographic History*, "The Chinese in California have contributed as much as, if not more than, any other single race to the State's early economic development and played a strong, vital role in the formative stages of many of California's major industries" (qtd. in Chen 108).

However, in this land of the free, the Chinese met with hostility and racial discrimination from white workers and local governments as soon as they came. "In the goldfields," Claire Jones wrote, "Chinese miners were robbed, beaten, and cheated. Miners of many other nationalities received similar treatment, but the Chinese were often picked on as a group. Their experiences in the goldfields gave rise to the expression 'not a Chinaman's chance.' In the 1850s and 1860s, someone who didn't even have 'a Chinaman's chance' for success in an undertaking was certainly doomed to failure" (39). From *The Shasta Republican* (California), Jack Chen dug out an entry of 18 December 1856: "Hundreds of Chinamen have been slaughtered in cold blood in the last five years by the desperadoes that infest our state. The murder of Chinamen was of almost daily occurrence" (127). Chen particularly mentioned these anti-Chinese violent riots and agitation: the continuation of the Tuolumne riot and the May 1852 county resolution banning Chinese from mining there, "an example followed in Marysville with the expulsion of 400 Chinese from Horseshoe Bar and another 300 from the North Fork of the American River," the attempt of 150 white workers in Folsom to drive 200 Chinese from their homes and to take over the claims they worked for the Natoma Ditch Company in 1858, the 1866 San Francisco riot of white workers that attacked the Chinese, leaving one dead and fifteen injured. "But up to 1870 this violence was sporadic. In 1870, it became a co-ordinated, sustained campaign" (137).

The discrimination took the form of expulsion, confiscatory taxes, and other legal obstructions. Jack Chen listed, among other, the following California local and state anti-Chinese legislations:

1852	Miners in Roster, Atchinson's Bar, Columbia, and other camps exclude Chinese from mining.
1852	Bond Act requires all arriving Chinese to post a $500 bond.
1854	California Supreme Court decision makes Chinese ineligible to testify in court against whites.
1855	A $50 head tax is levied on "aliens not eligible for naturalization." (The Chinese were singled out to be ineligible.)
1855	Head tax requires shippers to pay $50 for every Chinese passenger they bring to America.
1860	Chinese children are denied admission to general public schools. After 1866, they were allowed to attend if white parents did not object. Chinese are denied admission to San Francisco City Hospital.
1860	A Fishing tax is levied on Chinese activities in fishing.
1870	San Francisco prohibits hiring of Chinese on municipal works. City ordinance bans use of Chinese carrying-pole for peddling vegetables.

1870	Chinese are prohibited from owning land in the state.
1873	San Francisco taxes laundries $15 per quarter of a year for using poles to carry laundry, while the tax on horse-drawn vehicles is $2 a quarter.
1875	San Francisco Anti-Queue Law orders shaving off queues of all Chinese arrested.
1879	California state constitution prohibits corporations and municipal works from hiring Chinese and authorizes cities to remove Chinese residents from their boundaries to specified areas.
1880	Fishing Act prohibits Chinese from engaging in any fishing business. Act to Prevent the Issuance of Licenses to Aliens deprives Chinese of licenses for business or occupations. (137-39)

The anti-Chinese legislation was not limited to only the state of California. Shin-shan Henry Tsai gave these examples:

The Oregon Constitutional Convention in August, 1857, ruled that Chinese should not be allowed to own mining claims or land. Two years later, when Oregon achieved statehood, its legislature levied a $5 poll tax on every Chinese. In 1864, Washington Territory passed an act designed to disfranchise the Chinese in the mining field. A special quarterly capitation tax of $6, called the "Chinese Police Tax," was levied on every "Mongolian" in the territory. The sheriff in each county was responsible for collecting the tax and was entitled to keep 25 percent of the money he collected. Moreover, if there were disputes between whites and Chinese, the latter were prohibited from giving testimony in the courts. In Montana, Nevada, and Idaho, similar discriminations were imposed on the Chinese, while the California legislature, beginning in 1852, passed a series of laws against the Chinese miners. ... Most of these acts were later declared unconstitutional by state or federal courts. (13-14)

Thus, the discrimination and hostility started first from the grass roots, then, as Mary R. Coolidge argued throughout her *Chinese Immigration*, wily and demagogic politicians and legislators acted, in order to win the support of the working classes. The anti-Chinese hostilities resulted not only from labor competitions and economic considerations, but they were also, as Stuart C. Miller elaborated in the conclusion of *The Unwelcomed Immigrant*, a part of the general xenophobia of Protestant Americans, who believed that "Mongolian" blood was debased, that the Chinese mind was politically retarded, and that further Chinese immigration would threaten Caucasian dominance in America.

We should bear in mind that the early Chinese immigrants in the United States were not illegal. At the time of the Gold Rush, America and particularly California, Arizona, and New Mexico, which were ceded to the United States in 1848 as a result of Mexican War, welcomed immigrants from all over the world as long as they came on their free will. In February 1862, the U.S. Congress passed the Prohibition of Coolie Trade Act, but the Chinese laborers were not coolies by definition. The term "coolie" had connotations of servitude, slavery, or peonage and was used loosely in the United States to designate all Chinese immigrants. "But however restricted the rights of early Chinese immigrants in the United States may have been," Professor Shih-shan Henry Tsai contended, "the term coolie is an inaccurate name for them" (6), because they were voluntary contract laborers. Moreover, the 1868 Supplementary Article to the Sino-American Treaty of Tianjin, better known in the United States as the Burlinghame Treaty, repeated the American principle of free immigration. Article V of the treaty stipulated: "The United States of America and the Emperor of China cordially recognize the inherent and inalienable right of man to change his home and allegiance, and also the mutual advantage of the free migration and emigration of their citizens and subjects respectively from one country to the other for the purpose of curiosity, of trade, or as permanent residents" (Bevans 682). It was primarily the prejudice against the Chinese, their racial and cultural differences, and the competition among laborers especially during the financial and economic crisis of the "terrible seventies" that caused the anti-Chinese hostilities.

The early Chinese immigrants themselves were also responsible to a certain extent for their unfavorable position. They did not try very hard to assimilate since more than half of all the Chinese immigrants before 1882 returned to China within a few years, as Claire Jones reported (30). This was also the main reason why they kept their queues, which were the pledge of loyalty to the Manchu emperor. Without queues they could be beheaded when they returned. Many of the Chinese did not even learn how to speak English, which was, of course, much more difficult for them to learn than for European immigrants because Chinese belongs to a totally different language family. Unlike most other immigrants who arrived committed to a new life in the United States, they tried to preserve their old way of life by huddling together in Chinatowns. Since so many of them wanted to go back and could not express themselves well, the Chinese appeared to be uncomplaining, withdrawing, apolitical, and passive. They could compete with Irish and German immigrants, two other major labor forces along the West Coast then, only by being willing to do harder work or to take lower wages. In fact, only in building the transcontinental railroad did the Chinese have little competition with white workers, for the work was so hard that just one in ten white workers stayed on the job (Jones 34).

After the railroad was completed in 1869, however, 25,000 men, most of them Chinese, lost their jobs (Jones 36), and the goldfields were worked out at about the same time. While more immigrants kept pouring onto the West Coast, competition for jobs became increasingly intense, and so did the anti-Chinese hostilities. Denis Kearney, ringleader of terrorism in San Francisco and head of the Workingman's Party, "specialized in fiery speeches denouncing the Chinese as enemies of American workers. Roused by the slogan 'The Chinese must go, his mobs ransacked Chinatown, where 116,000 Chinese people lived in fear" (Jones 40). Many Chinese were murdered, driven out of small towns of California, and their houses and business premises were set on fire and gutted. Furthermore, Stuart C. Miller stated, "The most prominent labor spokesmen of the time---George McNeil, John Swinton, John P. Irish, T. V. Powderly, Samuel Gompers, Eugene Debs, Henry George, and William J. McLaughlin---were outspoken sinophobes." Their speeches incited the anti-Chinese agitations, and so did the mass media. Miller continued, "Virtually every labor newspaper and organization opposed Chinese immigration after 1870" (1969, 196), despite the fact that the Chinese never presented any threat. At the peak of their immigration, they numbered about one percent of California's population.

Since "the Chinese arrived during the middle of the slavery controversy and were never able to shake the 'coolie' label" (Miller 1969, 146), some politicians propagated the fear that the Chinese immigration was instituting a new form of slavery at the time when Black slavery had been just abolished. This was one of their arguments in the Chinese exclusion debate. The Chinese, Miller further pointed out, "also arrived during the period when the work of Holmes, Lister, and Semmelweis made Americans more conscious of the relationship between dirt and disease. ... The period between 1850 and 1882 was also one in which a pseudo-scientific rationale for modern racism developed" (1969, 146). The racist terms like "Chinese germs" popularized and became another argument for excluding the Chinese. Although one of the reasons of Chinese railroad workers' achievement despite the hard conditions was their healthy habit as Claire Jones described, "The Chinese bathed each night after work and changed into clean clothes before supper, customs which amazed their white fellow workers" (36), many Americans were so ingrained with the prejudice of filthy Chinese that one New York tourist in California found it hard to believe the immaculate appearance of Chinese immigrants: "They seem to come out of their filth as the eel from his skin, with a personal cleanliness that is marvelous, and to most, incredible" (Bowman 279).

Under such anti-Chinese circumstances, the popular fiction of some writers also distorted and derogated the Chinese and their culture. The novel *Almond-Eyed: The Great Agitator; a Story of the Day* [1878] by Atwell Whitney is an apologue about the conflicts between the Chinese and white workers in California. The Chinese are presented as a group with little individual characterization. Their heathenism is so solid that the special religious classes have no effect on them whatsoever. They remain brutal savages as the altercation Job Stearns witnesses in Chinatown among three of its people illustrates: "The two Chinamen had the woman pressed to the floor, and one of them was engaged in the elevating, Christianizing operation of decapitating her with a pick handle" (31). The Chinese are fierce competitors and they "can do anything. They follow our hard-working people close on their heels, steal their trades, cheapen labor, and then sit down to a dinner of rice and potato sprouts, such as a hearty white would starve on" (72). The Chinese are shown as filthy, unhealthy, and immoral people. Their slum is a noxious hilltop with a stream of refuse rolling down toward Aristocracy Street. They gamble, have smallpox, and smoke opium. Their sins are far beneath those of white men's as Whitney narrated: "Our immorality is out of reach of the young; theirs is of a different stamp, cheap---easily indulged in and unhedged by any remains of horror and conscientious scruples. Ours is hidden in gilded temples at whose doors one must knock and pay to enter; theirs is an open pool of filth in whose putrid waters the child may dabble his feet" (29). The conflicts eventually result in the unemployed white workers' riot, in which both Chinatown and the factories are burned. The owner Simon Spud leaves town, and the laborer Job Stearns stays to manage the new factories being built. They will employ only white workers, but Chinatown is also being rebuilt. Whitney concluded: "The stream of heathen men and women still comes pouring in, filling the places which should be occupied by the Caucasian race, poisoning the moral atmosphere, tainting society, undermining the free institutions of the country, degrading labor, and resisting quietly, but wisely and successfully, all efforts to remove them, or prevent their coming. Good people, what shall be done?" (168).

The rhetorical question, of course, needed no answering. It was a call to exclude Chinese immigrants. If Whitney's novel appealed mainly to the American working class and did not make enough impact among the better educated readers, Pierton W. Dooner demonstrated to them America's doom as a result of admitting the Chinese in his 1880 novel *Last Days of the Republic*. This is an apologue of the Yellow Peril. It describes Chinese immigration as a conscious maneuver toward final conquest of America and accuses the Chinese government of conducting the infiltration through the six companies in California. Dooner's Chinese characters, like Whitney's, are also portrayed as a group rather than individuals, but they are presented as a monolithic mass with a common ambition and they appear very efficient, "for it is their enterprise, their thrift, their industry---in short, their virtues, that have made them invincible and insupportable, and not the exercise of any degrading or vicious habit" (102). The apparent difference from Whitney's description is not to give the Chinese any credit but to warn Americans of the threatening danger from the deceitful Chinese. The novel illustrates that the Chinese infiltration can be so successful that they even control the state governments of California, Nevada, and Oregon, where the white working class opposes them in vain.

In contrast, the influx of Chinese laborers described in the novel is welcomed by the aristocracy of the South on account of the perceived racial and national characteristics they possess:

Compared with the Pacific Coast States, the progress of the Coolie throughout the whole territory known as the Slave States, might be said to have made without any obstacle worthy of the name. The inhabitants were delighted with them as a substitute for the negroes ... they could not have provided themselves with a model more suitable... than... the Coolie. He was so eminently stupid in great things, and so quick and keen in small; so obedient, so cunning, so ignorant, so unassuming, and so servile, that the Southern land-owners once more imagined themselves the masters of a race of slaves, ---but this time willing slaves---and a prospect of permanence to the institution. (130)

For the same reason, the Chinese are welcomed in New England to work in the big factories. Once naturalized, however, the Chinese begin their military conquest and the United States is doomed.

This paranoia of the Yellow Peril was echoed by Robert Woltor's *A Short and Truthful History of the Taking of Oregon and California by the Chinese in the Year A. D. 1899*, which is actually a novel published in 1882 that purports to be a history written at the turn of the century. Woltor's Chinese characters are even less individual than those of his predecessors; only Prince Tsa is more significant than others. He is the leader of the invasion and when "he stated his object and purpose, Prince Tsa bore less resemblance to a human being than he did to Milton's Satan" (58). The invasion is described as twofold. On the one hand, the Chinese act in automatic concert without visible leaders or organizations to move around and to push white workers out with their willingness to take lower wages for harder jobs under harsher working conditions. On the other hand, the Manchu government builds up its military forces and becomes a world maritime power by 1899. Then the invasion begins and the Chinese Americans rise throughout the cities along the West Coast as a fifth column. Woltor added two qualities to the Chinese characteristics:

Our enemy, moreover, possess two great elements becoming the most sanguinary warfare, which may well be the envy of warmer-blooded races, namely a stoic indifference to pain, which makes them fearless to deeds of blood, and a certain coolness in moments of excitement and danger, when calmness is invaluable. The Caucasian shudders at the sight of blood---the Mongolian, though his life blood oozes out, at sight of the vital fluid becomes stoic. Did they but possess the proper dash in action, with able leaders no troops on earth could stand on the same parallel, as warriors. Fortunately, "dash" is a natural gift of the Caucasian, and the Mongolian character cannot acquire it. (77)

At the end of the novel, the Chinese are victorious in Oregon and California and they even threaten the rest of America. This novel was written at the time when China had received numerous defeats since the Opium War, and European powers had forced one unequal treaty after another upon China and carved away their spheres of influence and extraterritoriality from the Chinese government. The message is never to relax vigilance and never to give Chinamen a single chance.

Indeed, the Chinese did not have any chance at all. On 6 May 1882, President Arthur signed into law the slightly revised bill introduced by Senator John F. Miller, Republican of California. The main provisions of the Exclusion Act of 1882 were to suspend the entry of Chinese laborers to the United States for ten years, State and Federal courts were forbidden to naturalize Chinese, and the term "Chinese laborers" was to include both the skilled and unskilled.[2] The "Chinese Exclusion Act" brazenly tore up the Burlinghame Treaty. "For Chinese Americans, the Exclusion Act of 1882 has become their ethnic Pearl Harbor," stated Shih-shan Henry Tsai. "But as infamous as the act was, it was only the first of a series of increasingly stringent laws against the Chinese" in 1892 (65). In spite of the negotiations of the Ching (Qing) government and the protest of the Chinese Americans, the Act was renewed for another ten years and several new provisions were added including the denial of bail to Chinese in habeas corpus proceedings. Moreover, the law was enforced so sternly that Dr. Poon Chew Ng wrote in 1908, "The exclusion law has been carried out with such vigor that it has almost become an extermination law" (1). According to the U.S. Bureau of Census, between 1880 and 1920 the Chinese population of the United States dropped from 105,465 to 61,639 (35). A decrease by a total of 43,826 was one of the results of the exclusion laws. Even President Theodore Roosevelt admitted in the Annual Address to Congress, 1905, "In the effort to carry out the policy of excluding Chinese laborers ... grave injustice and wrongs have been done by the nation to the people of China and, therefore, ultimately to this nation itself" (qtd. in Chen 194). Although some American congressmen and senators opposed the racist act and laws, the "Chinese Exclusion Act" was extended and reenacted again and again until its repeal in December 1943.

Shih-shan Henry Tsai attested in *The Chinese Experience in America*, "That the Chinese Exclusion Act was racially motivated is no longer seriously doubted by scholars" (65). It marked, as Stuart C. Miller acknowledged, "the first departure from our official policy of open, laissez-faire immigration to be made on ethnocultural grounds" (1969, 3). It was a mockery of the words written by Emma Lazarus and carved on the Statue of Liberty: "Bring me your tired, your poor, your huddled masses yearning to breathe free." It would have been difficult for the American people to accept such a departure psychologically, had not some writers justified the change by fictionalizing the necessity. Some popular fictioneers served this role best.

Besides the three novels mentioned above, two magazines in San Francisco, the *Overland Monthly* [1868-75, 1883-1935] and the *Californian* [1880-82] were chiefly responsible for the strengthening and continuation of the unfavorable American image of the Chinese by consistently publishing short fiction with Chinese characters as protagonists. The first editor of the *Overland* was Bret Harte who wrote the popular narrative poem, "Plain Language from Truthful James," better known as "The Heathen Chinee." The poem satirizes the white miners Truthful James and Bill Nye who try but fail to cheat the Chinese Ah Sin at cards. Although Harte took advantage of the growing anti-Chinese attitudes, he was not particularly racist, considering the poem as a whole and his other works. Most contributors to the magazines, however, were much more racially biased against the Chinese than Harte. Four stories, "The Battle of Wabash" [1880] by someone named only Lorelle, "The Sacking of Grubbville" [1892] by Adah F. Batelle, "The Year 1899" [1893] by William W. Crane, and "The Revelation" [1911] by R. P. Pearsall deal with Chinese invasions of the United States and bear strong resemblance to the three novels. The Chinese in these stories appear as a mob that is easily led, uncaring of human life, and diabolically clever. Other stories such as "The Dramatic in My Destiny" [1880] by Emma F. Dawson and "Chung's Baby" [1898] by Phil More present all the Chinese as dealers and users of opium and suggest the danger of being contaminated, should any white Americans befriend the Chinese. Most stories---including "Thoroughbred" [1895] by Frank Norris, "Baxter's Beat" [1910] by G. Emmerson Sears, "Ah Foo, the Fortune Teller" [1915] by Marian Allen, and "The Provocation of Ah Sing" [1922] by Gordon Grant---are about the crimes, mysterious activities, dark ways, and vain tricks of the Chinese. Such stories reinforce the notion that the Chinese are inscrutable, untrustworthy, and given to violence.

The two magazines also published some stories---such as "The Haunted Valley" [1871] by Ambrose Bierce; "The Chinese Ishmael" [1899] by Edith M. Eaton, otherwise known as Sui Sin Far, the earliest outstanding American writer with Chinese ancestry; "The Winning of Josephine Chang" [1920] by James Hanson---that deal with romantic love and are not anti-Chinese, but other love stories, especially those that involve miscegenation like "After Strange Gods" [1894] by Frank Norris, "The Canton Shawl" [1914] by Hazel H. Havermale, "Ah Choo" [1920] by Esther B. Bock, and "Sweet Burning Incense" [1921] by Jeanette Dailey indicate uncleanliness, disease, impropriety, and danger of the interracial marriage between the Chinese and white Americans. Only the stories that have Chinese immigrants as domestic servants to white Americans are close to reality, probably because the close association helped them get to know each other well, but it was a reality in which the Chinese were socially and economically controlled and therefore posed no threats to the white. In these stories, including "Sing Kee's Chinese Lili" [1897] by Mary Bell, "Ah Gin" [1907] by Eunice Ward, and "Sang" [1917] by Lucy F. Lindsay, the Chinese are portrayed, in spite of the condescending attitude, as loyal, efficient family servants and poor, sympathetic characters. However, these stories are few and they were overshadowed by those that depict the Chinese as invaders, revengers, smugglers, gamblers, and opium smokers with dark ways and vain tricks, or at best as comic figures who look silly, speak broken English, act cowardly, and are always penny-pinching.

Not so systematically some stories, novelettes, and novels were written about the Chinese in American Chinatowns, and like the works mentioned above, most of these writings did more harm than good to the American image of the Chinese. William Norr's *Stories of Chinatown: Sketches from Life in the Chinese Colony of Mott, Pell and Doyers Street* [1892] contains six stories about the relationships between white women and Chinese men. The author intended to illuminate evils of the Chinatown by these muckraking stories and to illustrate, as he said, "how young and comely women can cast their lot with the repulsive Chinese" (4). All the Chinese in these stories are gamblers and opium dealers who contaminate young white women with liquor, drugs, and immorality. Robert W. Chambers, one of the most popular writers from the mid-1890s to 1930, wrote a novelette "The Maker of Moons" [1896], again an allegory of Chinese invasion, but it has two new elements, the mysterious but immense personal power of an old Chinese man Yue-Laou and the use of grotesque beasts as a threat to America. Both of these elements would be fully developed in Sax

Rohmer's novels of Fu Manchu a decade later. Dr. C. W. Doyle's *The Shadow of Quong Lung* [1900] is a composite novel of five stories related through the crime lord Quong Lung, who is also a graduate of Yale and a barrister of London's Inner Temple. Doyle's Chinatown in San Francisco is full of criminal activities and inhabited exclusively by sly, cruel, and ruthless people except for one couple, Ho Chung and his wife. I cannot deny all he wrote, as those crimes were indeed acknowledged symptoms of the ghetto economy, but his selection of what to write is biased and without any balancing positive qualities. His attitude is clearly expressed in the preface: "Of course the best thing to do with Chinatown would be to burn it down; but the scheme is too Utopian to be discussed in a mere preface" (7). Moreover, Dr. C. W. Doyle also created a prototype of Fu Manchu as Chambers did. The Chinese in Jack London's two stories "White and Yellow" and "Yellow Handkerchief" from his collection *Tales of the Fish Patrol* [1905] are wild and nasty villains among the shrimp catchers. Their violent tendencies were described as racial traits, which manifest themselves much more threateningly in his story "The Unparalleled Invasion" [1906], another fantasy of the Yellow Peril.

The fantasy stories about American Chinatowns and the inassimilable Chinese developed in Frances A. Mathew's *The Flame Dance* [1908], Lemuel de Bra's *Ways That Are Wary* [1925], and Hugh Wiley's *Manchu Blood* [1927], but nothing compared with the novels of Fu Manchu and Charlie Chan in American popular culture about the Chinese before Pearl Buck. Although Sax Rohmer, the author of Fu Manchu, was English, "[m]illions of copies of his books have been sold in the United States, signaling a popularity that has led to adaptations in film, radio, television, and comics" making Fu Manchu one of the most influential figures of the fictional Chinese. The "image of Fu Manchu has been absorbed into American consciousness as the archetypal Asian villain" in American popular culture (W. Wu 164). Therefore, we must consider him in the discussion of the American image of the Chinese. Rohmer wrote thirteen novels, three short stories, and one novelette about Fu Manchu, and the first three novels *The Insidious Dr. Fu-Manchu* [1913], *The Return of Fu-Manchu* (1916), and *The Hand of Fu-Manchu* (1917) constitute a unit and are the most popular of his works. The character's name, as William F. Wu noted, was hyphenated only in the first three novels. The theme of these novels is that "Asian hordes are on the verge of sweeping through Europe and North America with only a few British heroes opposing them" (W. Wu 168). Fu Manchu is introduced as follows:

Imagine a person, tall, lean and feline, high-shouldered, with a brow like Shakespeare and a face like Satan, a close-shaven skull, and long, magnetic eyes of true cat-green. Invest him with all the cruel cunning of an entire Eastern race, accumulated in one giant intellect, with all the resources, if you will, of a wealthy government which, however, already has denied all knowledge of his existence. Imagine that awful being, and you have a mental picture of Dr. Fu-Manchu, the yellow peril incarnate in one man. (Rohmer 1913, 17)

This archenemy possesses mysteriously lethal powers and is capable of weird, complex, and original assassination techniques using a scorpion, an adder, belled mice, an Abyssinian half-man, half-baboon with the intelligence of a man and the strength and agility of an ape, the "flower of silence" that produces poison to affect the tongue, and so on and so forth. As William F. Wu pointed out, "Fu Manchu fills a power vacuum that had existed in the tales of Chinese immigration and infiltration; with his presence as "the yellow peril incarnate," the evils of Chinatown are seen as a clearly intelligent malevolence rather than as either a random one, or an inevitable one" (174).

The detective Charlie Chan, on the other hand, embodies all the good qualities of the Chinese: faithful, good-humored, well-mannered, submissive, intelligent, and as cool as a cucumber all the time---qualities that might be seen in the Chinese domestic servants. He was created by Earl Derr Biggers, who defined the character of the detective in three mysteries: *The House without a Key* [1925], *The Chinese Parrot* [1926], and *Behind That Curtain* [1928]. His other three Charlie Chan novels, *The Black Camel* [1929], *Charlie Chan Carries on* [1930], and *Keeper of the Keys* [1932] just give more stories. Although Biggers died in 1933, Charlie Chan was popularized "through a total of forty-seven serial and feature films produced during the 1930s and 1940s" (Chin 1). Fu Manchu and Charlie Chan seem to "represent the yin-yang symbol of Taoism that illustrates a dualist interpretation of the universe" But Charlie Chan is a Chinese Hawaiian whose assertiveness, sexuality, and variety of emotions are all eliminated by the author. This self-effacing figure's subservient behavior to white Americans indicates that he has been, in a sense, domesticated. As William F. Wu contended, "These two characters do not represent archetypal dualities such as good and evil, or even crime versus law. The duality they represent is racial, yellow versus white, with Fu Manchu embodying yellow power and Charlie Chan supporting white supremacy" (164).

The American image of the Chinese was thus formed by the reports of the traders, diplomats, and missionaries, by the comments and books of some scholars and politicians, and by the mass media, speeches of some politicians, and the fiction of popular writers. It is not my task to argue how truthfully the image mirrored the real Chinese people back then, but to demonstrate how and why the image was going, generally speaking, from bad to worse. My task is also to provide the background against which Pearl Buck wrote her early books, so that their historicity can be seen.

When the image of the Chinese people was so unpleasant, most American people naturally would not like them. Professor Shih-shan Henry Tsai recorded, "In 1927, social scientist Emory S. Bogardus surveyed 1,725 Americans and found only 27 percent who said they would accept Chinese as fellow workers, 15.9 percent as neighbors, and 11.8 percent as friends." In 1948, however, "E. Elmo Roper reported that 85.8 percent of the whites then surveyed said they would accept Chinese as fellow workers, 72 percent as neighbors, and 77 percent as friends or guests" (xi-xii). What made the change? The fact that Japan attacked Pearl Harbor and the United States and China became wartime allies certainly helped as Tsai suggested, but we should remember that the United States and China were also allies during World War I, but the U. S. government appeased Japan in the Peace Conference at Versailles in 1919 by letting Japan take over the German concession in Shandong province of China.   The American image of the Chinese was not improved to any perceivable degree by China's war effort including sending two hundred thousand laborers to France to dig trenches. China's economic growth, many scholars assumed, must have helped to bring about the change of its image. This factor was not the only one, nor the most decisive one, for Chinese industry developed most quickly between 1912 and 1920 when its annual growth rate, as John K. Fairbank mentioned in *China: A New History*, was 13.8 percent (270). Moreover, after World War II, China's economy was in a mess, and prices, Fairbank told us in the same book, "rose 85,000 times in six months" in 1948 (334). China was actually torn apart by its civil war at the time the survey was conducted. The change of the general American attitude toward the Chinese, I believe, had more to do with a dramatic improvement of the American image of the Chinese and a better understanding between the two nations. Pearl Buck played a singularly important role in the improvement and understanding.

The indication of the first survey was also seen in Pearl Buck's early publishing experiences. Her manuscript of *East Wind: West Wind* had been rejected by many American publishers before the John Day Company "decided to plump for it" (Day 309). Even *The Good Earth* was rejected by one publisher, who would ruefully tell the story of how the wrong decision was made "on the old ground that people did not want to read about China" (Day 310). This judgment was representative of most Westerners in the beginning of 1930s; as Lewis Gannett said, "Nobody thought a book on China would sell until Pearl Buck did one" (qtd. in Day 312). The popularity of Fu Manchu novels before *The Good Earth* did not prove otherwise because they were about the West and the Chinese in the West. Pearl Buck wrote a novel about genuine Chinese peasants and farmers in China to describe so realistically how they lived, how they loved, how they toiled, how they thrived, how they suffered, and how they endured that for the first time in history the majority of Western readers saw the majority of the Chinese as they were. *The Good Earth* broke down many of the racial prejudices and thus improved the American image of the Chinese.

The Good Earth was originally given the title *Wang Lung*, the protagonist's name, but at the publisher's suggestion, the title was changed (Harris 1969, 138). After all, the name would not have any meaning to most English readers. The significance of the name is suggested in a natural and hidden way in chapter 17, when Wang Lung has greatly increased his lands and yet often feels shame for his illiteracy in a grain shop,

he must say humbly to the haughty dealers in the town,

"Sir, and will you read it for me, for I am too stupid."
And it was a shame to him that when he must set his name to the contract another, even a paltry clerk, lifted his eyebrows in scorn and, with his brush pointed on the wet ink block, brushed hastily the character of Wang Lung's name; and greatest shame that when the man called out for a joke,
"Is it the dragon character Lung or the deaf character Lung, or what?" Wang Lung must answer humbly,
"Let it be what you will, for I am too ignorant to know my own name."

The dragon character Lung in Chinese is a complex one with seventeen strokes and the deaf character Lung is even more complex with an ear radical of six strokes under the dragon character. Of course, nobody would use the deaf character Lung as his name, but it is impossible for Wang Lung to tell the written difference of these homonyms, and so he has to swallow the humiliation. This episode contrasts sharply with another one in chapter 22, when Wang Lung has been able to afford his son some education.

Now there is a pride a man has when he sees his eldest son reading aloud the letters upon a paper and putting the brush and ink to paper and writing that which may be read by others, and this pride Wang Lung now had. He stood proudly and saw this happen and he would not laugh when the clerks, who had scorned him before, now cried out,
"Pretty characters the lad makes and he is a clever one!"
No, Wang Lung would not pretend it was anything out of the common that he had a son like this, although when the lad said sharply as he read, "Here is a letter that has the wood radical when it should have the water radical," Wang Lung's heart was fit to burst with pride, so that he was compelled to turn aside and cough and spit upon the floor to save himself. And when a murmur of surprise ran among the clerks at his son's wisdom he called out merely,
"Change it, then! We will not put our name to anything wrongly written."

These two episodes illustrate how Pearl Buck made Wang Lung alive in the novel. They also reflect that China, as an ancient civilization, highly values book knowledge and the knowledge of its language. No matter how rich a man is, he can be humiliated if he does not read and write, and some people, lowly as they are, will not hesitate to do the humiliating. Unlike the upstart in Molière's *Le Bourgeois Gentilhomme* who imitates the manners of aristocrats, that Wang Lung takes pride in his son's literacy is not ridiculous but natural.

Moreover, the readers who did not know Chinese by now should get the meaning of Wang Lung's name. Even though they might not know that "Wang" means "king," it makes little difference, for, like the English surname King, Wang is just a family name for people of all ranks and classes. What matters is that "Lung" is an expedient term for dragon, as mentioned before. This Wang Dragon is portrayed as anything but evil despite what the name might suggest to some Christian readers. Like any other ordinary human beings, he also has weaknesses. When he becomes rich by hard work and the jewels O-lan has given to him, he takes a concubine Lotus and ignores his wife, though she is well provided for. That is the worst thing he has done in his life. It is wrong but nobody would say Wang Lung is a devil because of it. Actually he is portrayed as common folk, a man who is honest, hard-working, vulnerable, and adamantly attached to the land. He is so believable that any farmer in any country can identify with him. The vicissitude of his life is so real and attractive that readers are soon absorbed in his fate and strife forgetting all the racial and cultural differences. As Mitchell Kennerly said, "After the first few pages I forgot that I was reading about Chinese men and women. ... It was as though I was living with these men and women, different from us only in the clothes they wear and the land they live in" (qtd. in Harris 1969, 194). And as the *Book-of-the-Month Club News* commented on the novel, "The People in this rather thrilling story are not 'queer' or 'exotic,' they are natural as their soil. They are so intensely human that after the first chapter we are more interested in their humanity than in the novelties of belief and habit" (qtd. in Harris 1969, 194). The people portrayed in *The Good Earth* "were not just Chinese," Paul Doyle commented, "they were representative of farming people the world over. They were universal in their struggle, in their joys, in their disappointments. This quality was immediately recognized by readers of the novel" (1980, 30). By the time readers have reached chapter 17, Wang Lung is so familiar to them that few, if any, would ever associate him with a Satanic monster despite the meaning of his name. Readers do not necessarily love or like Wang Lung but certainly understand him and are likely to sympathize with him, who dreams of prosperity, struggles to achieve his goal, endures hardships, enjoys a little bit of good luck, helps his neighbors and relatives, becomes rich, buys lands, indulges in lust, loses his peace of mind, faces domestic troubles and the danger of selling lands by his sons. Wang Lung is thus a typical farmer who lives in the circle of life on the seemingly timeless land of China, where people like to regard themselves as the "Offspring of Lung." He has no high ideals, nor does he have devilish intentions. He is just an ordinary man who "runs the whole gamut of human emotions" as best summarized by Paul Doyle in the following passage:

He can be gauche and timid, as on the first visit to the House of Hwang to claim his bride; he can be stubborn and resolute, as in his determination to buy more land; he can be servile and pusillanimous when he learns that his uncle is a member of the robber band; he can be tender and gentle to his mentally retarded daughter and to his child concubine Pear Blossom; he can be a complete fool in the hands of certain women, as in his first overwhelming passion for Lotus; he can be incredibly inconsiderate and unfeeling as when he deprives O-lan of her two cherished pearls; he can be snobbish and hard-hearted in his attitude toward the squatters in the outer courtyards of the House of Hwang; he can be crafty and calculating in his gift of opium to his uncle and the latter's wife; he can be idle and restless; he can be dedicated and industrious; he can in his old age seek only comfort and quiet, and humor his sons too much. In these and in other ways he becomes a complex and many-sided figure; and, although he is dominated by a ruling passion for the land, he is above all a human being with all the whims, emotions, quirks, inconsistencies, contradictions, and variable attitudes that make up a living individual. (1980, 35-36)

He is thus more like a "brother of a dragon" in Robert Penn Warren's sense than a descendant of a dragon in the Christian belief. His wife O-lan, a "sister of a dragon," is portrayed as an even more respectable and sympathetic figure. It was a challenging job for Pearl Buck because this heroine is required to be plain, not so repulsively ugly as the deformation of Hugo's romantic Quasimodo, but plain enough in a realistic world for everyone to ignore her. We first see her in chapter 1, where she is presented to Wang Lung to be taken home and to be married.

She had a square honest face, a short, broad nose with large black nostrils, and her mouth was wide as a gash in her face. Her eyes were small and of a dull black in color, and were filled with some sadness that was not clearly expressed. It was a face that seemed habitually silent and unspeaking, as though it could not speak if it would. She bore patiently Wang Lung's look, without embarrassment or response, simply waiting until he had seen her. He saw that it was true there was not beauty of any kind in her face---a brown, common, patient face.

No beauty, no coquetry, no romance, no sentimentality, no virtues of an "angel in the house," yet O-lan gradually wins readers' respect and sympathy with her strength, endurance, devotion, indefatigability, and passive resistance against unfair treatments. Besides cooking meals, cleaning the house, taking care of children and Wang Lung's father, she works side by side with her husband in the field, even after she has just given birth to a baby, as did the American women who went to open up the West with their men. She gives birth to babies and cleans up the mess all by herself. She takes up the knife when Wang Lung has decided to kill the ox during the famine but cannot do it himself. Ordinarily she is always silent, but when the villagers are driven by hunger to rob Wang Lung who actually has no food left either, it is O-lan who comes forward and speaks in her plain, slow voice to shame them and stop them from taking away the furniture. She tries every way to find edible things and always eats last. Yet, she is no saint but a practical woman. In the southern city, she teaches her children how to beg for food. When her second son has stolen a piece of pork and Wang Lung is angry throwing the meat on the ground and shouting, "Beggars we may be but thieves we are not!" she picks it up and says quietly, "Meat is meat" (chap. 12). She also joins the looters and gets the rich man's jewels.

Like most Chinese women in the past, O-lan is completely devoted to her husband and family. When Wang Lung decides to sell the jewels, she gives them all, except two small white pearls, to her husband so that the family is able to prosper more quickly. She obeys her husband completely even when Wang Lung asks for the two pearls to give to his new love, but she is not a woman without any will and personality. She insists on dressing her firstborn in finery and making special cakes so that she can go to the big House of Hwang to walk with pride before those who have looked down on her before. She decides that Wang Lung must marry Lotus so that he will be satisfied and all their silver will not be wasted in the tea house. She also protests the presence of Cuckoo in her house, Lotus's serving woman, who has been cruel and critical to her in the House of Hwang. Her passive resistance against Lotus and Cuckoo protects her family, and she triumphs in the end over her rivals. Thus, her value is not skin-deep like the beauty of many female fictional figures, but it lies deep in her ability to survive all sorts of hardship and adversity. In contrast with Lotus whose only skill is to please or enchant men, O-lan possesses valuable qualities of a human being disregarding sex. Those qualities are too often neglected in life as well as in art because sexual stereotypes have blinded most of us. Yet, people like Wang Lung and O-lan could be seen everywhere in China. They are the best realized Chinese farmers in English and have not been surpassed by the creation of any other writer. By her genuine portrayal of these ordinary Chinese people Pearl Buck bridged the cultural gap between Americans and the "Offspring of Lung," in Dorothy Canfield's words, "as if they were cousins and neighbors" (qtd. in Harris 1969, 194). If it is true, as E. M. Foster said, that the final test of a novel is "our affection for it," then *The Good Earth* is truly a great novel.

Pearl Buck did not bridge the gap of communication and understanding between China and America by glorifying the Chinese, whitewashing everything Chinese, or avoiding China's evil and ugliness. Just like Wang Lung, who is not a perfect man, China is not depicted as a perfect world. The good earth is also filled with misery: flood, drought, pestilence, famine, and poverty. The country is disturbed by robbers and warlords. Rich men idle away their time in the teahouse and visit prostitutes while poor men toil in the field and worry about the next meal. Some persons, like Wang Lung's parasitical uncle and aunt, are addicted to opium. People sometimes have to do horrible things including eating dogs and killing one's own baby. Unlike some missionaries who described such occurrences to prove their superiority over the "heathen Chinese," Pearl Buck presented the circumstances under which the townsmen eat dogs and O-lan kills her fourth baby in chapters 8 and 9: a long spell of draught, failure of crops, money used up, no proper food for months. Even grass and barks are eaten up and Wang Lung's family has to flee from famine by going south, but O-lan is about to go into labor. "The child in her body hung from her lean loins like a knotty fruit and from her face every particle of flesh was gone, so that the jagged bones stood forth rock-like under her skin. 'Only wait until tomorrow,' she said. 'I shall have given birth by then. I can tell by this thing's movements in me.'" Then the baby is born. Wang Lung is waiting outside. "'It would be merciful if there were no breath,' he muttered, and then he heard the feeble cry---how feeble a cry!---hang for an instant upon the stillness. 'But there is no mercy of any kind in these days,' he finished bitterly, and he sat listening" (chap. 9). Thus, O-lan herself has to do mercy to the baby.

It is in this kind of severe situation that the infanticide has happened. Pearl Buck did not resort to sentimentalism, but the ensuing description arouses sympathy rather than condemnation. Unlike the hearsay for a topic of gossip or the quasi-scientific statistics for cold-blooded judgment of a nation disregarding everything else, her rendering of the infanticide makes readers understand why it happens and feel the deepest sorrow for human sufferings. Moreover, something typical of Chinese culture is reflected in the famine scene of chapter 9, the respect for the old. "As for the old man, he fared better than any, for if there was anything to eat he was given it, even though the children were without. Wang Lung said to himself proudly that none should say in the hour of death he had forgotten his father." The Offspring of Lung are thus depicted as part of the suffering human beings in this troubled world. This was easily and well understood by American readers during the Great Depression.

If Pearl Buck only implied the relationship between the dragon and the Chinese in *The Good Earth* in 1931, she announced it a decade later with the publication of *Dragon Seed*, one of her best known and most popular novels. It would be a much better one if the romance between Lao San and Mayli were not inserted. Another translation for the "Offspring of Lung," the title, *Dragon Seed*, refers to the Chinese and connotes more fighting spirit. Ling Tan, the protagonist, just like Wang Lung, is much attached to his land and is living a peaceful and productive life with his extended family consisting of a mother, three sons, one of the two daughters, and some grandchildren. Yet, unlike Wang Lung's, his life is destroyed by the Japanese invasion. The mother and the third son are violated by several lust-crazed Japanese soldiers. Heavy taxation and restrictive regulations are imposed on the peasants and farmers. Innocent civilians are killed by the wanton bombing of the "flying ships." These peace-loving Chinese are shocked and awakened, and their spirit of Lung, which is an ancient totem that symbolizes force as well as benevolence, is invoked. They start to fight the invaders with all their weapons: hoes, swords, guns, and poison. Their heroic resistance, though a kind of primitive guerrilla warfare, is described with vivid imagination.

However, Ling Tan is saddened at the pleasure in killing shown by his third son Lao San, who has turned into a ruthless guerrilla leader. Instead of the enemy, Ling Tan poisons the fish in his pond so that the enemy will gain nothing from it. Thus, the dragon seed is nothing like the fictional figures such as Yue-Laou by Robert W. Chambers, Quong Lung by Dr. C. W. Doyle, or Fu Manchu by Sax Rohmer. Nor are the "Offspring of Lung" like the Celestrials described by some missionaries, including Edmund Roberts and W.S.W. Ruschenberger, as cowards or barbarians. In Pearl Buck's novel, the Chinese are realistically presented as they are, not angels, nor devils, but human beings, who do what they are compelled to do. Some are more merciless than others, some are conscientious, some are cowardly and have almost become traitors like Ling Tan's eldest daughter and her merchant husband. They are all understandable human beings despite some minor cultural differences including "Lung" or the

Chinese dragon, which is no longer seen as a symbol of evil as misunderstood by some narrow-minded missionaries.

Between *The Good Earth* and *Dragon Seed* was a lapse of ten years, in which American readers learned a great deal about Chinese culture and the majority of Chinese people through Pearl Buck's novels: *Sons, A House Divided, The Mother, The Patriot,* and through the Chinese philosopher Lin Yutang's books: *My Country and My People* [1936], *The Importance of Living* [1937], *The Wisdom of Confucius* [1938], and *Moment in Peking* [1939]. The former's books are stories of people, by which readers familiarize themselves with China and the Chinese. The latter's books, except the last one, systematically introduce Chinese culture and philosophy to Westerners and especially scholars. Their books satisfied the needs of both common and intellectual readers in the 1930s and 1940s as far as Chinese subject matter was concerned. What should not be forgotten is that it was Pearl Buck and her husband Richard Walsh who invited Lin Yutang to the United States to write.

Sons and *A House Divided*, the second and third books of the trilogy that begins with *The Good Earth*, labor under the handicap that all sequels to famous books must face but fall short of the first volume by far as novels, though they have much social and cultural value as illustrations of China's problems and zeitgeist. *Sons* is about the warlord career of Wang the Tiger, Wang Lung's third son, in the first half and his ambivalent relationship with his son Wang Yuan in the second half. The warlord experience of Wang the Tiger is initiated by his conflict with his father Wang Lung over the bondmaid Pear Blossom. So the title catches the essence of the novel. However, this appropriate title seemed to have lost critics' and reviewers' attention, indicating a loss of the theme. Had Pearl Buck experienced the life of brigands or warlords, she would have produced a much more interesting novel, but the characterization of Wang the Tiger is not successful. Compared with Hemingway's Pablo in *For Whom the Bell Tolls*, Wang the Tiger is pale and feeble. While it is true that not all the brigands and warlords are colorful and strong, he is not a sympathetic figure, either, despite his twice-failed love, his unrealized revolutionary ideals, and his strong affection and excessive devotion to his son. His portrayal, as Paul Doyle concluded, "contains little to bring reader identification; and even his ultimate despair, which is basically the result of his own foolishness and naivete, seems deserved and rather fitting. It is difficult to sense tragedy here, at least from the way the story and characters are presented" (1980, 55). His battles are more like an imitation of the battles described in *Shui Hu Chuan (All Men Are Brothers)* five hundred years before rather than an imitation of life in early 20th-century China.

The major value of *Sons* is that it demonstrates a fundamental change in China, the change of the family relationship and social system. If *The Good Earth* presents a timeless circle of the life of Chinese farmers: industriousness making Wangs rise, laziness making the Hwangs fall, and indulgence in wealth making the Wangs lazy and causing them to fall again, this slow but steady turning of the wheel of fortune is interrupted by the change described in *Sons*, which is set in a country where the last emperor had just been overthrown, and disturbances in the name of revolution occurred one after another. When the traditional relationship between a monarch and ministers had been broken in China, the relationship between a father and sons was the next to be questioned, as the Chinese concepts of "Zhong" (loyalty to the emperor) and "Hsiao" (filial piety to the father) had always been inseparable. Ministers were supposed to obey their monarch absolutely as sons obeyed their father, but *Sons* is a novel about Wang the Tiger's protest against his own father Wang Lung, his uprising over more powerful warlords, and in turn, his son's, Wang Yuan's, disobedience to him. Through their stories readers can see two of the most important problems of China, the instability of the country and the breaking down of authority, which are, of course, closely related with each other.

Moreover, Pearl Buck demonstrated in the sequels an important idea, which was unfortunately ignored until recent years. The idea is that monarchy itself, in the first half of this century, was not so important to the Chinese as the general recognition it represented for them, namely a certain order by which one emperor succeeded another. Her suggestion is that to overthrow monarchy is not so crucial as to establish a new order, and the Nationalist Revolution was too hasty in the sense that the Chinese people were not yet prepared for the Republic. This is a painful historical lesson that Chinese scholars including Liu Hsiao-po and Hu Ping recently drew from our modern history. Pearl Buck expressed this idea also in *My Several Worlds* discussing China's Nationalist Revolution without deprecating its leader: "Sun Yat-sen was an honorable and selfless man, whose integrity is beyond doubt. He deserves the homage of his people. He is not to be blamed that in his burning desire to serve them he destroyed the very basis of their life, which was order" (382). China abandoned its monarchy and established a Republic in 1912, but we failed to reach a new common recognition as how to find a legitimate leader. China paid dearly for it: President Sun had to resign and gave the office to the ambitious militarist Yuan Shih-kai; powerful war lords such as Chang Tso-lin and Wu Pei-fu started a civil war without any constitutional significance; and the radical warlord Feng Yu-hsiang violated the agreement with the Ching Royalty by driving them out of the Forbidden City, pushing the Nationalist Revolution of 1911 further away from its remote resemblance to England's Glorious Revolution. One of the consequences was the barefaced gangster logic later summarized by Mao Tse-tung (Mao Zedong) from China's chaos: "Political power grows out of the barrel of a gun" (1967, 33).

In *Sons* and *A House Divided*, we see warlords fight each other without any revolutionary sense. Even the "Northern Expedition" of the Nationalists joined by the Communists is marred by betrayal and lack of substantial improvement of the society and people's lives. Pearl Buck was no theorist, but her extensive experience of living among ordinary Chinese people and her strong intuition helped her produce these insightful novels. Without the general recognition of the people, the order was lost, and the warlords battled among themselves for power. The two parties fought over twenty years and two civil wars for sovereignty, and even today the stability of mainland China is threatened whenever an old leader is to be succeeded by a new one. In such disorders, the main characters suffer from the common fate of all the Chinese people. If new China was a baby being born at the time, *Sons* and *A House Divided* are novels about the pain of the difficult labor. Although the pain is not described well enough to arouse readers' strong sympathy, it is clearly presented, if somewhat detached, for them to see as a consequence of the China's revolution. Therefore, the novels may be more valuable to scholars than to casual readers.

Literature, unlike history, focuses on people rather than events. Through the portrayal of more and different walks of Chinese life, Pearl Buck improved the image of the Chinese people in the American mind and showed China as a rapidly developing country. *Sons* illustrates the historical change by the story of one family, and so we see mainly the conflicts between the sons and fathers in the novel. Unlike Wang Lung, who obeys his father, respects his father, takes good care of his father, coaxes his father, and gives a grand funeral to his father, Wang the Tiger, his son, rebels against him, and Wang the Tiger's own son then rebels against him. Wang Lung hates soldiering as a profession most of all, and yet his third son runs away from home to be a soldier and becomes a warlord. Wang the Tiger tries every way to make his son Wang Yuan a good soldier, but Wang Yuan just wants to be a farmer. He loves nature and poetry and hates the art of killing. In contrast with his father, he runs away from the military academy. Their stories reflect the new family relationship and China's zeitgeist. The traditional virtue "Hsiao" is being replaced by new ideas including freedom, equality, and the realization of one's own value. All Wang Lung knows is to make his father happy and his family prosper, to enjoy himself, and to let the Empress Dowager or whoever the new rulers are worry about state affairs. But Wang the Tiger has been enlightened by the new ideas and so he feels oppressed at home when the bondmaid he loves is taken by his father for a concubine. This is more than just "sexual frustration" (P. Doyle 1980, 53); it is a denial of his personal value. That is why he must leave home to seek a military career, although near the end of the novel he acknowledges that he is too weak to be a warlord. His real tragedy, however, lies in his inability to see his own son's same need for freedom, equality, recognition of his value, and moreover, his duty to his country as every individual should perform but was not encouraged to in the old China. This last idea is further developed in *A House Divided*. I can understand why *Sons* was Pearl Buck's personal favorite of all her books about life in China (Spencer 1964, 172), for it manifests the rebellious spirit so generally felt by the young people including herself at the time.[3] It is a pity that this tragedy is not intensified enough to arouse the same feelings in its readers, most of whom were so far away from the changing land. Or had the novel been published in the uneasy 1960s, it would have been better received in the United States. It is worth noticing that China's problem she presented in the book is one of the results of the rebellious spirit she advocated. It grew strong in the sixties and nineties again. "Where are we going?" is a question that serious Chinese readers would naturally ask.

A House Divided, an epitome of a country divided, also has its pros and cons. Its major problem is that Wang Yuan, the hero of this bildungsroman, appears even more pallid than Wang the Tiger and holds less reader interest. Although Wang Yuan is a typical Chinese young man caught between the past and the present, the old and the new, East and West, not enough introspective probing is done to reveal and dramatize his dilemma. The basic elements of the novel are, in fact, very good and certainly have the potential to be developed into a great book about China. Pearl Buck already gave us a young intellectual who is a truth seeker groping around for his goal of life. His feeling for his warlord father is ambivalent. His attitude to revolution is ambivalent. His feeling for America is also ambivalent. I do not agree with Paul Doyle that "his chameleon-like shifts of mood lessen our respect for him and weaken our belief in his reality" (1980, 60), for these shifts are only natural for youths in their formative years, especially for Chinese youths at the time when traditional values including filial piety still lingered on while new Western ideas were beckoning to them, when revolutionists dreamed so beautifully but revolutions resulted in such disappointment, and when Wang Yuan and the like first saw with their own eyes that China's power and prosperity had been surpassed by the West in almost every way. Wang Yuan is definitely a representative of Chinese intellectuals who were concerned with their country and their people. Following his journey through life readers could learn much about the changing China, not only its small towns and villages but also its big cities like Shanghai and Nanjing, not only the farmers and peasants but also rich and upper class people, not only students at home but also scholars abroad. It is a pity that the novel has too much breadth in its setting but not enough depth in its protagonist. Like *Sons* it does not arouse strong affection from readers. If *The Good Earth* is a great book, *Sons* and *A House Divided* are just good books. They are good at introducing to the West many different aspects of China and the desire and endeavor of many Chinese youths to modernize their country.

The Mother comes back to the rural life where Pearl Buck was most at home and, in my opinion, is as great a novel as *The Good Earth*, if not greater. Wang Lung and O-lan attract our attention partly by the vicissitude of their life from rags to riches and from the toil without to the quarrel within. The mother arouses our sympathy by her fate, which is the common fate of all women in a male-dominated society, demonstrated in her rather insipid life. It was therefore a more challenging novel for Pearl Buck to write successfully. The plot of this novel is much less complicated than that of *The Good Earth*, but the reader's interest, affection, and identification are equally strong. As Isidor Schneider said, "It is so direct in its appeal to the emotions that it draws tears to the eyes. And it has a certain quality common to some of the world's finest books and peculiarly satisfying in whatever book it appears, of presenting its characters safe, in the integrity of their destinies, from envy, scorn and censure" (136). The novel touches us not by sentimentalism but by intensifying life itself, simple as it is. G.R.B. Richards made this remark when comparing *The Mother* with *The Good Earth*: "The simplicity of the peasant mind stands out in bolder relief and the conflict of opposing natures is less dramatic and more real. Poetic but not sentimental, distinguished by sympathetic understanding and appreciation of unseen struggle, it is essentially artistic, essentially commonplace, essentially and universally human in its conception and in its execution" (1934, 1). Many critics have remarked that the mother is a "universal portrait of the eternal mother" (P. Doyle 1980, 62), but she is at the same time unique. Mark Van Doren commented, "Mrs. Buck's refusal to name characters and her selection of a wholly unaccentuated style are doubtless proper for the kind of novel she has written," and he continued, "But it is worthy of note that she has not been able in the end to avoid individualizing her people. The mother, the father, each one of the children, the cousin, the landlord's agent who seduces the mother, the village gossip---not one of these but has his uniqueness and picturesque clarity" (1934, 78). Let us see how it is achieved in the characterization of the protagonist.

The mother is uniquely herself, typically Chinese, and also so universal that there "is no mother of whatever race," the reviewer for the *New York Times* said, "who will not recognize some measure of herself in the Chinese peasant woman" (qtd. in Harris 1969, 197). Her personal uniqueness is seen mainly in her quarrels with her husband. Unlike O-lan who never raises her voice in speaking to Wang Lung and obeys him even when he asks for the two pearls, the only thing she has ever requested for herself, the mother has many more edges and is filled with such vigorous zest for life and for a better future of her family that she does not put up with her handsome but vanity-loving husband when he wastes her money. She is unique also in her strong sense of honor, which is manifested in her strenuous endeavors to cover the shame that her husband has abandoned his home and family.

Like O-lan, the mother is typically Chinese: hardy, frugal, industrious, full of energy to work both at home and in the field. She compares favorably with the toughness of Bertolt Brecht's Mother Courage and John Steinbeck's Ma Joad. She also shares Chinese women's common shortcomings: valuing boys more than girls, favoring younger and more handsome boys, disliking and distrusting daughters-in-law. Paul Doyle criticized the novel for the mother is "too neglectful of medical care for her sickly daughter" and "rather arbitrarily favors her younger son over her much more stable and deserving elder son" (1980, 64), but I believe it was better that Pearl Buck did not make the mother a perfect "angel in the house." A real person with weaknesses does not necessarily diminish readers' sympathy as Doyle assumed.

The mother is universal in that she rejoices briefly over the birth of children and grandchildren, suffers like an eternal *mater dolorosa* in a harsh world, and weeps as if she were a modern Rachel for the untimely death of her son. She works hard but life gives her little in the male-dominated society. She suffers from the double standard for men and women and has to pay so much including a painful abortion for a little pleasure and comfort that any woman would naturally need in her situation. If O-lan arouses a reader's sympathy for the unfair treatments she has received from Wang Lung, the mother awakens the reader's realization of the unfair treatment that women all over the world, including many of the readers themselves, have received from men, from society, and from conventions. The only weakness of *The Mother* is that it lacks a climax, and yet the novel was not meant to be dramatic but naturalistic. As far as learning about China is concerned, a naturalistic novel is probably better than a dramatic one.

    The Patriot is a far more successful bildungsroman than *A House Divided*. This time the hero I-wan is the son of the Shanghai bank president, one of the richest men in China, and yet readers can easily identify with him, for he has experienced things that are common to us all: disillusionment in revolutionary ideals, reconciliation into a peaceful life ignoring world affairs, and choices between love for one's family and love for one's motherland. More vividly realized than Wang Yuan, I-wan springs to life and assumes reality. His fate and choices in the critical moments of China's recent history easily grab the reader's attention. Had more exploration of his internal world been made, the unlikely military training of the workers he conducts been canceled, and the obvious narrative maneuver to bring Chiang Kai-shek into the story been altered, this novel could have been a masterpiece, but as it is, its value for the insight into and illustration of China's recent history is more considerable than its artistic value.

    The Patriot is one of the first and foremost novels to deal with Chiang Kai-shek's betrayal and massacre of the Communists in 1927 and to deal with the Japanese invasion of China. It was wise of Pearl Buck not to have mentioned the Chinese Nationalist party or explained the cooperation between the two parties in the "North Expedition" in the book so that the novel was made less offensive to certain persons and the Chinese government, less partisan but more political, and less regional but more universal. The reader does not have to be told about the events in order to appreciate the formative story of the young hero. It is sufficient to know that the revolution is betrayed, the status quo is maintained, and he is disillusioned, jeopardized, and has to flee. The interesting point is that the author implied that the revolution would not do much good to the country and people even if it were not betrayed by Chiang Kai-shek this time. En-lan (the name suggests Zhou En-lai), the Communist who indoctrinates I-wan with the revolutionary ideas, is portrayed as a firm and ruthless fighter filled with hatred for the rich. Communist readers might like Pearl Buck for that, but the Western readers were likely to suspect this kind of revolutionist whose primary interest was fighting and achieving power rather than construction and administration. Unfortunately, what the Chinese Communist Party did later proves this suspicion to be more than reasonable.

Pearl Buck was faithful to truth despite her disagreement with communism. She depicted the Communists as brave and effective at fighting the Japanese and described their guerrilla warfare as the only practical and successful tactics in 1939, at about the same time that Edgar Snow wrote his reports about Red China's resistance. On the one hand, she admired the Communists for their willingness to unite with the Nationalists in the war against their common enemy, forgetting the wrongs Chiang Kai-shek had done to them. On the other hand, she showed her distaste through I-wan for their killing of Japanese captives, even though the Japanese had committed horrible atrocities in China. She also predicted through the dialog between I-wan and Chiang Kai-shek that the war would be long and hard before Japan could be finally defeated. Her prediction proved to be right and the war lasted eight years from 1937 to 1945. Moreover, her analysis and portrayal of Chiang Kai-shek as a chameleon and an opportunist are penetrating. In the novel he is seen to betray the revolutionary cause, to offer a bribe and execute the man who takes the money. His conversion to Christianity is ridiculed by even I-wan's serious father. Yet readers can feel the impressiveness of Chiang's bearing and ability to dominate and to inspire his followers. A clear suggestion is made in the book that such a leader is worthy of cooperation but cannot be trusted and the Communists should be further supported in the war against the Japanese. It was a pity that the Roosevelt Administration ignored it as it ignored the suggestions of Joseph Stilwell, John Service, and Edgar Snow.

However, *The Patriot* is not a novel of argument or war propaganda. It is a novel of human beings, and in Katherine Woods's words, "of human passions and frustrations and valor and patience and strength. It must have been written at white heat, under stress of intense feeling; yet its intensity is not of bitterness and hate, but of insight and compassion" (1939, 2). Some critics said that part 2 of the novel, I-wan's ten-year life in Japan after the failure of the revolution, is most striking and "presents one of the most realistic and convincing portraits of the Japanese character found in literature. Japanese attitudes of love of country, duty, and endurance are particularly well delineated; and Japanese qualities of delicacy, mannerliness, and love of beauty contrast sharply with their stoicism, militarism, and cruelty" (P. Doyle 1980, 96). This may be true, but this part is not trying to show, as the *Springfield Republican* reviewer asserted, "why Japan has become a strong nation while China lacks the vital elements making for strength" (7e). This part is a preparation for the hero to wake up from his hibernation, to decide between his family and country, and to develop into a mature patriot. It is an important part of his characterization. The first and second parts of the novel have obvious flaws, but they do not obscure its splendor as an artistic miniature of a Chinese patriot, whose growth suggests Chinese nationalism in the making.

Compared with Pearl Buck's novels, Lin Yu-tang's books are more scholarly. Dr. Lin systematically introduced to the West every aspect of Chinese life, culture, society, and politics in beautiful English. *My Country and My People* was an immediate success in 1935, enjoyed seven impressions within four months, and received favorable reviews by R. E. Kennedy, Nathaniel Peffer and some other authoritative critics. *The Importance of Living* was specially recommended by Book-of-the-Month Club in December 1937 and became a best-seller in 1938. *The Wisdom of Confucius* was included in the Modern Library of Random House in 1938. His novel *Moment in Peking* was the Book-of-the-Month Club selection for December 1939. In those years, Lin lived mainly in New York and was active in American literary and art circles meeting with Eugene O'Neill, Robert Frost, Thomas Mann, Edna St. Vincent Millay, George Jean Nathan, Carl and Mark Van Doren, J. Donald Adams, the dancer Isadora Duncan, the actress Lillian Gish, and the photographer Carl Van Vechten; giving lectures on themes of China everywhere; publishing articles in major American magazines and newspapers including *Time* and the *New York Times*. Lin was so influential that in 1938, the *New York Times* even held a "Lin Yu-tang Contest" based on the second section of the first chapter of *The Importance of Living*, and in 1939, Clifton Fadiman's book *I Believe: The Personal Philosophies of Certain Eminent Men and Women of Our Time* included Lin's essay, along with those of Einstein, H. G. Wells, Pearl Buck, Thomas Mann, John Dewey, Bertrand Russell, Beatrice Webb, and George Santayana, among others.[4]

Lin Yu-tang is mentioned here not only because he was invited to the United States to write by Pearl Buck and her husband Richard Walsh, but also because Lin's books were edited by them and published by John Day Company where Walsh was the chief editor. Pearl Buck also wrote a long and influential introduction to *My Country and My People,* Lin's first success in the United States, and in his own preface to the book, Lin acknowledged, first of all, the help of Pearl Buck and Richard Walsh in the form of editing, criticism, and encouragement. And of course, it was she who introduced Lin to the American public and literary circles, not to mention that Lin's family of five had lived in her home in Pennsylvania for quite some time before they settled down in New York. Lin Yu-tang was only the first of many Chinese writers, scholars, and artists whom Pearl Buck invited to the United States to introduce Chinese culture to the American people. Such endeavors to bring about new and better understanding among the peoples of the world took form of her founding the East and West Association, a nonprofit organization, in 1941. She "carried on the work of this association throughout the war, handling particularly the educational material of the organization" (P. Doyle 1980, 102). Among its many activities was the bus tour performance given by a troupe of young Chinese actors and actresses including the famous movie star Wang Yung (Ying), and the opening performance, as recalled by Pearl Buck in *My Several Worlds,* was given for Mrs. Roosevelt and some friends at the White House (374). The association had greatly promoted the cultural exchange between America and Asian countries until Joseph McCarthy killed it in 1950.[5]

Pearl Buck was heartsick and in her disappointment she confided, "In addition to the McCarthy business, the discontent with Americans about Asia makes me feel that Americans do not want to see or hear about people from Asia. This has made me begin to believe that we in America will have to reach our maturity by the hard road of personal and material experience" (qtd. in Sherk 137). While these words are somewhat prophetic, we must not underestimate, as she did herself, Pearl Buck's achievements in a basically single-handed crusade to change the image of the Chinese people in the American mind.

As those two surveys conducted in 1927 and 1948 indicated, the general American attitude toward the Chinese changed within these two decades. The repeal of the Chinese Exclusion Act in 1943 was an earlier indicator of the change, which came about partly because of Pearl Buck's books. Her convincing portrayal of Chinese characters of many walks of life showed Americans what the majority of the Chinese were really like. They were not heathen barbarians, or children of Satan or Lung the evil monster any more. They were no longer the yellow peril threatening the Western civilization, nor were they a bunch of criminals headed by Yue-Laou or Fu Manchu. Not all of them were cowards without a sense of honor or dignity. Not all of them were sick men and women smoking opium and gambling against each other. Not all of them were sneaky, tricky swindlers and ruffians trying to cheat and corrupt good American citizens. Every Chinese was not either a man with a queue or a woman with bound feet. Every Chinese was not an obedient domestic servant speaking broken English any more, nor was he a polite westernized retainer quoting conveniently "Confucius say ... " now and then.

Since 1931, the Chinese in the American mind were no longer cheap, dirty coolies or any of the above types but honest, hardworking peasants and farmers like Wang Lung, O-lan, Wang Yuan, the mother, and the Lings. They were peace-loving but they could fight to the death to defend their own land just like American farmers. They were tough, frugal, and persevering. They feared gods might take their happiness away when they were enjoying some good luck, and they dared to curse gods when luck was too tough. They were perhaps more superstitious and less religious than most American farmers, but they were certainly not evil or stupid. They were friendly and hospitable human beings with human weaknesses, who love eating and chatting perhaps a bit too much. They had no ambition to conquer the world but just wanted to be left alone even by their own rulers. Some of their rulers were selfish, treacherous, and incompetent, and there were bandits and warlords that plagued China. There were also well-educated people like Wang Yuan and I-wan who were trying to modernize China, taking the United States as its model. They were, at the same time, trying to avoid erasing China's national identity. Thus Pearl Buck showed to the West that there was nothing mysterious or peculiar about the Chinese, who were basically the same as any other people, no better, no worse. We peoples of the East and West had the same dream for a better life. We had the same fear for mishap and death. We felt the same pain and sorrow at loss of life and property. We enjoyed the same pleasure, physically or spiritually. We suffered from the same weaknesses and wrongdoings. In a word, we were all human beings.

This simple truth was not so simple in the early 1930s, when Arthur H. Smith's book *Chinese Characteristics*, for instance, was still one of the most influential books on China among Western intellectuals, according to Charles W. Hayford's studies (19). The Chinese, as this book tried to prove and make the reader believe, were a people who had no sense of time or accuracy, who had the talent for indirection and misunderstanding, who were intellectually turbid, physically nerveless and indifferent to comfort and convenience, and who had no sincerity, no sympathy, no public spirit whatsoever.[6] Among the masses, the anti-Chinese stories and novels mentioned in the first half of this chapter were blooming and culminating in Fu Manchu books and movies well into the 1940s. Edith M. Eaton was the only Chinese American writer with some influence who complained of the unequal treatment for the Chinese in "The Land of the Free" [1909], but her voice was too weak at that time. The opposition was too strong for the writers who did not know the Chinese well enough, and no Americans who had lived in China from childhood had the talent and courage to write about the Chinese truthfully before Pearl Buck.

If history helped her succeed in the sense that the Great Depression made Americans more easily share the sufferings and better appreciate the struggles described in *The Good Earth,* and that the Japanese invasion of China drew the attention of the West to the victims, then Pearl Buck's success helped to shape history, too. The realistic portrayal of the Chinese characters in her phenomenally successful novels gradually improved the American image of the Chinese. Millions of Americans who did not read even *The Good Earth* saw the Oscar-winning movie of the same title. *Dragon Seed* was also adapted into a popular movie seen by millions. The only two American actresses who won the Academy Award for Best Actress twice in a row, Louise Rainer and Katharine Hepburn, starred in the two movies respectively. The image improvement paved the way to ending the anti-Chinese laws in 1943. Many scholars including Jack Chen and Shih-shan Henry Tsai acknowledged Pearl Buck's participation and her important function in the efforts of appealing for the repeal of the Chinese Exclusion Act, but we should know that the much more important work had been done before the direct appeals and arguments.

Moreover, the improvement prepared the American people to support China in fighting the Japanese invaders. Americans were used to ignoring things happening on the other half of the globe, and many even thought, as most traders, missionaries, and diplomats did, that foreign invasions would help China modernize. In 1895 after Japan invaded Korea, Taiwan, Northeast China (Manchuria), and even part of China proper, "sentiment in Washington and among the concerned public generally, was pro-Japanese" (Cohen 41). As William Rackhill, the most respected authority on Chinese affairs at the time, put it, "a good thrashing will not hurt China in the least. ... It is the only tonic which seems to suit [her]" (M. Young 22). The American Minister to China even advised the Secretary of State that "Japan was only doing for China what the United States had done for Japan bringing Western civilization" (Cohen 41). America's appeasement of Japan's aggression against China was further shown after World War I in the Paris Peace Conference as mentioned before. After Japan invaded the inland of China in 1937, China fought Japan for four years without any substantial support from the U. S. government, which, however, had been feeding Japan's war machines by selling them oil, iron, petroleum products, and providing them with war supplies for all these years before the bombing of Pearl Harbor. Between 1937 and 1940, the total value of American exports to Japan was $984 million, 4.5 times as much as American exports to China ($219 million) in these years (Cohen 149).

However, many Americans were much more concerned with the issue of China than the U. S. government was. They thought the Japanese were invading the homeland of Wang Lung and O-lan, killing their children, and I-wan and En-lan were fighting hard. The Chinese were no longer just an abstract concept for them but had taken concrete shapes in their minds as the characters created by Pearl Buck. "In the spring of 1939, a Gallup poll indicated that the overwhelming majority of the Americans questioned favored an embargo on war supplies to Japan. Sanctions were now politically possible---had the Administration desired to impose them" (Cohen 146). Several bills for economic sanctions against Japan were introduced in Congress and various organizations friendly to China lobbied intensively, but "these efforts came to naught. ... In the United States, the friends of China began to oppose government policy, for the most part unable to comprehend Roosevelt's evaluation of the relative importance of the European and Asian wars" (Cohen 148). The different opinions between the people and the government in 1939 were just the reversal of those in 1882 when President Garfield at first vetoed the Chinese Exclusion bill. "There was no shortage of sympathy for China among Americans" (Cohen 150), and they supported the Chinese by donating money, materials, and even by voluntarily taking part in their fight. The best example was, of course, the Flying Tigers under Claire Chennault, a retired American airman. Even though some of them were no more than mercenaries, we Chinese remember them dearly because their help was much needed. They came to the rescue of Chungking, harassing Japanese communication lines, destroying nearly three hundred Japanese airplanes over Burma and South China, and transporting army supplies for China across the Himalayas. Of course, Pearl Buck herself also actively took part in such war activities as raising funds, giving speeches, and writing articles for China's cause, but the cognitive and artistic functions of her novels helped the Chinese far more than did her direct involvement. She was to the Chinese much more than what Harriet Beecher Stowe was to the black slaves.

NOTES

1. This is the incident that started the second Opium War (1856-60), also known as the "Arrow" War, or the Anglo-French War in China. *The New Encyclopaedia Britannica* says in the entry of Opium Wars, "In 1856 the British, seeking to extend their trading rights in China, found an excuse to renew hostilities when some Chinese officials boarded the ship *Arrow* and lowered the British flag." Then the second Opium War broke out. "The French joined the British in this war, using as their excuse the murder of a French missionary in the interior of China."

2. For detail see *United States Statutes 1881-13*. Washington, D. C., 1883. Vol. XXII. 58-61.

3. In 1932 Pearl Buck defended and praised the Laymen's Foreign Mission Inquiry, which criticizes the missionary work. See her essay "The Laymen's Mission Report," which marks the beginning of her breakup with the church.

4. For detail of Lin Yu-tang's publications and activities in the United States see chapters 12-14 of *Lin Yu-tang: A Biography* by Lin Tai-yi. Beijing: Chinese Drama Press, 1994.

5. For details of the East and West Association see chapter 13 of *Pearl S. Buck: Good Earth Mother* by Dr. Warren Sherk, the national Field Secretary of the organization. Drift Creek Press, 1992.

6. Just a glance at the contents of Smith's book is enough to see that these misconceptions were only some of the prejudices against the Chinese, and as Charles Hayford said, the book is now best known as an example of Sino-myopia.

4

A MULTICULTURAL MEDIATOR

One of the biggest events in the cultural contact between the East and the West was undoubtedly the establishment of Christian missions. The American missionary movement in China lasted more than a century; thousands of missionaries spent the best part of their lives far away from their own country, and tens of millions of dollars were spent in the oriental land. These generations of endeavor and generous enterprises were all for the sole purpose of bringing the Gospel and salvation to the Chinese. Judging from the number of the Chinese who were converted, everyone admits that the missions failed. As Jessie G. Lutz informed us, "At no time did the number of Christian converts exceed one per cent of the Chinese population, and by the mid-twentieth century the missionary effort had been halted" (vii). The saddening fact is that most of the converts were mere "rice Christians," that is, they became Christians for material benefits rather than spiritual needs. Moreover, some of the converts were even "friendship Christians," that is, they became Christians not because they were converted but because they did not want to hurt the feelings of their Christian friends. However, the number of converts should not be the only measure by which we evaluate the missions. Nor should it be the most important measure. Their failure is much more apparent than their achievement. The lessons that can be drawn from their failure and the experience that can be summarized from their achievement are still beneficial in today's cultural exchange.

Pearl Buck was one of the first influential writers who dealt with the issue of Christian missions in China. Being a daughter of American Presbyterian missionaries who, unlike many of their condescending colleagues, were genuine friends of Chinese peasants and farmers and won love and respect with their good deeds as well as kind intentions, she grew up among ordinary Chinese people. She learned Chinese before English, took Chinese lessons from a tutor, Mr. Kung, as well as English lessons from her mother, made many Chinese friends, did some missionary work, and experienced much as both an insider and an outsider, as both a beneficiary and a victim in China and America. Although she was not a scholar and did not systematically study the causes of the failure or discuss the achievement and impact of the missions, she personally knew the missionaries and their objects better than most scholars did. Her intuition, sensibility, knowledge of Chinese, and close contact with the Chinese helped her see what many scholars neglected, and she wrote many stories that illustrate the lives, efforts, failures and achievements of some missionaries long before a few scholars evaluated them abstractly in the fields of history, religion, philosophy, sociology, anthropology, politics, and economics. Thus, she served and may still serve as a multicultural mediator. Some of her books, especially *The Exile, Fighting Angel, Pavilion of Women, Kinfolk*, and *Peony* were valuable in helping readers reconsider Christian missions when they were failing in China, and her books are still valuable today to help us deal with cultural differences and to advance human civilizations with a tolerant attitude. Her books are particularly valuable in helping the Chinese learn about missionaries as human beings rather than argue about Christian missions as an abstract issue, so that we may reconsider this "imperialist cultural invasion" from all sides.

Over the issue of Christian missions two opposite hard feelings existed and still linger across the Pacific Ocean. On the one side, many Americans were saddened by the failure and felt strongly that the Chinese were incorrigible and ungrateful. Indeed, in order to save the souls of the Chinese, Americans donated great sums of money to help China, established many colleges and schools, hospitals and clinics, and sent so much relief to the famine and disaster areas. Many noble men and women devoted the best part of their lives to China, and some even lost their lives there. What was the reward? Some converts, a few churches, and a lot of hatred. The Boxers killed innocent missionaries and their families in 1900. The Nationalists forced several thousand missionaries to evacuate their posts in the interior of China, looted the Christian section and killed six Westerners during the Nanjing ransack in 1927. The Communists kicked all the remaining missionaries out of mainland China for good in 1949. China was eventually "lost" politically and spiritually.

On the other side, Chinese authorities imbued young Chinese, including myself, with the idea that sword and cross were two weapons with which Western powers tried to conquer China. Indeed, Napoleon "declared early in the 19th century that 'the religious missions may be very useful to me in Asia, Africa, and America, as I shall make them reconnoiter all the lands they visit. The sanctity of their dress will not only protect them but serve to conceal their political and commercial investigations.' This became, often unconsciously, the policy of all Western powers" (qtd. in De Riencourt 147). To prevent it Christian missions had been banned by the government of the Ching (Qing) dynasty for a century until China's defeat in the first Opium War. The unequal Nanking treaty guaranteed free importation of Indian opium and Western missionaries, who then returned in droves. It was now that American missionaries began to pour into China, too. In the later conflict with the West, Peking was taken and the magnificent Summer Palace ransacked and burned to ashes by the British and French troops headed by Lord Elgin. It was true that the Boxers killed some innocent Westerners in their fight against the imperialists, but was it not also true that the Western powers retaliated with hundredfold cruelty? As the editor of the *San Francisco Call* said, "For every woman missionary sacrificed by the Boxers five hundred Chinese women have gone to torture and death. For every man ordained for martyrdom a thousand Chinese men have atoned with their lives. For every missionary child cut down in its innocence a hundred Chinese babies have been tossed and impaled on Cossack spears. For every missionary compound burned or sacked value a hundredfold has been looted in Tientsin and Peking" (qtd. in Miller 1974, 275). As more and more unequal treaties were concluded, Christian missionaries enjoyed more and more privileges in China. As Amaury de Riencourt said, "The poison of opium, extraterritoriality and Christianity became inextricably mixed with Western imperialism in Chinese minds" (148). Of course, American missionaries were innocent of the crimes committed by the Europeans, but the physical and cultural similarities made them indistinquishable to the Chinese. At any rate, backed by the gunboats and garrisons of the Western powers, they all enjoyed extraterritorial rights and they frequently interfered in local politics. "Never had the contrast with the peaceful missions of the Buddhists of old been so blatant" (De Riencourt 148).

Besides, it was the American missionary Issacher J. Roberts who tutored Hung Hsiu-chuan (Hong Xiuquan) in the Christian doctrine[1] and "gave him examples of how to pray, preach, sing hymns, catechize, confess one's sins, baptize, and otherwise practice fundamentalist Protestantism" (Fairbank 1992, 207). Using these methods Hung organized people to worship God and to rebel against the government. Although the "Tai Ping rebels never ceased proclaiming their Christian faith, and they treated missionaries extremely well" (De Riencourt 148), the Western powers not only gave them no substantial support but also helped the Ching government crush them. The American Frederick T. Ward, as the Englishman Charles G. Gordon, played a major role in the suppression.[2] The rebels and the later revolutionaries who identified themselves with the Taipings, such as many Nationalists and Communists, hated Westerners including American missionaries for betraying the revolution. The Manchu royalty was not really grateful to the Western powers even though they stood by the government in the rebellion, for after all, it was the missionaries who initiated, no matter how indirectly, the whole disturbance that had considerably weakened the dynasty. The Chinese people hated the missionaries even more because little good came out of Hung's "Supreme Peace Heavenly Kingdom" where God was worshiped. At least twenty million people were killed during the thirteen years of rebellion from 1851 to 1864, and it was "almost as terrible a business as the Great War" (Russell 65). In a sense, the Boxer Rebellion of 1900 was the inevitable counterpart of the Taiping Rebellion.

Both sides of the Pacific have much to learn from our past experiences of the cultural exchange, and Pearl Buck's books record the experiences and shed light on our learning. The biographies of her parents, *Fighting Angel* and *The Exile*, vividly demonstrate that American missionaries went to China not only to save the souls of the heathens but also to save their own souls, if not more so. It was primarily out of their own need, not the need of the Chinese, that they left home and became "exiles." In chapter 1 of *Fighting Angel*, Pearl Buck described her father Andrew as a shy and frightened lad of seven, and she mentioned a revealing dialog between his mother Deborah and a kindhearted neighbor Mrs. Pettibrew about him:

"He don't hardly seem like yours, Deborah," Mrs. Pettibrew said solemnly. "He don't even look like yours. I don't know where he gets those light eyes and that red hair. Hiram especially is as handsome a boy as ever I saw---but all your nine children are big and handsome and a sight for sore eyes, except Andy. But then---most families have a runt in 'em."

And this was kind Mrs. Pettibrew! His heart began swelling in him like a balloon. It would burst and he would begin to cry. He wanted to run away and he could not. He sat, his mouth full of dry apple, scuffing his toe back and forth in the grass, caught in agony. His mother released him. She said, kindly enough, "Well, he isn't so handsome, maybe, but he's awfully good, Andy is. None of the others is as good as he is. I always say likely he'll be a preacher, too, like Dave is and like Isaac talks to be---and if he is, he'll be the best of them." (4-5)

These are the "words which he never forgot so long as he lived. They remained not so much words as wounds, unhealed." These two women on "that June day, in a farmhouse in the West Virginia hills, set his feet on the path that was to lead him across plains and seas to a foreign country, to spend his years there, to lie at last in a distant grave, his body dust in foreign earth, because his face was not beautiful. ... On that day he made up his mind he would always be good" (5). Faithful Christians would say, "God works in mysterious ways." Psychologists would say it was the sublimation of his libido. Anyway, China did not call him.

Moreover, Pearl Buck said in chapter 2, there were other reasons for young men to want to be preachers: "aside from the opportunity it gave them to exercise personal authority over other people's minds and lives. At that time it was a calling of high social position. The preacher in a community was also the leader in other ways, and an ambitious young man wanting power could scarcely find a more satisfactory way of getting it" (15). As for Andrew's decision to go to China, she told us that it had to do with his rigorous personality, strong sense of divine duty, dislike to work his father's fields and take hold of the land, and the commanding demand of a "tall gaunt" missionary who had just come back from China (16). At that time, missionaries like Andrew considered China as the key to world-wide salvation. In their thinking China, as Stuart C. Miller said, "was Satan's chief fortress, and the conversion of her huge population would topple pagan defenses elsewhere throughout the world and usher in the millennium" (1974, 281).

If Andrew's determination to be good was initiated by his lack of beauty, Pearl Buck's mother Carie's determination was initiated by her love of beauty. In chapter 1 of *The Exile*, the episode of being stung by "a colored spider, gay in red and black" (40), when observing and touching it, shows her love of beauty and sense of fair play, for she did not blame but just watched spiders thereafter. She was witty, joyous and fun-loving, but sometimes when she "stopped a moment to look through the open door into the garden and to wonder if heaven could be more beautiful, the sharp fear rushed into her mind, "But I am not saved---will I see heaven?" (44). The price for her to see the beauty of the spider was a swollen arm for some time, but the price to see the beauty of heaven was many sorts of misery and suffering for most of her life: lack of love and companionship from her husband, a hard life in a foreign country without much spiritual fulfillment, and the deaths of four of her seven children.

Carie decided to be a missionary also because she was extremely honest and had a strong personality. She would have to see a sign before she could really believe in God, and unlike most of her facile-hearted friends who were easily "'converted' and took communion, ... Carie, sitting mutinous and agonizing in the little church, shook her head above the bread and wine. She would not deceive herself or anyone" (45). She was miserable with the restlessness of this search. She often went out into the woods, threw herself down, and cried to God for a sign, but it never came. At last, her mother was dying, and Carie "could not bear the fear in her mother's eyes" and vowed to herself that she would give her whole life to God---she would be a missionary, if she could have a sign. Then the final moment came as described at the end of chapter one. "She saw her mother's dim eyes lighten. A faint smile of surprise broke over her white lips and she gasped, 'Why---it's---all *true!*'" (48). This Carie took as the sign and steadfastly she set herself to the fulfillment. Her belief was strengthened after several years' studies in West Virginia and in Bellewood Seminary, near Louisville, Kentucky, where she was enchanted by the charm of self-sacrifice, especially by that of the Jewish queen Esther, and gained, as we see in chapter 2, "a delightfully naive assurance that those who do right and trust in God will surely have their reward" (53). When she broached to her father the idea of becoming a missionary to China, she met with unexpected strong objection, which, however, made "what had been a high resolve ... also an obstinate determination" (55).

Carie's motives to be a missionary thus seemed to be less selfish and more noble than Andrew's, and both of their motives were divine rather than worldly, unlike many other missionaries', because the life of American missionaries, hard as it was, was still "the life of the upper class in China." John Fairbank further imparted to us in *Chinese-American Interactions*, "All these Americans, for instance, had servants. They were affluent compared with the masses of the Chinese common people. They had a chance to travel around the country. They went to summer resorts developed by foreigners in China---to Kuling in the lower Yangtze region or to Peitaiho (Beidaihe) north of Tientsin on the coast." They enjoyed many privileges but had few responsibilities. Fairbank continued, "It was very different from life in America, where you walked down the street as one of the people. In China you were a marked man. You might be nobody back home, in fact, maybe you were shipped out to get rid of you. But in China you were somebody. Socially speaking, you were highly visible, you stood out in a crowd" (1975, 66-68). Despite their more noble motives, it still remains true that China did not need Carie and Andrew, nor did any Chinese invite them to come. It was they themselves who thought that China needed them. As Fairbank stated, "The Americans of the late eighteenth century had a very special view of the world, ... they had a special message for mankind, that they were a new breed of people, ... They believed in egalitarian democracy. They believed in small government, ... They believed that their free enterprise promised a superior way of life both materially and spiritually, ... With these beliefs, the Americans were very expansive. Undoubtedly, they were also self-righteous" (1975, 11-12). These aggressive, self-righteous Americans included missionaries, who, along with the merchants and naval diplomats, imposed their own beliefs, despite their good intentions, upon the Chinese by trying to improve their spiritual welfare. Besides, "Good Christians," Fairbank continued, "not only believed all the things in the Bible in rather literal terms, including hell and damnation; many of them also believed that the millennium was about to come, the Day of Judgment when Christ would reappear" (1975, 19). So what they were doing was also to prepare themselves for the Second Coming.

The difference between the novelist's description and the scholar's generalization is that the former may not be so penetrating and truth-revealing as the latter, and yet while it illustrates the not so altruistic motivation, it also presents something noble in these missionaries. We learn about them as human beings in the former and study their missions as a historical phenomenon in the latter. We may gain understanding of the missionaries from the former as particular cases and soften the hard feelings. We may see insight into the cultural interaction from the latter as a whole event and draw some lessons. Both are needed if the Chinese and American peoples wish to bury the hatchet and dig out something valuable for the present and future.

Pearl Buck's biographies are great tragedies about two admirable persons who are engaged in a no-win "holy" cause. They are tragic heroes in the sense that they are both good persons with higher than average human qualities, but they misjudge the nature of their cause, sacrifice a great deal, and die without much accomplishment. Carie also mistakes Andrew as a soul-mate, and the tragedy is clearly felt by herself as she realizes the stern truth later in her life. Andrew, however, does not feel the tragedy so much as his wife does or as the reader may see, for he lacks common sense, and is too devoted to the divine work to see the reality. Having read these books, if we do not admire the heroes, we certainly do not despise the protagonists, as Chinese readers might despise Christian missions after studying their history. Pearl Buck's biographies are likely to arouse our pity and fear, as all great tragedies do, and cause a cultural as well as emotional catharsis that is healthy to the complex of Christian missions.

Andrew is portrayed in *Fighting Angel* as a person who has little desire for material comfort---not that he does not enjoy comfort, but that he has a principle against luxury of any sort. "He would never own more than two shirts---if he had more he gave them away to someone who needed clothing---and those suits he wore to threadbareness, but he was always fresh and clean" (27). When he was traveling, which, being an evangelist, he did very often, he always plodded on foot or upon a donkey or a mule. Later when railroads were built in China, he always rode in third-class until he was very old. "He loved good food as well as any man, but he would not eat more than he thought necessary for strength to do God's work. ... Plain food, eaten slowly and sparingly, was his rule." Yet he was madly generous "when it was to buy Testaments and tracts and books of biblical research, or if it was to help a struggling divinity student toward graduation from seminary" (71). He was critical of many of his colleagues for being lazy, living too well, playing too much chess, quarreling too much among themselves. He expected missionaries to be more like saints than weak humans.

Unlike many other missionaries, Andrew was so dedicated to the work that he plunged into Chinese with ardent enjoyment on the ship to China and "spoke the language as few white men ever do, with feeling, and literary precision. It came at last to be more native to him than his own tongue---he spoke it far more" (29). He was able to preach "his first sermon six months after his arrival" (35). The following anecdote in chapter 3 illustrates not only his habit of speaking Chinese, but also his good command of it:

Once in an American pulpit, when he went back on a furlough, he rose before a great audience to pray. As he always did, he stood a long moment in silence, to empty his mind of all except God. Then, feeling no one there except himself and God, he began to pray---and the prayer came in Chinese. Only when he was half through did he realize what he was doing. He stopped and then went on in English. But the prayer became nothing. He was conscious of others there now, and God was gone. (29-30)

In order to be close to the people he was trying to convert, Andrew was willing to do much more than most other missionaries wished. In chapter 6, we see that "he put on Chinese garments and let his hair grow long and braided it into a queue" (83). When the long hair became intolerable, "he cut it off and bought a false queue which Carie sewed firmly inside his round black satin Chinese cap" (84). In his numerous preaching tours, he was robbed, beaten many times, and almost killed once, but nothing could stop him, not even the Boxer Rebellion. When all other white men had left, he stayed with Ma, a Chinese Christian, all through the hot summer, preaching and handing out his tracts as usual. Ma told Pearl Buck, "Many times I stood near, thinking I must, like Stephen, be witness to the death of a martyr. There were stones flung at him---once a stone cut him on the cheek, but he did not even put up his hand to wipe away the blood. He did not seem to feel it" (105). All these qualities and endeavors are admirable and heroic, but they also make the reader feel pity for their waste in an impossible cause.

In spite of all his efforts, Andrew could not convert many people into the kind of Christians he wished them to be. One of the most important reasons, as Pearl Buck demonstrated in chapter 5, was the different attitude the Chinese held toward religions. Their first reaction to this foreign priest was friendly: "Well, it was a good thing---all religions were good---all gods were good. ... But Andrew shook his head. Not all gods were good, he said firmly. There were false gods---gods of clay and stone---but his was the one true god. They listened, humoring him. After all, he was a foreigner---he could scarcely be expected to know manners" (56-57). This tolerant attitude toward religions made his work both easy and difficult: easy for him to get some listeners, difficult for him to make them listen to him alone. When he was trying to argue with a Chinese priest that the Chinese god was false and even to use a twist of humor in his argument, he met with this kind of rebuff:

He would point his stick at a bowl of food set before a god and remark gently, "I suppose he will eat that when nobody is looking?" And the priest would grin and nod or he would say comfortably, "He sees it and takes the essence of it and he does not mind if we poor priests take the worthless matter that's left and eat it."

Then Andrew would go on and talk a little about the true God, and the priest would listen and murmur, "Every man has his own god, and to each his is the true one, and there are enough for us all." (150)

Nevertheless, Andrew could never understand that "one religion more or less meant nothing to the [Chinese] people. There was always the possibility that there might be an extra god somewhere of whom they had not heard, and whom they should propitiate for benefit. To add a white man's god could do no harm. Buddha himself had been a foreigner, though black" (150). This is a vivid illustration of the greatest obstacle to the missionaries' progress. As Charles P. Fitzgerald admitted, "The Chinese people did not reject the Christian faith, but they were unwilling to grant it the exclusive title to belief which to the European seems so natural" (98). This kind of tolerance inevitably ran counter to the fighting angel's attitude. "It was only when Andrew preached boldly that his god was the one true god that hostility arose. It was when Andrew told them that they must leave the worship of ancestors in their family halls because to bow before a man was to give what belonged to his god only, that many went away and ceased to follow him" (83). The tragedy was whatever Andrew did

he would have done with that swordlike singleness of heart. As it was, born of the times and of that fighting blood, he chose the greatest god he knew, and set forth into the universe to make men acknowledge his god to be the one true God, before whom all must bow. It was a magnificent imperialism of the spirit, incredible and not to be understood except by those who have been reared in it and have grown beyond it. ... But to Andrew spiritual imperialism was as natural as the divine right of kings was to Charles the Second. Andrew, too, had that same naive and childlike guilelessness of the king. (31)

However, belief was a matter of free choice. The Chinese could not be forced, nor did they care to argue with him. They simply left. Pearl Buck also discussed that it was unfair for a missionary, who lived a much better life than average Chinese farmers did, to go around telling them their gods were no good. Although Andrew lived a more simple life than most other missionaries, he might have been more militant than they were. And it is well known that Christianity has been an exclusive religion, and many Christian missionaries were fighting angels to a certain degree.

Besides, the Chinese did not think they were sinners to be saved, but instead, thought Andrew was possibly a penitent trying to purge his sins: "He must have made a vow to a god to do a good deed, else why leave home to wander over the earth? He was laying up merit for himself in heaven, it must be. Perhaps he had committed a crime in his own land. Well, he was an ugly fellow ... but a good man, doubtless, selling his little books to buy his rice on his journey" (57). Later when they knew him better, some were converted because they had chronic diseases, they needed inner peace, or they wanted to please him in order to get a job, to learn English, to see foreign lands. The idea of original sin simply could not get into their minds.

Discussing the difference between the Eastern and Western thought in *China as I See It*, Pearl Buck asserted, "Undoubtedly one reason is that Chinese philosophy has on the whole believed that the heart of man is good, ... this simply said thing has had a very far-reaching effect." On the one hand, although most Chinese are poor, "in that poverty they are not degraded, and they walk with a sort of inner freedom and gaiety which I do not feel among us here" (68). Bertrand Russell also attested to this point of view in *The Problem of China*: "The average Chinaman, even if he is miserably poor, is happier than the average Englishman, and is happier because the nation is built upon a more humane and civilized outlook than our own" (196). On the other hand, the belief in goodness of human nature led to the concept of "saint within and king without," which means, as John Fairbank interpreted, "ethical conduct was the root of good government" (1992, 140). Therefore, unlike the United States where power was shifted downward by means of new constitutional arrangements, China has always sought ways of reforming and perfecting the rulers. At best we had efficient governments in which, as Fairbank said, "Never have so few ruled for so long over so many" (1992, xvi). In late Ching dynasty, the government officials and the people were in the ratio of one to ten thousand (Fairbank 1975, 33), as opposed to the ratio of one to five hundred in the United States today. However, China sometimes suffered disastrous consequences, when the emperor, minister, or magistrate was a tyrant, or when he was feeble, foolish, or incapable. The examples abound particularly in this century. In contrast, the Western concept of original sin, of the inevitable human vulnerability, had positive political results. No statesmen, no matter how good and capable they may be, are fully trusted and given absolute power. The power of the U. S. government, for example, is so counterbalanced that no one man could severely damage its function or become a dictator. The Chinese government makers could benefit the nation by learning this from Christian culture. On the other hand, she implied that American people could benefit themselves by learning something from Chinese culture, since too many Americans, as Pearl Buck maintained in *China as I See It*,

though we be comfortable enough, are not really free. That is, we have inside us a little core of gnawing worry, ... a vague unlocalized sense that perhaps we are not doing all we ought about something or other---a sort of unfocused conscience. We live in an inner unease which makes us restless or weary or overexcitable, or gloomy or too nervously pleasure-seeking. It is really an abortive sense of duty, ... inherited perhaps from our Puritan forefathers, and fostered by Sunday Schools, ... we still have with us the atavistic memory of the wicked human heart. (68-69)

However, the two countries did not learn from each other the best part of their cultural heritages, and the Christian missionaries' preaching in China was the right medicine given to the wrong patient. Ordinary Chinese people did not need to add any more bondage to their souls.

Moreover, the Chinese gentry and literati, as John Fairbank said in *Chinese-American Interactions*, "regarded Christianity as outright superstition and were constantly getting after the missionaries. When told about the Virgin Birth, the literati asked, 'How do you account for that? Could you do that again; if not, how do you know it happened? It's not common sense'" (1975, 23). As far as ethics was concerned, they argued that the Confucian reciprocity "not to do to others as you would not wish done to yourself" (Legge 157) was as good as the Ten Commandments, if not more comprehensive. What was worse was that some stiff and narrow-minded missionaries, when failing to convert others, would bear a grudge against them. They hated Chinese intellectuals including Confucians for their ability to think and to question just as the later Communists did. In chapter 8 of *Fighting Angel*, Pearl Buck criticized this kind of stiff narrowness possessed by some missionaries, particularly some from the South:

To this day they maintain an incredible narrowness of creed which accepts in entirety the miracles of virgin birth, water changed into wine, the dead raised to life, and the second appearance, hourly expected, of Christ. Their judgment upon those who do not or cannot so believe is inhumanly cruel---such persons simply do not exist for them---no friendship is possible, no acquaintance desired. But within their own group of sympathizers they are friendly and kind enough, endlessly helpful in illness or need. Religion in their case, as in so many another, has hardened their hearts and made it impossible for them to see, except through the dark glass of their own creed, what life is or ought to be. (121)

Throughout the two biographies, Pearl Buck was suggesting that human beings are more important than whatever beliefs they might hold, spiritual or political. Love of humanity is the embodiment of love of God or of any Truth, or to be more precise, it is not real love of God if it hurts human beings.

Another cause of the failure of Christian missions, Pearl Buck suggested in *Fighting Angel*, was the unjust policies of the missions, of which Andrew was completely intolerant: "If any individual missionary had a clash with a convert or a Chinese preacher, all the missionaries upheld the white man, regardless of right or wrong. 'It wouldn't do,' it was often said, 'to allow the natives to undermine the authority of the missionary.' For then what would become of the authority of the church?" (81). It is not to say that there was no injustice in the practice of Buddhism, but the fact is that the Buddhist church has never been so institutionalized as the Christian church, and during the dissemination of Buddhism, no Indian priests racially discriminated against the Chinese. Nor did Indians have gunboats and garrisons behind them. As Pearl Buck said in *China as I See It*, people are more likely to be convinced by what one is than by what one says:

I have seen it in China when Westerners were trying to impress their religion upon people. With much speaking, by prayers and sermons and schools they have tried to interpret their religion. But the only time it has been interpreted and understood has been when people observing these Westerners, knowing their lives and understanding their spirit, understood something at least of what they were trying to interpret. I have heard people say in China, "This foreign religion is no good. See what a bad temper the missionary has!" I have heard people say, "This foreign religion must be true and good. See how good the missionary is who preaches it, how kind!" (13)

Indeed, it is just that simple with the common folks. They are not scholars and do not study the Bible so much as they observe the behaviors of the preachers. This lesson is more than historical when we think of what John Fairbank said about exporting Western democracy in *China: A New History*: "And until Western democratic regimes have a more effective way of curbing corruption and maintaining public morale, these examples of democratic government may fail to win public approval in China. We outsiders can offer China advice about the overriding need for human rights, but until we can set an example by properly curbing our own media violence and the drug and gun industries, we can hardly urge China to be more like us" (1992, 432).

Of course, Pearl Buck also mentioned the negative effects of China's being opened to the Gospel at lance point. She described in chapter 8 of *Fighting Angel* that even some Chinese converts would use "the name of the power of the white man and the white man's religion to further their own ends. For in that time it was enough for a man to boast before a magistrate, 'I belong to the white man's church, and I have his protection,' for the magistrate to fall silent and give him his way without regard for justice" (116). This historical factor was later fully discussed by both Chinese and American scholars. But it was courageous of her in 1935 to present the other side of the Boxer Rebellion. She agonized in chapter 7 over the tragedy:

The mind can acknowledge the force of the Chinese right to refuse foreigners upon their soil, it can acknowledge the unwarranted imperialism of such men as Andrew, righteous though they were and honorable in intent and of good meaning. The mind says people have a right to refuse imperialism. But the heart shudders. For those who were martyred were the good and innocent, none the less good and innocent because they were blind. For the glory of God had made them blind. They were drunk with love of God, so that they saw nothing but His glory, could only see the one necessity, that all others should become like themselves. And so forsaking all else they went out as blind men do, trustful, not able to see danger, or if seeing, not believing.

There is no reconciling these two, the mind and the heart. The mind may say a thousand times, and rightly, "They had no right to be there. They provoked what they received." But the heart answers, "They were innocent, for they believed that what they did was of God." (104-105)

It should not be too hard for many voluntary Vietnam veterans to identify themselves, to some extent, with the missionaries, if they liken their political belief to the spiritual belief of these fighting angels. If the lesson is not learned, the tragedy may yet be repeated, only for different causes and with different characters and settings.

Pearl Buck showed us in chapter 4 of *Fighting Angel* still another cause of the failure of Christian missions, which was largely neglected by scholars. It was the foolish fight over trivial differences among too many religious denominations, "well over a hundred different types of the Protestant Christian religion alone. This has been in China, more than a spiritual imperialism---it has been physical as well" (43). They divided their spheres of influence as Japan, Germany, England, and France divided China into areas for trade and power. They quarreled over minor things and belittled each other. She did not gloss over her father's blemishes in this respect. "If some irate Methodist missionary pointed out that in a certain town there was already a Methodist chapel and that therefore Andrew had no right there, he pshawed and preached on briskly." But "illogically, he could be merciless on any who stepped into his preserves" (44). A war that went on year after year between Andrew and a one-eyed Baptist missionary was whether immersion or sprinkling was right in the baptismal service.

After thirty years of strenuous warfare, the situation was settled one morning by the one-eyed missionary being found dead in his bed of heart failure. Andrew felt he was completely vindicated. He was at the breakfast table when the sad news was brought in by the compound gateman. He poured tinned cream into his coffee and put in a little extra sugar before he answered. He secretly loved sugar and was very stern with himself about it. But this morning he stirred it up. Then he looked around at us all and said in a voice of calm and righteous triumph, "I knew the Lord would not allow that sort of thing to go on forever!" (45)

This reminds the reader of the dispute about how to break an egg that Jonathan Swift ridiculed in *Gulliver's Travels,* but the reader probably does not feel any biting satire here. One of her achievements in *Fighting Angel* is that Pearl Buck was able to reveal many of her father's shortcomings, some of which are rather shocking, without making the reader hate him, for the shortcomings are always tempered with humor in the revealing. This is, of course, the humor of a daughter who loved, respected, and understood her father, especially at the time of writing the book. It is not hard to imagine that it would be rather difficult to remain good-humored after living with such a fighting angel all one's life and Carie's tragedy makes the reader wonder how real Andrew's love of God is. If it hurts people closest to him, does it not mean that it is actually a selfish love, even though it is love of one's spirit not flesh, of one's work not comfort? Of course, being a daughter, Pearl Buck would not spell out the scathing truth against her father, whom she grew to love when he was old and became dependent on her. She showed it with understanding and forgiveness through many anecdotes.

In his devotion to his work, Pearl Buck told us in chapter 3 of *Fighting Angel*, Andrew "ruthlessly and unconsciously dedicated all those lives for which he was responsible" (28). First of all, his marriage was mainly for the need of the mission. Without any emotions he told Pearl Buck, "You might have had Jennie Husted to be your mother." His father opposed his intention to be a missionary to China, but his mother compromised, under the condition that he could find a wife to go with him together. He had never considered "such a thing" as a wife before, but his mother said, "There's always women willing to marry any two-legged thing in pants" (23). Then he began to observe young ladies and asked them if they had ever considered the foreign field. Miss Jennie Husted was one who wrote to him and warmly supported his views in his published trial sermon, "The Necessity of Proclaiming the Gospel to the Heathen, with Especial Reference to the Doctrine of Predestination," but she turned out to agree with him only in words. Carie was the first to agree with him in deeds, and so they were married. What Carie told Pearl Buck in chapter 8 of *Fighting Angel* also suggests theirs was a marriage of religious convenience:

Once, in a romantic adolescent moment, dreaming over Tennyson's *Princess*, I looked up to ask her, "Mother, were you and Father ever in love?"

She was sewing at some everyday garment, and for a moment I could not fathom her sudden look at me. It was---was it pain, shock---what was it? But it was not surprised enough for pain or shock. It was as though I had opened a secret, unconsciously. Then the look closed.

"Your father and I have both been very busy people," she said, her voice practical and a little brisk. "We have thought of our duty rather than how we felt." She turned a hem quickly and went on sewing. (125)

Had their marriage been a combination of two souls craving for each other, the lack of love in the usual sense would have been compensated. But Andrew did not see a woman, not even his wife, competent to be companion to a man. "Among men he heard a crude scorn of women as creatures full of notions and whimsies, necessary to man and to be respected only in the simple functions of mating and housekeeping, and this scorn was slacked only by the brief aberration of courtship, to be resumed once it was over. It did not occur to him to look for or desire intellectual companionship or spiritual understanding in a woman" (89). They seemed to be married to the work rather than to each other. He was definitely more excited at the realization of his dream than at the consummation of the marriage. Their honeymoon was to be spent on the journey to China, but he even forgot to buy her a train ticket. Pearl Buck recorded his older brother's reproof in chapter two of *The Exile*: "'You must remember you have a wife now,' ... But he never could quite remember it" (59).

Nor could Andrew quite remember his children, not even at Christmas time. To the day Pearl Buck wrote *Fighting Angel*, she still remembered a doll. "The legend underneath read 'life-size.' ... But it cost three dollars and ninety-eight cents and was of course hopelessly out of possibility. ... She prayed resolutely for years that some Christmas---but there never was such a Christmas. ... Santa Claus---or God---might give it, but not Andrew who needed all the money. And Carie had no money of her own" (100-101). Andrew did not think that his wife should have a checkbook, let alone share a joint bank account. In chapter 9 a strife is described:

Nevertheless, there was that war between them, and it went on for forty years, when suddenly, for no apparent reason, Andrew gave up one day and handed her a checkbook to a joint account. Carie by that time was past the need of it. The children were grown and her great desires were over. Nevertheless, for victory's sake she took it and under direction made out a check or two and then put the book away. But it was a comfort to her. She could draw a check if she wanted to, at last. (139)

Of course, Andrew did not want anything material for himself, but what he wanted also cost money. "Money was the power to save souls---money to rent chapels, to open schools, to buy Bibles. ... So there was always a little ache about Christmas. And then he would murmur doubtfully, 'No one knows the authentic date of Christ's birth. Besides, there is evidence that the festival is mixed with heathen traditions.'" He could not understand Carie's exclamation: "The point of it is to give the children a good time." Pearl Buck defended her father by explaining that it was because "no one had ever troubled to give the child Andrew a good time" (98), but we can also argue that Andrew cared about only his work because it satisfied his soul and gave him pleasure, for which his daughter's pleasure was sacrificed. Moreover, the sad truth was that the Chinese might not need most of his help---the Bible pages were often used to make shoe soles, but his daughter so much wanted that doll.

Andrew was a strict father, and his children were distant from him when they were young. He was always away from home doing his work, and whenever he came back, "nothing seemed quite natural until he was gone again. They tiptoed about, because he was tired, they fetched his slippers and books, they gave up Carie to him," and since Carie was too softhearted to whip the children, "major punishments were reserved for Andrew's coming" (128). Andrew's hand was hard and the punishment severe. All this might be one of the reasons why Pearl Buck did not quite believe in Freudian explanations of Oedipus complex and she certainly had not experienced any Electra complex. She did not apply much psychoanalysis in her books, though one of her majors in Randolph-Macon Woman's College was psychology.

Carie actually regretted having married Andrew although she openly expressed it only once. Pearl Buck revealed it in *My Several Worlds* that when she was trying to leave home and to live on her own, Carie wept and reproached her for disobedience. She answered, "But you left your home when your father did not want you to do it. Grandfather even forbade your marriage." Carie's eyes darkened and said, "I know it, and I did wrong. I wish I had obeyed him" (110). She regretted not only because Andrew did not take good care of her and the children but also because she could not participate directly in his work. In chapter 4 of *The Exile,* Pearl Buck related that when they had grown up and gone to school, Carie "plunged with all her old gay vigor into this new period of her life, ... It seemed to her that these were the years for which she had really left her country; these were the years which were to make that sacrifice worthwhile. She said to herself that surely Andrew would gladly use her strength, as she could use his, each supplementing the other." But Andrew did not want her help, nor did he give her any help. "He was imbued, moreover, with the Pauline doctrine of the subjection of the woman to the man and to him it was enough if she kept his house and bore his children and waited on his needs" (193). Thus, much injustice was done to their own women when the missionaries were attempting to save the souls of other men. The achievement of their attempt was not so real, to Pearl Buck, as the hurt of injustice, and she reflected this nearly thirty years before Betty Friedan published *The Feminine Mystique* in 1963.

Andrew was so much devoted to his work that even Pearl Buck did not know for sure how much he cared about Carie in their busy life of saving others. In chapter 10 of *Fighting Angel,* we find Carie was dying and unconscious, but Andrew "was almost glad, for he would not have known what to say to her. It was strange he could think of nothing he would have said," strange, I believe, because he had watched so many die, soothed their souls, and condoled their families. "He did not speak of her again, and none of us saw him weep. Whether he was widowed or not, none of us knew. ... He stood tearless beside her grave, his face set in utter gravity, his eyes sealed in gravity." After the funeral, he went into his study and shut the door. Fearing he might be grieving alone too much, Pearl Buck went to look through his window and found him "working over the pages of the Testament, the Chinese brush in his hand, painting the characters one by one down the page. ... And he never once visited her grave. But something broke in him, some strength of stubbornness. There was no one at home to contradict him, praise him, blame and scold him into energy" (162). The description of a hard-hearted man who cared about nothing but his work is tempered by the last two sentences. But the reader will still ask, "If this was how he treated his wife and children, what was his heart made of? How could he save others with such a heart? Wasn't his devotion to God too abstract? Was it possible that he was too bookish, or his mind was too innocently divine to do missionary work among people? What was his work after all? How successful was he? Was his success worth the sacrifices?"

Not surprisingly, after Carie's death, when some righteous young missionaries attacked him again, "for the first time in his life doubt began to creep in. Perhaps they were right---perhaps nothing he had done was any use" (163). Carie used to warn him often that some of his converts were corrupt. "She was nearer the common people than he could ever be. Women were not afraid of her and they gossiped and told tales, ... and he refused to believe anything." His answer was simply, "I merely sow the good seed---he will separate the tares from the wheat" (116). Now the proofs of everything were presented before him: "Bills for opium stamped with the church seal, signed confessions, sworn statements. ... Without knowing what he did, he signed the paper and gave away his work" (163). Although he soon recovered from this blow and with Pearl Buck's help got the job to teach in the Nanking seminary and to establish the Correspondence School, he was not quite the same thereafter.

Nevertheless, Andrew was one of the best missionaries. He regarded China as his spiritual country. Actually, he was far more at home working in China than spending his furlough in America, whereas many other missionaries could not even bear the hardship and monotony of living in an alien country although their living standard was much higher than that of the average Chinese. "In the pages of *The Chinese Recorder* a few writers testified that they (missionaries) lived in more comfortable homes in China than they had in the United States. Others belabored the fact that, by living in compounds, they shut themselves off from the Chinese" (Varg 316). In comparison, Andrew always lived and worked among the Chinese peasants and was much more successful than the average missionary. "At one time," his daughter mentioned in chapter 8 of *Fighting Angel*, "Andrew had over two hundred churches and schools in his diocese" (115). He translated the New Testament from Greek into Chinese in the vernacular style and published it with his own money. He never obeyed any rich men or church authorities when he believed that he was right. He tried his best to protect Chinese converts and bore much persecution from his colleagues and church. He steadfastly visited the sick and stayed by the dying, and no one knew how often he did these things, for he never told anyone. "They were simply part of his work. Most of all the Chinese loved him because he knew no color to a man's soul and he took the part of the yellow man again and again against the white man---the lonely convert's side, the poorly paid native preacher's side, against the arrogant priest, the superior missionary" (158). At last, his new school in Nanking "met with remarkable success. In the course of the ten years Andrew was to see the student roll mount into hundreds and upon it were men from every country in the Orient and some of the South Sea Islands and a few were among Chinese in the United States" (172).

Pearl Buck did not say whether or not these achievements were worth the sacrifices. This kind of expenditure and income can hardly be measured, but one of her implications was that one should not involve others' happiness into one's own sacrifice no matter how noble and divine the cause might be. Her sympathy was definitely with her mother, and more important, in the portrayal of her mother, she showed us other achievements of American missionaries: medicine, health, education, ideology, sexual equality, famine relief, and setting good examples by being good. These were, of course, not the ends of Christian missions. As Griffith John said, "We are here, not to develop the resources of the country, not for the advancement of commerce, not for the mere promotion of civilization; but to do battle with the powers of darkness, to save men from sin, and conquer China for Christ" (qtd. in Lutz xix). But Pearl Buck showed the opposite was true.

Some scholars later studied the first six of these seven achievements including: George H. Danton's *The Culture Contacts of the United States and China,* Kenneth S. Latourette's *A History of Christian Missions in China,* Jonathan Spence's *To Change China,* Evelyn S. Rawski's "Elementary Education in the Mission Enterprise," and John Fairbank's *Chinese-American Interaction.* Some of them maintained, as did Pearl Buck, that the means, such as schools and hospitals, the missionaries used for the end of converting the Chinese were actually what the Chinese really needed. But as scholars, they discussed the achievements only in terms of institution, influence, and various statistics. Inevitably, they could not summarize many of the good deeds individual missionaries had done, nor could the influence of such deeds be measured properly. Literature, particularly biography, seems to be the only means of reflecting them, and especially, the seventh aspect, setting good examples by being good. As a by-product of a genuine portrayal of Pearl Buck's mother, *The Exile* does the reflecting.

Carie's life consisted of following Andrew around, taking care of him and the house---his base---trying to keep the children alive, and educating them. However, simply by being a good woman she probably changed more Chinese people for the better than Andrew did, even if she did not convert as many into Christians. Pearl Buck did not record her mother's good deeds, so to speak, but they were described in the characterization of Carie and her relation to other persons. Unlike Andrew, who was reserved except when preaching and had no intimate friends all his life, Carie was easygoing and got along with ordinary

Chinese very well. In chapter 3, Pearl Buck said, "Stronger message than her words was the swift and native sympathy of her nature when she listened to their sad stories." They called her "The American of Good Works," and many women, whom she had never met before, came to her home to tell her their troubles because she would listen and try "to do something about it." Pearl Buck remembered that "her mobile face twisted with sympathy, listening earnestly to a broken voice that went on and on. ... Many of these women were among the most downtrodden of their kind and had never in all their lives had the comfort of having one sit down to hear the burden of their poor hearts, and it seemed they must tell her over again and again for the relief it gave to speak to a listening ear." And once a woman said to her, "I have been despised all my life because I am a woman, ignorant and ugly. Yet, you, an American and a stranger, pay heed to me. Therefore what you believe I will believe, for it must be true to make you like this---kind, even to me!" (104).

One of these women, Wang Amah, lost "her little girl child the morning it was born" because her man did not want it. "Carie, passing the wretched hut on the same day, heard the desperate moaning from within and her quick ear detected more than usual suffering and it was a call to her at once to see what was wrong" (91). The woman wanted to leave the cruel man but had nowhere to go. "Never did Carie ask another question of the woman. She received her into her home" (92). The woman became the amah (foster mother) of the children, took good care of them, taught Pearl Buck Chinese, told her many stories, and was well looked after when she was old. When Carie was very sick after giving birth to Faith, Wang Amah nursed her back to health with "a dish of special broth made from a particular fish and herbs the Chinese use for puerperal fever" (143). When Wang Amah caught cholera one summer, leaving the children to Andrew's care and interrupting his long morning prayer (usually a whole hour) for the first time, Carie treated her, bathed her, and cured her. Later Carie confessed, "I am afraid I did not do it for the Lord's sake" (155), and when Andrew said that she should remember to do things in His name, she protested, "When somebody is dying you haven't time to think why you save them---you have to start doing it right away!" (156). Yet she was not so sure whether she had given up the quest after God in mere service to people, for which, she was afraid, God had taken some of her children away, and she always thought Andrew "better" than herself. Modern readers, however, should know better.

While portraying her mother as a kind and generous woman, Pearl Buck further illustrated that being a good person and doing good deeds were probably more important and certainly more effective in changing others' lives for the better than just preaching the Gospel. While Andrew was preaching outside, Carie opened her small clinic at home, treating sickly mothers and babies, teaching women how to read and to sing and to knit, imparting the simple essentials of Christian living and conduct, and looking after her own children at the same time. Andrew gave his message, we find in chapter 4 of *The Exile*, "as one who comes a stranger to a strange land, bearing a letter from the king of his own country. It was his duty to read the message that all might hear it. That duty done, his responsibility ended" (191). Carie did more. For instance, when she was soothing a dying woman, the woman was so touched and said to her, "There has never been one who cared for me as you have. ... Why have you loved me, who am not of your blood and bone?" (146). Then she entrusted her daughter Precious Cloud to Carie's care. Carie took Precious Cloud as her Chinese daughter, brought her up, sent her to a Chinese boarding school, and married her to a decent Chinese young man. Later their children called Carie grandmother. One psychologist suggested in the Pearl Buck Centennial Symposium that she adopted nine children later in her life because she had not been able to get the life-size doll when she was a little girl. I wonder why her mother's example was not considered as a more influential factor.

In China Carie was not helping only the Chinese. Knowing some American sailors disgraced their country by visiting brothels and beating up prostitutes, she was ashamed and "began to do something she continued for many years" when she lived by the Yangtze River. She made cakes, pies, cookies, and "invited the boys to tea. ... When they were fed to capacity, she sang to them and sometimes just sat and let them talk to her, woman-starved as they were. When they were gone, she had a triumph in her that for at least one time she had kept them safe---had protected them and given them a little of America" (99). Carie did much more than she preached. She said to those who came to her house "not a great deal beyond the practical, merry talk she made of this and that in common affairs, for she was never any good at preaching." But people always left her house "clean and fed and heartened" (145). Once an American tramp, who used to be a tradesman, came and stayed a week. The world had dealt with him harshly, and "he could scarcely speak without oaths. ... When he left us, rested, clean, wearing a suit of Andrew's clothes and Andrew's shoes on his feet, he hesitated at the door and at last he muttered, 'Never reckoned I'd see America again---have, though, and right here, ma'am!'" (146). Pearl Buck rightly concluded Carie's biography by saying, "To the thousands of Chinese whom she touched in every sort of way she was America. ... To all of us everywhere who knew her this woman was America" (218).

This is an appropriate evaluation of missionaries like Carie. Whenever there was a famine, she would help Andrew administer relief and tell people, "'It is from America, for you---from America!'" Pearl Buck recalled, "Over and over again I have heard her say those words. She became to those hopeless folk a living embodiment of America" (168). One year the famine was so bad that Carie canceled even Christmas. The day was "spent in cooking great vats of rice and distributing it bowl by bowl through a crack in the gate until none was left and we had done all we could. It was a long, silent day. She could not even sing at evening. As reward there was less weeping in the night and she slept a little more" (171). Carie was, of course, only one of thousands of American missionaries who gave the Chinese the kind of help they really needed. Even before the relationship between China and the United States was normalized, some Chinese had told their children, as my mother told me, that Americans were good people and America was a generous country. Indeed, individual missionaries like Carie represented the best of America.

Thus, Pearl Buck's biographies of her parents are valuable in that they bring two missionaries to life. One was a typical fighting angel with all the good intentions, which did not prove to be enough for the cause in which he was engaged. He sacrificed much of his comfort as well as the happiness of his family for primarily his own spiritual needs and made some achievements on rather shaky ground, a truth he never seemed to have quite realized. His characterization is vividly realized as his daughter describes his unique righteousness, bookishness, stubbornness, fearlessness, self-confidence, and his lack of common sense and human consideration. His portrait is of a hermit among the crowd, a man who lives within himself, having no companion, communicating with no one but his God, unconcerned about no one's opinions but his own or supposedly God's. No wonder he was compared to a modern St. Paul; his attitude toward women were the same as the saint's, too.[3] In his endeavors and personality we can see more causes for the failure of Christian missions in China than for their achievements.

Another character was a typical missionary wife who was not able to preach much but by simply being a good woman and doing good deeds probably changed more people than she might have by preaching and taught many Chinese about medicine, health, language, and the moral principles shared by all human beings. She was also unique: a witty, humorous, warmhearted, courageous, and emotional woman who was searching for God with doubts all her life, loving beauty and material refinement with guilty feelings, and giving practical help to people with the fear that she was forgetting their souls. She appeared to be a much more sympathetic figure than Andrew, for she suffered so much more in losing four of her seven children and regretted her choice after being disillusioned with her saint-like but not so humane husband. In her life we can see some achievements of Christian missions in China that are almost impossible to be reflected otherwise.

Pearl Buck's artistic achievement in these two biographies has been discussed by others, and I have been emphasizing their cognitive function. She saw the faults as well as the merits of the American missionaries, and in portraying her parents she also presented some achievements and causes of the failure of Christian missions that should be further studied. As Henry S. Canby commented, "Her biographies of her parents are unquestionably the best studies ever done of the unique personal traits developed by the missionary fervor of the nineteenth century, which, some day, will be recognized as a very important part of the social history of Western civilization in that departed epoch" (8). These two books should be rediscovered and treasured, in Paul Doyle's words, "not only as examples of excellent biographical writing but also as pictures of two completely rendered Americans and of a historical phenomenon characteristic of a particular time and place" (1980, 76). This part of the chapter, I hope, is only a beginning of the rediscovery.

Pearl Buck also presented an ideal Christian in *Pavilion of Women* although it is not artistically so successful a portrait as are the portraits of her parents. Father Andre or Brother Andre, depending on who is speaking of him in the novel, bears a similar name and some physical similarities to her father, but he is different in many ways: he belongs to no church but makes his living by teaching languages and sciences; he does not talk of God to people who do not wish to listen; he does not go around telling people their gods are false; he does good deeds to the best of his ability; he influences people around him with his behavior, knowledge, and reasoning. Andre is a humanitarian, not a fighting angel. This Italian Christ-figure has been cast out by his church as a heretic because he thinks men and women are divine, a great sin in his generation. He is not exactly a missionary but he has brought more blessings to the Chinese than most missionaries. Even after his death, his spirit lives on in Madame Wu, the protagonist, who becomes wiser and kinder because of him, runs her big household more humanely, takes care of the homeless girls who have been brought up by Father Andre, and thus begins her own new and meaningful life.

As a foil to Andre is the funny figure Little Sister Hsia, a plain and kindhearted English missionary spinster who speaks Chinese with mispronunciations that often result in malapropism. She is dead serious, however, once she starts preaching, and only to be polite Madame Wu listens to her preach of the Gospel with patient disinterest. Andre's way of Christianity is different, not in preaching but, as he tells Madame Wu, "in cleaning my house and making my garden, in feeding the lost children I find and take under my roof, in coming to teach your son, in sitting by those who are ill, and in helping those who must die, that they may die in peace." He has also adopted the tolerant Chinese attitude toward other religions, as shown in his reply to Madame Wu's worry about a religious conflict in a funeral: "I would not have kept your priests away, ... I never forbid anyone who can bring comfort anywhere. We all need comfort" (chap. 8). His attitude is further expressed in the following dialog with Madame Wu in chapter 10:

"Is our Heaven your God, and is your God our Heaven?" she inquired.

"They are one and the same," he replied.

"But Little Sister Hsia told me they are not," she retorted. "She always told us to believe in the one true God, and not in our Heaven. She declared them not the same."

"In a temple there are always a few foolish ones." he said gently.

"There is only one true God. He has many names."

"Then anywhere upon the round earth, by whatever seas, those who believe in any God believe in the One?" she asked.

"And so are brothers," he said, agreeing.

"And if I do not believe in any?" she inquired willfully.

"God is patient," he said. "God waits. Is there not eternity?"

Unlike Andrew who always preached to people around him and gave or sold them religious tracts, Andre does not impose his belief upon others. He regards belief as an individual ability like senses and intellect that can grow within everyone. When other persons have the need to learn about it, he tries to help them cultivate it with common sense and reasoning, instead of reading out of the Bible or giving a serious sermon. On another occasion when Madame Wu asks him about the existence of the soul, Andre explains that the soul is a residue neither male nor female, it is not inherited from any other creature, but it shapes one a little different from all others. "It is that which is given to me for my own, a gift from God." She again inquires, "And if I do not believe in God?" Andre answers thus:

"It does not matter whether you believe or not, ... You can see for yourself that you are like no other in this world, and not only you, but the humblest and the least beautiful creature also has this precious residue. If you have it, you know it exists. It is enough to know that. Belief in its giver can wait. God is not unreasonable. He knows that for belief we like to see with the eyes and hear with the ears, that we like to hold within our hands. So does the child also know only what its five senses can tell it. But other senses there are, and these develop as the being grows, and when they are fully developed we trust them as once we trusted only our senses." (chap. 12)

Madame Wu is a good, capable, and highly intelligent lady, but she has been proud and despised others including her husband until Andre makes her realize it. As a result, she is improved, and so are the lives of people around her.

By the portraits of her parents and the success story of Brother Andre Pearl Buck actually negated the sermonizing of Christian missionaries, if not the whole missionary movement itself. Although she did not declare this standpoint, readers are likely to come to this conclusion themselves. Furthermore, she suggested in these books, particularly in *Kinfolk,* what the Chinese needed was the knowledge of natural sciences rather than God.

Since the late 18th-century the study of Orientalism, as Edward Said and many other scholars have attested, has basically been the cultural reinforcement of Occidental self-righteousness. It tells no more truth about the East than it confirms the belief that the West is superior. The time demarcation is important here because it indicates the decisive function of the economic power in such matters. Before and during the 18th-century, China had been seen by most Western scholars as an ideal country, the model of the world, basically because it was economically strong compared with most Western countries. Marco Polo's exaggerations of the "advanced" Chinese civilization were well known, and even in the 17th-century sinophilism was at its height in England. Take the Chinese language for instance. Francis Bacon took Aristotle's notion that words are "images of cogitations" and letters are "images of words" and asserted that the Chinese "write in characters real, which express neither letters nor words in gross, but things or notions" (1: 146-47). The inference was that Chinese was the "primitive language"---primitive in the sense that it was the first language

God created and the antediluvian people used, a pure language unaffected by the confusion of tongues at Babel. Sir Walter Raleigh claimed in his *History of the World* that Noah's ark finally landed somewhere between India and China, and so Thomas Browne assumed that "the Chinese ... may probably give an account of a very ancient language" and so they are still able to "make use of the workes of their magnified Confutius many hundred yeares before Christ, and in an historicall series ascend as high as Poncuus (Pangu, the first man in Chinese mythology), who is conceaved to bee Noah" (427). Eventually in 1668, John Webb, though he did not know Chinese, wrote an octavo volume, *An Historical Essay Endeavoring a Probability That the Language Of the Empire of China is the Primitive Language,* in which he also proved to his own satisfaction that the legendary Chinese king Yao was Yaus, Jaus, Janus, and finally, Noah. Therefore, he found China a country where both Christian and Platonic ideals were realized, for the Chinese were "of the City of God" (32).

Jesuit missionaries propagated this belief, and based on their fabulous reports from China and inaccurate translations of some Chinese classics, "many eighteenth-century philosophers found in China and the Chinese the model of a nation well organized on the basis of lofty reason and good conduct" (Zhang 117) even though they were beginning to belittle the culture of the Middle East. Voltaire admired the Chinese for they had perfected morality and he "greatly admired Confucius for counselling virtue, preaching no mysteries, and teaching in 'pure maxims in which you find nothing trivial and no ridiculous allegory'" (Zhang 118). European philosophers discovered, as Longxi Zhang continued to demonstrate, "that in great antiquity in China---a country whose material products had won the admiration of the average people in the market--- Confucius had taught the philosophy of a state built on the basis of ethical and political *bon sens*, and that the Chinese civilization had developed for centuries on principles different from, yet in many respects superior to, those of the West" (118). Adolf Reichwein even proclaimed, "Confucius became the patron saint of eighteenth-century Enlightenment. Only through him could it find a connecting link with China" (77). All these misconceptions were only the products of subjective idealist thinking. None of these scholars knew much about Chinese culture, but they assumed that a strong country must have had superior ethics and philosophy, and vice versa. Daniel Defoe was probably the first notable writer who questioned and despised the "advanced" Chinese civilization through *Robinson Crusoe*:

What are their buildings to the palaces and royal buildings of Europe? What is their trade to the universal commerce of England, Holland, France, and Spain? What are their cities to ours for wealth, strength, gaiety of apparel, rich furniture, and an infinite variety? What are their ports, supplied with a few junks and barks, to our navigation, our merchant fleets, our large and powerful navies? Our city of London has more trade than all their mighty empire. One English, or Dutch, or French man-of-war of eighty guns would fight and destroy all the shipping of China. (I: 2: 256-57)

What he said was much closer to China's reality than the favorable reports of Jesuit missionaries, and China's material inferiority also caused him to look down on the Chinese and their culture. Defoe found Chinese people "a barbarous nation of pagans, little better than savages" (I: 2: 257) and Confucianism "really not so much as a refined paganism" (II: 3: 127). Dr. Samuel Johnson also called the Chinese "barbarians," for he thought it was a sign of "rudeness" that they had not formed an alphabet as all other nations had (Boswell 929). Later when the colonialists, like Robinson Crusoe, found China lagged far behind the West in science, technology, and economy, they began to despise Chinese culture, to blame Confucius for everything, and to assert that China's backwardness was the result of the absence of Christianity.

Bertrand Russell was right when he concluded after comparing Greek culture with Taoism, Jewish religion and ethics with Confucianism, and modern science in the West with the lack of it in China, "The distinctive merit of our civilization, I should say, is the scientific method; the distinctive merit of the Chinese is a just conception of the ends of life. It is these two that one must hope to see gradually uniting" (194). Pearl Buck's novels illustrate this point of Russell's. Dr. James Liang, the hero of *Kinfolk*, having earned a medical degree in the United States, goes to China to treat the sick and the wounded. His brother and sister also join him there to serve their motherland and to search for their roots. When they realize that they are more needed in the rural area than the city, they go to Anming, a backward and incredibly primitive village of their ancestors. By building a bathhouse, a small clinic, and a primary school, they are gradually improving people's lives there and at the same time, they have found their own value. What they have done is only the means by which the missionaries attempted to convert the Chinese into Christians, but in *Kinfolk* the means is shown, rightly, as an end by itself.

Nevertheless, Pearl Buck was not suggesting in these books that nothing in Chinese culture needed changing or that China could learn nothing from Christian culture except science. She constantly depicted the need to do away with the social hierarchy and with sexual inequality, which were relatively more serious in China than in the West and prevented China from progress and caused much injustice to Chinese women and girls. Dr. Liang Wen Hua in *Kinfolk* is a typical member of Confucian elite, who knows both Chinese and Western cultures very well but knows nothing about the majority of Chinese people, the peasants. He is a snob who sneers at the ordinary Chinese and assumes that only he and his like can represent China. His nationalism makes him deceive himself and his children and students by exaggerating the old glory of China and by denying the existence of ugly Chinese customs such as footbinding of women in the 20th-century. Pearl Buck argued in *China as I See It* that partly it was the gap between the intellectuals and peasants and the refusal of an intellectual like Dr. Liang Wen Hua to work with the peasants that kept China backward. In *Kinfolk* she demonstrated that progress can be made only if intellectuals are willing to approach the peasants and farmers, to understand them, and to help them as James Liang and Mary Liang have done. Chinese intellectuals should learn from American missionaries in this respect. The Christian idea that men are created equal was crucial and most needed in China, and the idea that men and women are equal must yet be accepted by both the East and the West. Almost all of Pearl Buck's books expose sufferings inflicted on women. However, she never attributed the injustices to lack of religion, for she had seen them among Christians, too. She never assumed, as most missionaries did, that China's problem could be solved once the Chinese accepted Christianity. She never equated Chinese cultural differences including concubinage and arranged marriage to evil, barbarism, or something Christian angels must fight. On the contrary, she illustrated the raison d'etre of these cultural differences in her novels, which helped Western readers discern some Orientalists' misconceptions.

On the one hand, she imparted through Rulan, in *Pavilion of Women*, that young Chinese intellectuals were working hard to abolish concubinage. They were trying to drive the idea of "one-wife system of marriage" into people's mind by marching "in procession in the Shanghai streets in hottest summer" and waving blue banners that "bore in white letters the words, 'Down with concubinage.'" Their endeavor was related somewhat comically. They were obviously students who had been affected by Western education, as Rulan said concubinage was "a thing so old-fashioned, so---so wicked" (chap. 2). Indeed, concubinage caused women's sufferings and many domestic troubles, as Madame Kang exclaimed, "Why, when my father took a concubine my mother cried and tried to hang herself, and we had to watch her night and day, and when he took a second concubine the first one swallowed her earrings, and so it went until he had the five he ended with. They all hated one another and contended for him" (chap. 5). On the other hand, Pearl Buck revealed, through Madame Wu's decision to find her husband a concubine, some reasons that Westerners and modern Chinese did not know for the marriage system, which was more than simply a product of men's degeneration or their insistence on male progeny. First, since no effective contraceptives were available in the past, Madame Wu was tired of giving birth to one baby after another and she had no sexual desire any more. Second, she knew that her husband still had sexual needs, and it was better for the family to let him marry a concubine under her control than to visit the brothel or to commit adultery. These were the reasons why when Rulan proclaimed, "I believe in the equality of man and woman," Madame Wu replied, "Ah, two equals are nevertheless not the same two things. They are equal in importance, equally necessary to life, but not the same" (chap. 2). Third, it was a better way of life for a poor woman like Chiuming to be a concubine than to be a courtesan or to remain destitute. Being a novelist, Pearl Buck did not argue for or against concubinage; she just presented the reality as it was. Readers may come up with the above reasons, and they may also ask, "How about individuality? How about romantic love?"

Indeed, in America two lovers can embrace in public and let the world go by. In the name of love, judges refused to dissolve underage youngsters' marriage that had been contracted against their parents' wishes, and a school board retracted its dismissal of a teacher for romantic attachment with his pupil. "All of these attitudes and decisions are perfectly in order in a culture where individual predilections are accorded the highest value and the play of emotions is given more and more of a free hand" (F. Hsu 36-37). In China, however, these attitudes and decisions would be unthinkable now, and much more so half a century ago, for collectivity was and still is valued more than individuality. One is supposed to put individual happiness below the happiness of one's family, which always include one's parents. Likewise, the community should be considered above the family, and the country above the community. Therefore, "individual feelings must be subordinated to the requirements of the group, while sex and all activities associated with it must be restricted to the compartments of life where it is socially appropriate" (F. Hsu 37-38).

Because of this fundamental difference, the forms of love and marriage in the East differ from those in the West, and both have their pros and cons. In China marriage and family have been stable, and the divorce rate has been low. On the whole, children have been brought up in healthy environments, and old people have been well looked after at home. However, there have been many tragedies in which individual happiness was sacrificed for the benefit of the family or the country. Lu You, for instance, could not marry the cousin he loved and lived in sorrow all his life. Jiao Chong-ching's (Jiao Zhongqing's) mother, another example, domineered his wife so much that she committed suicide. As for concubinage, when Western ladies attacked it saying that then a woman should also have several husbands, Gu Hongming defended it by a witty repartee: "You have seen a tea-pot with four tea-cups, but did you ever see a tea-cup with four tea-pots?" But the truth was best described in Pan Jinlian's retort: "Do you ever see two spoons in the same bowl that do not knock against each other?" (qtd. in Y. Lin 1935, 165). As for romantic love, Chinese youngsters eighty years ago had no chance to develop it, for they were separated once they reached the age of puberty. Then their parents would arrange the marriage for them, in which they hopefully would learn to love each other. They usually did not experience any vehement emotions for each other but often shared a life-long commitment to family responsibilities. Marriage was the necessity for regeneration and the well-being of children, and love between husband and wife was only the added grace to a couple's happiness. Therefore, in Chinese literature prior to this century, love always refers to lust, and lovers always mean people involved in an affair. Deep feelings are described more often between parents and children than between husbands and wives. Friendship is usually found between persons of the same sex, for they naturally have more in common than persons of different sex.

In the West, romantic love is also a relatively recent concept. It took deep root "a few centuries after it was given currency by the troubadours, who flourished in southern France, northern Italy and Spain between the 11th and 13th centuries" (F. Hsu 38). It has aroused much imagination of young men and women to create, stimulated their motivation to strive, urged them to perfect themselves, and brought happiness to millions of men and women. However, it also resulted in irresponsible behaviors that caused much misery and suffering: broken families, disputes over alimony and custody, teenage pregnancy, illegitimate children, single parenthood, and solitary old age. Worst of all, children's well-being is sometimes sacrificed to the happiness or predilections of the parent or parents. As for the lovers themselves, they often hurt each other's feelings deeply as James Liang is hurt by Lili in *Kinfolk*. Tennyson's famous line, "Tis better to have loved and lost / Than never to have loved at all," represents only one opinion. Even many Englishmen preferred not to let their reason be affected by emotion for women. For most Chinese people marriage was just to "take a daughter-in-law for the parents" or to "get along" and to "raise kids." Since young people often make mistakes as did Pearl Buck with her first marriage, their parents could help them especially in the past when to marry at the age of twenty was generally thought late. Besides, love often gradually developed in an arranged marriage as illustrated in the case of James Liang and Yumei. It might not be so passionate but it was usually steady and enduring.

Of course, Pearl Buck was not suggesting in *Pavilion of Women* and *Kinfolk* that arranged marriage was preferable to freedom of marriage or that a concubine was better than a mistress. She was just demonstrating that China's marriage system was not as bad as many Westerners thought. It was not simply a "wicked" social evil. Before we changed or abolished it, we should study its raison d'etre, its advantages and drawbacks. Individualism or collectivism, romantic love or arranged marriage, one can hardly say yet which is better. Nowadays monogamy is the mainstream marriage system all over the world. It is doubtlessly a manifestation of sexual equality. It certainly has saved a great deal of "knocking against each other" in a polygamous household. Yet it has its own problems. Many people have fallen in love with two men or two women simultaneously and wished the social institution would tolerate their love. In China in the past, if a woman fell in love with a married man, she could be willing to marry him and serve his wife with respect. Is it better now for women to drive one another out and to take one another's place by turn in the name of monogamy? In Nepal, a woman could marry a man and all his brothers if they were happy to share her and to keep the family unity. Is it more civilized for men to fight and even to kill one another for romantic love of a beautiful lady? Is the marriage of the Mormons and the Moslems immoral or is it just different from ours? Don't we all have strong points as well as weak points? Human nature is imperfect, and so are our institutions, Eastern or Western. The important thing is to understand each other rather than to judge. In understanding we can learn from each other and possibly even work out something better.

The value of *Pavilion of Women* and *Kinfolk* lies primarily in such cognitive function, which also includes Pearl Buck's exposure of some old and obviously unhealthy ways of life and thinking that are going through a gradual change with the help of the people educated in the West. Artistically, however, the novels have some considerable flaws. Madame Wu, the heroine in *Pavilion of Women*, is far less vivid than some minor characters including Madame Kang. The latter's words, weeping, and laughter give her so much more life than the former, who is supposed to be, I admit, graceful and elegant but instead is rather pale. Brother Andre seems too good to be true, and he is like an ideal model existing only in the writer's dream. In Paul Doyle's words, he "appears as a fanciful dream, a wish-fulfillment, a strange, exotic creature who belongs more appropriately in the fantastic world of James Hilton's Shangri-La than in real life" (1980, 121). Similarly, the hero James Liang in *Kinfolk* is pale compared with his mother, Mrs. Liang, who is vividly realized with lively gossip and vigorous energy. Dr. Liang's affair with Violet Sung stands out as an unnecessary Hollywood dessert in a Chinese country meal. Although the plot, as many critics remarked, is contrived, it is flat and lacks a climax. On the whole, however, *Kinfolk* is still, in Mary Ross's words, "a richly human story, with humor and pathos as well as the larger emotions." It casts light on China and Chinese people and is also "far from flattering" to Western readers by reflection (1949, 6).

As far as cognitive function is concerned, Pearl Buck's *Peony* is unique and most valuable. The novel illustrates the assimilation of Jews in the city of Kaifeng in the northern Chinese province of Honan (Henan). As we know, Rome destroyed Jerusalem nineteen centuries ago, and the Jewish uprising under Bar Kokhba was defeated by the Romans in A. D. 135. Then the large-scale Diaspora began and from then on Jews scattered all over the globe, but they rarely assimilated anywhere in the world. Wherever they went, they brought their religion with them, built a synagogue, formed a Jewish community, and always managed to maintain their cultural tradition. In 1948, many Jews even went back to Palestine from different parts of the world and reestablished their country. However, China was a big exception. Jews went to China, as described at the beginning of *Peony*, "in a small steady human stream" to trade or "in a sudden crowd of some hundreds at a time" to seek shelter from persecution. If they settled down there (they tended to do so), usually within a few generations they assimilated themselves into Chinese culture. Even the largest Jewish community in Kaifeng disappeared by the end of Ching dynasty (Shapiro 125). As Michael Pollak, the authoritative scholar of Chinese Jews, attested, "Physiognomically, linguistically, and culturally they have all become as Chinese as their neighbors" (xiii), and Lawrence I. Kramer confirmed, "Photographs taken by Brown in 1933 show that the K'aifeng Jews were indistinguishable from other Chinese."[4] Although some of them preserved some Jewish tradition, they also "used their sacred books in casting lots," as James Finn, the author of *The Jews in China*, an early influential book on the subject, observed in 1843, "and their literary men pay the same homage to the memory of Kung-foo-sze (Confucius) as their neighbors do. ... and in writing Chinese they render that name by Teen (heaven), just as the Chinese do, instead of

Shang-te (Lord above), or any other ancient appellation of the Deity" (23-24). Their religious enthusiasm slackened, their synagogues were not well attended to, and they "had by now [1850] no teacher and almost no knowledge of their religion, even less of Hebrew" (Leslie 56).

Judaism in Kaifeng was mingled with Chinese religions and philosophies as shown by the words carved on the vertical tablets in their synagogue: "From the time of Noah, when beauteous creation arose, until now, talented men of Western India have sought the principal that produced Heaven, Earth, and Man / From the time of Abram, when our religion was established, and subsequently, men of China have diffused instruction, and obtained complete knowledge of Confucianism, of Buddhism, and of Taoism" (W. White 138). What should be explained here is that "Noah" is, in the original language, "Nu Wa," the goddess who creates the first human beings according to the Chinese myth.[5] William White translated the name into "Noah" in order for English readers to understand without explanation. Another pair of vertical tablets that he recorded and translated demonstrates that the religious ceremonies of the Kaifeng Jews were mingled with Chinese customs: "The Spring Sacrifices have to do with selecting and growing, and the Autumn Sacrifices with harvest thanksgiving; for we dare not forget the goodness of Heaven and Earth in the matter of growth and harvest / We reverence the ancestors in the Temple, and sacrifice to the Forefathers in the Hall; by which also we express our desire to fulfil the offerings to the Ancestors" (W. White 149). Still another pair illustrates that the Jews' God was no different from Tao or the Way and their religion was more social and ethical than supernatural, like Chinese religions, or rather, philosophies: "In using the Way as the coordinator of Heaven, Earth, Man, and Things, we do not think of its name or form / In establishing the Religion for the harmony of Prince, Parents, Master, and Friends, we are not concerned with abstractions" (W. White 151). The Jews in Kaifeng were "totally integrated into the Chinese population and a 1900 attempt to organize these Jews and to create an aid society with their aid and for their benefit (by E. M. Ezra) failed" (Dicker 67). Zionists were so few in China that even though Dr. Sun Yat-sen wrote a letter in 1920 to N. E. B. Ezra, the founder and editor of *Israel's Messenge*, to support the Zionist movement, and so did the Nationalist Chinese government thereafter, only the Jewish war refugees in Harbin, Tientsin (Tianjin), and Shanghai left China and emigrated to Israel or the United States after World War II (Dicker 68).

Why and how did the Jews assimilate in China? Scholars wondered about this unique social phenomenon, and offered basically four factors for the assimilation: 1) China's racial and religious tolerance, 2) the similarities between Chinese and Jewish cultures, 3) the Jews' isolation in Kaifeng, and 4) the flooding of the synagogue. "Persons unfamiliar with Chinese history cannot readily believe," as Sidney Shapiro said, "in view of the sad record in the Western world, that the Jews in China were never persecuted for racial or religious reasons. Actually, it has been Chinese tradition to welcome foreign religions and cultures, and to utilize what is best in them" (xviii). The Jews' own inscription records the Song dynasty emperor's welcome and tolerance: "You have come to our Central Plain. Preserve your ancestral customs and settle in Bianlinag (Kaifeng)." The inscription also demonstrates, after more than three hundred years since they erected the first synagogue in 1163, "the friendly relations the Jews enjoyed with their hosts, and the gratitude they still felt for the freedom of religion which had been granted to them" (Shapiro 165). Most scholars mentioned this first factor too, and comparing the Chinese Jews with the Egyptian Hebrews, Michael Pollak well summarized it in the following passage:

In China, no ruler ever singled out the Jews for persecution, and they were never enslaved. The numbers of the Chinese Jews, unlike those of the Hebrews, remained always small; and, again unlike the Hebrews, they never departed from the country to which their forefathers had come. The parallel their stone inscriptions of 1489 had tacitly drawn, whether by chance or by design, between the two arrivals---theirs at the court of the Sung (Song) and that of the Hebrews at the court of the Pharaohs---did not extend beyond either event. In the final analysis, however, the Hebrews who said, "Let us be Egyptian in all things," did not prevail. As for the Jews who said, "Let us be Chinese in all things," they, it would seem, carried the day. (345-46)

Some scholars including Lawrence Kramer mentioned the second factor, and a few including Donald D. Leslie mentioned the last two factors. However, one cannot help but ask: "Are the similarities between Chinese and Jewish cultures more than those between Christian and Jewish cultures or even more than those between Arabic and Jewish cultures?" As for isolation, Kaifeng was the capital of Northern Song dynasty (960-1127) when Jews first came to China in large groups, and it has always been a major metropolitan of China connected by the Silk Road with Chinese Turkestan, the Middle East, and Europe. Surely it cannot be more isolated than the tiny village of Anatevka in Czarist Russia depicted in *Fiddler on the Roof*. And as for flooding, one may retort that any church, temple, or synagogue is subject to natural deterioration and destruction. So long as people have faith in it, they will repair or rebuild it. Shapiro also included in his book, *Jews in Old China: Studies by Chinese Scholars*, Gao Wangzhi's presumption that Chinese Jews assimilated because China's examination system kept them so busy reading Confucian classics that they had no time to study Hebrew and Judaism (126). Since Gao did not give any statistics concerning their occupations or, at least, the number of the Jews who pursued the career from scholarship to officialdom, his remains a presumption only. Furthermore, it is well known that many Chinese scholars and officials were Confucians and Buddhists or Taoists at the same time, and their career did not interfere with their religions. Gao's presumption is not convincing. Pearl Buck's novel *Peony* published in 1948, no coincidence with the Jewish revival, precedes most scholars' discussions of the assimilation issue, emphasizes the first factor, mentions also the kindness with which the Chinese treated the Jews and even allowed intermarriage, and demonstrates vividly how the assimilation happened through the story of Ezra's family.

Highly recommending *Peony*, H. R. Forbes commented on the novel: "The conflicts inherent in the Chinese and Jewish temperament are delicately and intricately traced with profound wisdom and compassionate understanding in this tale. ... This is an enchanting story, the theme of which is tolerance" (1948, 651). Some other critics seemed to have missed this theme. The reviewer for *Kirkus* suggested the theme to be Peony's devotion and self-abnegation to the man and his family she loves. The reviewer for *New Yorker* did not regard the Jew's assimilation as the theme of *Peony* but just one of the secondary reasons for the not "very stirring love story" to be "quite interesting" (121). The love story is not very stirring, in my opinion, because the novel is not so much about love as about the cultural conflict and confluence. The love failures are the result of the conflict, and tolerance is the key to the confluence.

Therefore, the emphasis of the novel is on the development of the young master David's cultural awareness rather than on love between David and Peony, Leah, or Kueilan. The conflict is not so much between their love for David as between the Jewish and Chinese cultures. For the sake of his business Ezra wants his son David to marry the Chinese merchant Kung Chen's daughter Kueilan. For the sake of her religion Madame Ezra wants David to marry the Rabbi's daughter Leah. David's bondmaid Peony, despite her own love for him, serves as a go-between for David and Kueilan with the hope that she can become his concubine if he marries Kueilan. At first Leah's feeling for David, on top of her sweet childhood memory, is more religious than worldly. Before moving to Ezra's house upon Madame Ezra's request, she thinks if she could marry David, she "would move David's heart to rebuild the synagogue and to fulfill all her father's dreams. The remnant of their people, who were so scattered, would be brought together again in the new synagogue, and David would be the leader of them" (chap. 3). David is attracted to Leah only for one day when he has been awakened from his pleasure-filled life by Kao Lien's report of the persecution of Jews in other countries. His awakening, however, makes him more interested in knowing about his own people. Why are they different? Why are they persecuted?

David begins to learn why after listening to the argument between Kung Chen and the Rabbi, who has insisted on calling Kung "the son of Adam" and calling David "the son of God."

Kung Chen was much surprised. "I am no son of Adam," he declared. "Indeed, there is no such name among my ancestors."

"The heathen people are all the sons of Adam," the old Rabbi declared.

Now Kung Chen felt his own wrath rising. "I do not wish to be called the son of a man of whom I have never heard," he declared. ... "Moreover, I do not like to hear any man call only himself and his people the sons of God. Let it be that you are the sons of your god if you please, but there are many gods."

"There is only one true God, and Jehovah is His name," the Rabbi declared, trembling all over as he spoke.

"So the followers of Mohammed in our city declare, " Kung Chen said gravely, "but they call his name Allah. Is he the same as your Jehovah?"

... But the Rabbi would not have his pity. "Beyond this earth we can know!" he cried in a loud firm voice. "It is for this that God has chosen my people, that we may eternally remain mankind of Him, Who alone rules. We are gadfly to man's soul. We may not rest until mankind believes in the true God."

All the anger faded from Kung Chen's heart and he said in the kindest voice, "God--- if there is God---would not choose one man above another or one people above another. Under Heaven we are all one family."

When the Rabbi heard this he could not bear it. He lifted up his head and he prayed thus to his God: "O God, hear the blasphemy of this heathen man!"

... David was torn between pity and shame, and he ran after Kung Chen and caught him at the gate.

"I beg your forgiveness," he said. (chap. 6)

Thus, the two grown-ups cannot change one another, but the young listener is changed. David has begun to doubt if his people are right to assume the cultural supremacy. After the following dialog with Kao Lien, his father's trusted partner who has also given much thought to the Jews' fate, he finally realizes that this claim is partly why his people are not loved everywhere else but are often persecuted:

Kao Lien's small eyes grew sharp. "I will tell you what I dare not tell another soul," he declared. "But you are young---you have the right to know. They were hated because they separated themselves from the rest of mankind. They called themselves chosen of God. Do I not know? I come of a large family, and there was one among us, my third brother, who declared himself the favorite of my parents. He boasted of it to the rest of us---'I am the chosen one,' he boasted. And we hated him. I would gladly see him dead. No, I would not kill him. ... But if he died I would not mourn."

In the big, silent, shadowy room David stared at Kao Lien with horror. "Are we not the chosen of God?" he faltered.

"Who says so, except ourselves?" Kao Lien retorted.

"But the Torah---" David faltered.

"Written by Jews, bitter with defeat," Kao Lien said. (chap. 6)

Most Jews are grateful that the Chinese are tolerant, seldom argue with them, and have never persecuted them. On the contrary, the practical Chinese find Jews a clever people, full of energy and wit, and "often a Chinese, indolent with years of good living, employed a Jew to manage his business. Almost as often he gave a second or third daughter to the Jew for his wife" (chap. 1). The Chinese are not deliberately trying to change them but to get along with them so that all can be prosperous and happy. Only a fanatic like Madame Ezra is tired of kindness the Chinese showed to them and blames the Chinese for destroying them by enticing them into good living and intermarriage, and only a fanatic like her, as depicted in the novel, would like to give up the comfortable life in China and go back to Palestine, a small dry land (chap. 3). As Kao Lien said, the Chinese could be cruel to a man because of the wrong thing he did, but they are never unkind to a man because of his race (chap. 5). The Chinese are curious to learn about other peoples but the Chinese are not so religious as to be self-righteous. This is the life experience of Kao Lien and David.

As for book knowledge, David compares the teaching of Jehovah with that of Confucius and finds the former hard to accept:

the Rabbi had demanded that he learn by heart the curses that Jehovah put into the mouths of the prophets against the heathen: "Thou shalt surely kill him, thine hand shall be the first upon him to put him to death and afterwards the hand of all the people. And thou shalt stone him with stones that he die, because he sought to thrust thee away from the Lord thy God."

Such words David learned, and he hated them even while he knew them to be the words of Jehovah. He dared not speak his hatred, and he found comfort by going to the little house of his tutor and sitting with the mild old man in his quiet court. There he listened to other words that the gentle Chinese read all day:

"To repay evil with kindness is the proof of a good man; a superior man blames himself, a common man blames others.

"We do not yet serve man as we should; how then can we know how to serve God?" (chap. 5)

Anyone like David who has not experienced maltreatment and injustice will naturally find the Confucian teaching more reasonable. Anyone like David who has not experienced any racial discrimination or genocide will be unlikely to feel the need of a spiritual force so powerful as the Jews' jealous God to sustain his cultural supremacy, a symptom of an inferiority complex. For some people, not David though, to serve God was the only way to serve themselves because they had not much else left.

Furthermore, David sees the injustice of Leah's self-righteousness when she refuses to admit her brother Aaron's wrongdoing. David also sees the tragedy that Leah's self-righteousness causes---her own death. Thus he marries Kueilan and is assimilating into Chinese culture as he later says to his father:

"We cannot live here among these people and remain separate, Father," David argued. "In the countries of Europe, yes, for there the peoples force us to be separate from them by persecution. We cling to our own people there because none other will accept us, and we are martyred and glorified by our martyrdom. We have no other country than sorrow. But here, where all are friends to us and receive us eagerly into their blood, what is the reward for remaining apart?"

"Indeed---indeed, it is so," Ezra said. "All that has happened to us is inevitable."

"Inevitable," David agreed.

"And your sons, my grandsons, will proceed still further into this mingling," Ezra went on.

"It will be so," David said.

Ezra pondered. "Shall we then disappear?"

David did not reply. It was inevitable, as he himself said, when people were kind and just to one another, that the walls between them fell and they became one humanity. (chap. 12)

Many Jews had assimilated before them. Their holidays coincide with Chinese festivals. "Thus the rites of Passover and of Purim had mingled with the Chinese Festival of Spring, and the Feast of First Fruits with the Feast of the Summer Moon, and the sacred ten days of penitence before Yom Kippur came often at the Feast of the New Moon Year, so that even David escaped too easily from the penitence to pleasure" (chap. 6). The Jews in China have carved on the stone in the synagogue these words as Pearl Buck translated in chapter six: "*A braham, the patriarch who founded the religion of Israel, was of the nineteenth generation from Panku Adam.*" Here Panku (Pangu), the first man in Chinese mythology, is blended with the first man according to the Jews' religion.[6] They have also carved: "*From the time of Abraham, when our faith was established, and ever after, we the Jews of China have spread the knowledge of God and in return we have received the knowledge of Confucius and Buddha and Tao*" (chap. 6). The two cultures thus have been blended together.

However, David is not yet completely changed. His early religious education still works against his natural feelings. He cannot *happily* take Peony as a concubine although he loves her and knows she loves him and Kueilan would not mind. "That which his mother had pressed into his unwilling soul had taken root there. He had defied it and crucified it, but it was not dead. It lived in him still, the spirit of the faith of his own people. It had risen from the dead and claimed him. He could not free himself" (chap. 13). Even when Peony is in danger of being taken away by the licentious Chief Steward of Tzu Hsi's court, he still locks her out and leaves her no choice but to become a nun. Fortunately, David and Kueilan continue to have close contact with Peony after she has entered the nunnery, and she later becomes a wise mother abbess. This ending is a small tragedy of the cultural conflict to some readers and a great triumph to others. As human beings we wish all the lovers of the world become united in wedlock. As moralists we will not allow polygamy to be practiced by good people. Nothing can satisfy all.

Nevertheless, all human beings can, at least, live in peace, as the novel demonstrates, if we are not so fanatic about religious beliefs, and by implication, political beliefs as well. Jews assimilated in China mainly because they met with kindness and tolerance instead of discrimination and persecution. This implies that any culture, any social system, and any human institution can change without violence. Civilization develops in cultural exchange. We can learn from one another what is better for ourselves if we take a tolerant attitude toward our differences. We should have confidence in humanity that we are all able to improve and to progress without killing, fighting, or bloodshed. A change may come about more quickly without them. Even if it takes longer, it is still worthwhile. It may be more fundamental because nothing changes if the mind does not. And the mind is reluctant to change when the body is forced. Such is the case of communism in Russia and China. Such will be the case of Western democracy and individualism, too.

Moreover, *Peony* suggests that intermarriage is the key to the future of humanity, the great harmony of the world, the international concord and multicultural confluence. One of the most fundamental reasons that human races are different now is that humans scattered all over the globe and lived in different places without much contact and communication. No matter whether we believe in creation or evolution, we have at least one viewpoint in common, namely that human beings have one and the same origin from which our ancestors separated and migrated to where we are now. Our biological and cultural differences are the results of the separation and segregation, so are the prejudices and hostilities. We cannot go back in history to the "Original Way" or the "Garden of Eden" or the "Golden Age," which, if it ever existed, might not be so fabulously harmonious in the first place, but we can come in contact with one another with modern means of transportation and communication. We can understand one another more easily than before with our knowledge of social and natural sciences. But all this is not enough. Only by intermarriage can people of different races be united and their differences diminish. As many literary works, including Pearl Buck's *Come, My Beloved*, suggest the final test of our belief in racial equality is intermarriage. We may sincerely declare that all races are equal and all should be friends because we are theoretically convinced so, but emotionally we may still have a little dislike for a certain different race, so little that we usually do not feel it until our daughter is dating or wants to marry a man of that race. Are we going to separate them as Mr. and Mrs. MacArd separate Livy and Jatin in *Come, My Beloved*, or are we going to let them be united as Ezra and Kung have done? This is a provocative question readers are likely to ask themselves.

Pearl Buck showed us that nothing is more effective in eliminating racial differences and promoting cultural exchange than intermarriage, and assimilation is often completed with intermarriage in China. Intermarriage between Jews and Chinese is not just in her fiction or a rare phenomenon. "In fact," Donald D. Leslie acknowledged, "the Memorial Book makes quite clear that intermarriage took place on quite a large scale in Ming dynasty (and, we may assume, in the Ching). ... But it is fairly certain that by the end of the 19th Century, intermarriage was the rule rather than the exception" (105). Indeed, by intermarriage the Chinese have become the largest race on earth. Chinese culture has absorbed many different cultures, and it has been enriched by them. No races or cultures are destroyed, but we may all improve. At the end of *Peony*, we see both Jewish and Chinese features in the children of David and Kueilan, and we find that on the ruins of the synagogue they have built a new Jewish church, on which "are carved 'The Temple of Purity and Truth,' and beneath the words are carved the history of the Jews and their Way," together with the Taoist teaching: "The Way has no form or figure, but is made in the image of the Way of Heaven, which is above."[7] It sounds idealistic, but this kind of assimilation had been achieved because China had been religiously tolerant and had little religious restriction and no religious persecutions or wars except the Taiping Rebellion and the Communist regime. Among the similarities between Christianity and communism, one of the few bad things in common is intolerance, which has led to many tragic movements in the contemporary history of China. Now Chinese people have waked up from the frenzy of the Cultural Revolution, and China is again open to the world. Novels like *Peony* can help both Chinese and Americans find better ways to deal with racial and cultural problems.

We are both big countries with multiple races and cultures. Racial and cultural problems are, in the end, not only the business of the legislators or policy-makers but the business of every citizen. Communism has failed in Eastern Europe and is failing in China, but this is not yet the "end of history" as Francis Fukuyama so joyously heralded. Amost every social problem of the United States indicates that class struggle and ideological struggle are by no means the only struggles among human beings, that racial and cultural conflicts, among many others, will die hard before the confluence can happen, and that the way to freedom is still long and arduous. Thus, history even in Hegel's definition will not end very soon. On the way to achieve freedom and democracy everyone shares the responsibility, for the conflict is not so much between countries as among people. We need to advocate tolerance and intermarriage. We also need to take the lesson that to understand one another is more important than to impose our belief upon other people, no matter how much better we think ours may be. We can always learn from one another and from our past experiences including Christian missions and the history of Chinese Jews. Literature serves as an appropriate medium by which students and scholars as well as general readers can learn about the past, not only the historical events, but also the people in those events, so that a fuller picture can be unfolded. Pearl Buck's books are particularly valuable in this respect.

NOTES

1. For more details see chapter 16 of *A History of Christian Missions in China* by Kenneth S. Latourette.

2. For more details see chapter 3, "Ward and Gordon: Glorious Days of Looting," in *To Change China* by Jonathan Spence.

3. For more details see "Two-World Success Story: Pearl Buck" by Stephen Vincent and Rosemary Benet.

4. Kramer's essay is included in *Studies of the Chinese Jews* edited by Hyman Kublin and listed in the bibliography. The essay is originally published in *Jewish Social Studies*. XVIII, no. 2: April 1956: 125-144.

5. See Rudolf Lowenthal's "The Nomenclature of Jews in China" included in Hyman Kublin's *Studies of the Chinese Jews*. 59, or *Collectanea Commissionis Synodalis*, Peiping, vol. XVII, May/December, 1944.

6. See Herbert A. Giles's *A Chinese Biographical Dictionary*. London-Shanghai: 1898; reprinted in Peiping, 1939. p. 1607, no. 603, or briefly, see Lowenthal's "The Nomenclature" in Kublin's *Studies*, 58.

7. According to Taoism the Way of Heaven is shapeless and it is the abstract universal law that can be found everywhere. Therefore, it is in accordance with Jews' invisible but omniscient God.

5

A HISTORIC MIRROR

If the cognitive and educational functions are the primary value of Pearl Buck's literary works, as I have emphasized in my discussion, then critics may challenge the purpose of reading Pearl Buck for learning about China and East-West cultural issues with these questions: "Why must we read *her* instead of Chinese writers? Are her books in any way more valuable than the books of her contemporary Chinese writers? Even though she opened the eyes of Americans and other Westerners to what the majority of Chinese people are really like, what is the significance of her description of the Chinese peasants' life to the Chinese readers themselves?" What most American critics do not know and most Chinese critics are reluctant to admit is that Pearl Buck's novels are indeed more valuable than those of her contemporary Chinese writers in at least one sense--- her novels serve as a historic mirror that reflects the Chinese peasants' life more truthfully than do the mirrors held by the other writers, because theirs are tinted red with communist ideologies.

If we break the barrier of national pride and the traditional classification by nationality, it will not be hard to see that Pearl Buck's literary creation indicated a new direction for Chinese writers, who, consciously or unconsciously, followed her lead. When we examine the Chinese novels, which have a history of at least six centuries if we regard Shih Nai-an's *Shui Hu Zhuan* (*All Men Are Brothers*) as the beginning, we find no novels were written about the life of ordinary Chinese peasants and farmers. In discussing the significance of Lu Hsun's literary works in the history of Chinese literature, Hsujee Huang made a statement which I translate into English as follows:

For thousands of years in ancient agricultural China, the position of peasants was the lowest, and therefore, they were never portrayed in classical Chinese literature except some poems which pitied them. Although *Shui Hu Zhuan* is about the peasants' uprisings, yet the genuine peasants who are engaged in agricultural work are very few in the novel. ... It was not until after the May Fourth New Culture movement that Chinese peasants became the major subject represented in literary works. And Lu Hsun was the first writer in the history of Chinese literature to describe ordinary peasants. ... What he did was certainly great pioneering work! (59)

Indeed, Lu Hsun wrote some stories about ordinary Chinese people early this century including "The True Story of Ah Q" [1918] and "The New Year's Sacrifice" [1926], but they are not long enough to be novels nor are they about genuine peasants and farmers who work the field and represent the majority of Chinese population. Ah Q is a village lout who does only some odd jobs from time to time, and Hsian Lin's wife, the protagonist of "The New Year's Sactifice," is a nurse plus servant in a rich man's house. Lu Hsun's literary creation using the vernacular Chinese marked the beginning of China's modern and democratic literature, but he lived among scholars and students most of his life and did not know peasants well enough to write a novel about them. It is true that the writers of the "Rural Literature" in the mid-1920s including Wang Renshu (better known as Ba Ren), Peng Jiahuan, Wang Sidian, Pan Hsun, Hsu Chinwen, and Hsu Yunor did describe some incidents in the country and stories of the peasants, but their works are all short stories, and as Hsujee Huang said, their influence was limited even within China.[1] Undoubtedly, in 1931 Pearl Buck was the first writer who published a successful and influential novel about the life of Chinese peasants and farmers. However, since she was not Chinese, the historic landmark of *The Good Earth* has not been mentioned in any book on Chinese or American literature. The injustice of the traditional classification by nationality is most clearly seen here. It is high time that we did her justice with multicultural approaches.

We should notice that after the phenomenal success of *The Good Earth*, several prominent Chinese writers began to publish works about the life of ordinary peasants and farmers. Jiang Guangtsih's (Jiang Guangci's) novel, *The Wind of Farmland* [1932], describes the class conflict and struggles in the countryside. Mao Dun's short story "Spring Silkworms" [1932] commences his countryside trilogy, which is completed with his later stories "Autumn Harvest" and "The Remains of Winter," depicting the life of Old Tongbao and other villagers and revealing the causes of their miserable life in a harvest year. Wang Tongzhao's *The Mountain Rain* [1933] unfolds a panorama of the country of North China and reflects, through Hsih Dayou's spiritual growth and the maturity, pursuit, struggle, and awakening of the peasant. Zang Kojia's collection of poems, *The Brand* [1933], expresses the feelings of Chinese peasants in hardship and misery and describes their perseverance and industriousness. Hong Sen's play, *Wukui Bridge* [1933], which also forms a countryside trilogy with two other plays---*The Fragrant Rice* and *The Green Dragon Pool*---depicts the class struggle between the peasants and landlord. Hsiao Jun's novel, *The Village in August* [1935], describes the local color of the northeast of China (Manchuria) and people's resistance against the Japanese invasion there. Apart from Jiang's *The Wind of Farmland,* whose first thirteen chapters were originally published under the title of *The Roaring Land* in 1930, all the other works might be influenced, one way or another, by Pearl Buck's trilogy that starts with *The Good Earth*. This assumption can be challenged on the ground that all these Chinese writers' approaches are different from Pearl Buck's and are marked by Marxist theory of class struggle and Lenin's teachings about imperialism. However, since *The Good Earth* enjoyed at least eight different translations in the early 1930s, and Lu Hsun, the founder and the greatest man of letters of modern Chinese literature, expressed the wish that Chinese writers should be able to do a better job writing about Chinese peasants than Pearl Buck did (Yao 39), it is not too bold to say that at least they must have been stimulated by her success to see the new horizon of subject matters and try their hands in the then unexplored field. The assumption remains to be proved by research, which will be a very difficult task, for the writers made no open acknowledgement, and most of their diaries and private letters were almost certain to have been lost through the wars and upheavals of half a century.

The large-scale literary creation of the life of Chinese peasants took place, of course, after Mao Tse-tung's "Talks at Yenan Forum on Art and Literature" in 1942. Mao's talks discuss the relationship between art and politics, the standard of art, and the problems of inheriting classic Chinese literary heritage and foreign heritage. His talks advocate the position that art and literature must serve the needs of the people and politics and expound the problem of how art and literature can serve them. His talks are the manifesto of the so-called proletarian revolutionary art and literature and have encouraged the writing of peasants, for peasants, and even by peasants. The representatives of such revolutionary works include Zhao Shulee's novelette *The Rhymes of Lee Youtsai* [1943] and his novel *The Changes of Village Lee* [1945], Sun Lee's short story "The Lotus Lake," Lee Jee's narrative poem *Wang Guei and Lee Hianghsiang* [1945], Ding Yee and Ho Jingzhih's opera, *The White-haired Girl* [1945], Ouyang Shan's novel *Uncle Gao* [1946], Liu Ching's novel *The Story of Sowing the Millet* [1947], Zhou Leepo's novel *The Storm* [1948], and Ding Ling's novel *The Sun Shines upon the Sanggan River* [1948].

Clearly Mao's influence on modern Chinese literary movements has been much greater than Pearl Buck's. However, Mao's influence was more political than artistic and it is now fading whereas Pearl Buck's influence is probably gaining ground, or at least her portrayal of Chinese peasants and farmers and her description of their relationship with land and with each other are being confirmed, enriched, and reinforced by the literary works of Chinese writers after the Cultural Revolution. The fundamental difference between Pearl Buck and her contemporary Chinese writers is that she saw life as it was with little ideological guidance and wrote about life without any obvious political purpose, but they saw life through Marxism, Leninism, and Mao's theory of class struggle and wrote about life with the purpose of driving away imperialism and overthrowing the ruling class. We do not see any class struggle in *The Good Earth* or *The Mother* but many conflicts of men and women against various natural disasters, against their own desires, against one another, and most often, against their own family members. The relationship between the landlord and tenants can be friendly as shown by that between Wang Lung and Ching. Certainly there are some people more evil than others such as Wang Lung's uncle and the robbers who prey on the farmers; Cucoo and Lotus who live on men's lust and stupidity; and the agent of the landlord who takes advantage of the Mother in distress, but they are individuals, not a class. The pattern suggested by Pearl Buck is that poor peasants gain property and dignity through hard work, frugal living, and some good luck. This may sound like Horatio Alger's packaged message of success, but her rendering of the truth is so convincing that it can hardly be denied, and the pattern does not stop there. The rich farmers then lose property and dignity because of 1) idleness, 2) physical indulgence, and 3) social upheavals. In both the case of a poor man's gain (e. g., Wang's) and the rich man's loss (e. g., Hwang's), the first two causes are shown as more certain and decisive than the last one. Often the wheel of fortune is fully turned in about four generations. This pattern, well-known as it might be to American readers, was not found in any prominent work of her contemporary Chinese writers.

However, a major and constant theme of class struggle and anti-imperialism is seen in all the representative works of modern Chinese writers that are mentioned in any history of contemporary Chinese literature published in mainland China. Mao Dun's trilogy of stories blames the sufferings of the peasants on foreign industrialists' manipulations in China. Wang Tongzhao's novel illustrates the landlord's exploitation and the peasants' realization of and struggle against it. Zang Kojia's poems express primarily the peasants' sorrow, anger, and complaints under the yoke of the ruling class. Their works certainly reflect some truth of the realities of China in the early period of this century and express their heartfelt feelings, but the strong sense of a mission to save China from imperialism and to liberate Chinese peasants from the landlord class in the works makes them somewhat like political propaganda. They do not have the appeal to readers of different ages or countries, for they have not reflected the most basic needs and desires of the peasants. They read like studies or reports of some sociologists who went to live in the country for a brief period of time and learned something about the peasants but did not quite understand them.

The literary works about Chinese peasants created after Mao's "Talks at Yenan Forum on Art and Literature" are even more political. They were used as political tools, of which the authors were proud, and the historians were proud to record as such. This can be clearly seen in the creation of the opera, *The White-haired Girl*, which is short to summarize and is the only product of the 1940s that was not killed but revised during the Cultural Revolution, indicating its political longevity as well as its artistic achievement. The opera was collectively created by the teachers and students of Lu Hsun Arts Academy with Ding Yee composing the music and Ho Jingshih writing the libretto. It was based on the "White-haired Sorceress," a folk tale popular in the early forties in Hobei, a northern province of China. The Communists discovered that the so-called sorceress was actually a country girl who could not bear the abuse of a despotic landlord, ran away, and lived in the mountains alone for years until they saved her. Her hair turned white because she lacked salt and sunshine, and she was regarded as a sorceress because she was spotted several times when she came to steal and eat the offerings in the local temple which was supposedly responsive to people's prayers. After some discussions, the teachers and students of the academy decided that the folk tale could be adapted into a modern opera that would illustrate a profound theme: "The old society changed a human being into a ghost, whereas the new society changed a ghost into a human being" (Tang and Yan 3: 260). Guided by the communist ideology, the story line of the opera was made as this: the girl's father owes money to the landlord, who comes to dun him on New Year's Eve and presses him so hard that he commits suicide after selling his daughter to the landlord. The landlord then takes the girl to his house as a bondmaid, rapes her, and makes her pregnant. The girl runs away, keeps alive by her hatred. She once scares the landlord half to death in the temple and eventually avenges herself when the Communist Army liberates her village. Musically the product is a harmonous combination of Western grand opera and Chinese national music and folk songs.

The opera was first performed at Yanan in May 1945, and it was an immediate success. However, it underwent many revisions according to the guidance of the Communist leaders and the demand of the audience. For instance, in order to make the opera more revolutionarily logical, the girl's hope to marry the landlord was cut out, and later more characters were created including the girl's fiance, who beats up the landlord, joins the Red Army, and returns to lead the struggle against the landlord class.[2] The opera became the most influential and popular theatrical product in the Communist "liberated areas." The audience often "burst into a prolonged thunderous applause," and the opera often "made the audience sob. Some people would weep from Act 1 to Act 6, their faces wet with tears from beginning to end, ... After the performance, everybody was praising the opera." But responses to the opera were more than an aesthetic catharsis. "After seeing the opera, people of some villages were aroused to fight the landlord class. Many soldiers wanted to revenge the girl and her father by volunteering to go to the battle field. Some bourgeois intellectuals wrote articles to describe the impact the opera had on them and the awakening to class consciousness they experienced" (Tang and Yan 3: 268-69).

If *The White-haired Girl* only praised the Communist new society and awakened the audience's class consciousness, Zhou Leepo's *The Storm* and Ding Ling's *The Sun Shines upon the Sanggan River* taught readers as well as Communist cardres how to arouse peasants' hatred for landlords and how to carry out the class struggle in the country. These two novels are supposed to be the best of China's proletarian literature. Both of them won the Stalin Prize for literature in 1951 and took the most important places in modern Chinese literature until five years ago, when Hsiaobing Tang, Zaifu Liu, and Gang Lin began to publish critical essays challenging their cognitive and aesthetic values and exposing the negative effects they had exerted on life and literature. These two novels are now seen by more and more Chinese critics as typical examples of political modes of writing. *The Storm* is a literary illustration of the revolutionary method and policy of the Chinese Communist Party during the land reform---how the peasants are mobilized and organized to fight the landlord. They are made to realize that the landlord exploits them, to awaken to the "truth" that the landlord class is their enemy, and that only by overthrowing the landlords can they ever live a better life. Their hatred for the landlord is aroused and the revolutionary storm breaks down the old productive relationship that has existed for two thousand years. The peasants gain the courage to take the landlord's property and divide the land among them. The landlord is beaten up, conquered, and even physically eliminated. The novel is full of violence and violent language, and worst of all, such violence is justified in the novel. Zhou Leepo did try to use the peasants' language but his excessive use of the northern dialect is criticized as no more than a decoration to cover up his scant understanding of the peasants and at the same time causes difficulties in reading (Tang 85).

Similarly *The Sun Shines upon the Sanggan River* celebrates the so-called revolutionary violence and describes the relationship of people in the country as nothing but class oppression and struggle between the landlord and peasants. The landlord lets his son join the Communist Army in order to protect his class interests, makes his daughter marry a Communist in order to corrupt the key cadre of the new power, and encourages his niece to have an affair with a peasant leader in order to set up a sex-trap. The peasants are taught by the Communists to rise against the landlord. Everyone is shown as the tool of class struggle, and the peasants' victory in the struggle is shown as the sole drive of historic progress and agricultural productivity. Hatred, cruel revenge, and even killing are demonstrated, rationalized, and hallowed as the indispensable sacrificial rite of the revolution that will supposedly improve most people's lives (Liu and Lin 99). These novels among others, including Zhao Shulee's *The Changes of Village Lee*, are not without certain artistic achievement. Like the opera, they vividly portray some peasants, farmers, and landlords, poignantly describe their psychological activities as well as their daily lives, and successfully use their language in speech representation along with the authors' own language of narration. However, these novels all took class struggle as the key link, aimed at serving the proletarain politics, and literally became the revolutionary manuals for other Communists to follow in the land reform as well as the models of China's proletarian literature for later writers to imitate. As a result, millions of landlords and rich farmers were killed, persecuted, or reduced to utter destitution, and their children were made to pay for their parents' "debt" and to suffer for their parents' "crimes."

Such injustice was justified not only by the media of the Communist propaganda but also in Chinese literature from 1949 to 1976. The representative novels of this period about the Chinese peasants and farmers include Ouyang Shan's *Bitter Struggle*; Liang Bin's trilogy, *The Saga of the Red Flag*, *The Legend of Setting Fire*, and *The Picture of Fighting the Enemy*; Feng Deying's *The Bitter Rape Flower* and *The Winter Jasmine*; Liu Ching's *The History of Our Cause*; Zhou Leepo's *The Great Changes of the Mountain Village*; and Hao Ran's *The Bright Sunny Day* and *The Golden Broadway*. Such novels again and again take class struggle as the major theme; portray the peasants and rich farmers as class enemies; justify, advocate, and glorify violence against and oppression of the class enemy in the name of revolution. These novels do not lack charms, but their charms did more harm than Plato and Confucius ever feared literature could do to human beings and society. Two generations were affected by the so-called proletarian revolutionary literature since Mao's talks in 1942. We Chinese readers were enchanted by class struggle, by the description of the poor peasants' sufferings, and by the portrayal of the hateful class enemies in those novels. Our "class hatred" was stirred and directed to the landlords and later to the intellectuals themselves. Our "class love" was aroused and directed to the Communist Party and the leaders and eventually to Mao alone. Humanities were replaced by the theory of class struggle, against which we measured everyone and everything. Spouses criticized each other. Children exposed their parents' "counter-revolutionary crimes." Young students sacrificed themselves trying to save a few desks and chairs from fire because those were the property of our proletarian state. Our literature praised and depicted such "heroic deeds" and encouraged others to wish and dream to do the same. But no one would save a drowning man because he might be a counter-revolutionary committing suicide. Kant's absolute order was "rightfully" disobeyed in China during the Cultural Revolution!

Until after the Cultural Revolution, in which not just Chinese intellectuals but almost all the Communists themselves were persecuted by turns, the faint voice of anything different was hardly ever heard, the image of the majority of Chinese people was indeed distorted, and life imitated art in the largest scale ever in the four thousand years' history of China, but sadly, to the worst effect. If Chinese intellectuals have experienced three awakenings (first, the awakening to nationalism after being defeated first in the Opium War by Britain in 1840 and then in the sea war by Japan in 1895; second, the awakening to the value of human beings including women and children during the May Fourth New Culture movement in 1920s; third, the awakening to the class struggle theory from the 1930s to 1940s), then after the Cultural Revolution in 1976, we have been experiencing the fourth awakening, the awakening to the impossibility of communism, to the harm of the class struggle theory, and to the value and dignity of individual human beings. In this awakening, we also challenge the literary theories which maintain, on the one hand, as Mao advocated, that literature and art must serve the proletarian politics, and on the other, assert that literature and art can and even should disregard truth as Vladimir Nabokov expressed in metaphor, "the magic of art was in the shadow of the wolf that he deliberately invented, his dream of the wolf; then the story of his tricks made a good story" (1112). We have seen that the damage of the shadow or the dream of the wolf could be much greater than the loss of a few sheep. We know what terrible consequences could result from the tantalizing world created by the magic of artistic writers, if they were also political fanatics. The artistic charm and rhetorical eloquence of the proletarian revolutionary writers, just like those of McCarthyites, made us realize that art and literature ought and must be measured by truth, weighed moral values, and advanced by humanitarianism.

China has finally awakened from the nightmare of the anti-Rightist movement, in which Pearl Buck was severely criticized along with five hundred thousand Chinese intellectuals, and from the nightmare of the Cultural Revolution, in which a tenth of the Chinese population suffered from persecution or criticism to different extents and China was completely closed to the Western world. China is also waking up from the beautiful dream of communism as it has failed in Eastern Europe and is dramatically changing its nature in China itself. When Chinese writers and scholars are reflecting on China's modern literature, we wonder what the relationship between the landlord and peasants was really like before the Communists changed it by force? Did a peasant ever become rich under the landlord's oppression and exploitation? If so, how? The Communist writers distorted all this. Our Confucian ancestors despised the peasants, and no one found the peasants' life interesting enough to write about. In Pearl Buck's novels, however, we find a completely different picture of the lives of the peasants and farmers. Did she reflect more truth and realities?

It is not too late to learn, for many pre-revolution peasants and farmers are still alive. After the Cultural Revolution, Chinese writers began to publish works that were different from the mainstream of the proletarian revolutionary literature, and these works of dissidents are quickly becoming mainstream. Surprisingly, the literary works set in the country echo, enrich, and reinforce Pearl Buck's portrayal of Chinese peasants and farmers and her description of their lives and their relationship with one another. Novels and stories including Zhou Kechin's *Hsu Mao and His Daughters*; Gao Hsiaosheng's *Lee Shunda's Attempts to Build a House*; Leė Rui's *The Rich Earth*; Liu Heng's *The Cursed Food*; Mo Yan's series of stories, *The Family of the Red Sorghom*; Zhang Wei's *The Ancient Boat*; Su Tong's *The Family of the Opium Poppy*; Jia Pingao's *Impetuosity*; and Chen Zhongshih's *The White Deer Plain* all demonstrate much fewer and less severe class conflicts between peasants and landlords or rich farmers. All depict more conflicts between people and nature, peasants and wars or political movements, reveal the conflicts of the farmers' dreams, desires, or greed with bureaucracy, regulations, and conscience, or illustrate the conflicts between the traditions and new ideas. Some of these works also present the friendly relationship between the landlord and the tenants like that between Wang Lung and Ching. Some illustrate the process of poor peasants becoming rich through hard work and frugal living just as that in *The Good Earth*. In a word, I find more and more similarities in post-Cultural Revolution Chinese literature on old China's peasants and farmers to Pearl Buck's novels on the same subject. One obvious difference is that in these realistic novels of the much later Chinese writers I frequently find certain legendary colors. After all, they only heard of but did not experience directly what they wrote about. Pearl Buck's function as a cultural bridge is thus not only beyond political ideologies but also across an important time span because no other writers had written novels nearly as realistic as hers about the Chinese peasants' life before the 1940s when the ownership of land shifted hands and later became mostly public in China.

With the commercialization of modern technologies of transportation and communication, more and more people are exposed to the superficial differences of many races and cultures. The need to understand the differences historically and culturally is crucial for the harmonious coexistence of human beings. Pearl Buck's novels are indeed a historic mirror that is not only truthful but also unique. *The Good Earth, Son,* and *A House Divided* reflect what Chinese peasants wanted and trusted, why Chinese warlords fought, and where Chinese intellectuals were going by realistically depicting their lives and personalities. These novels mirror, without the distortion found in most other novels on the China scene, the real relationship between peasants and land, peasants and landlords, fortune and industriousness, farmers and literati. *The Mother* reveals the unequal relationship between men and women in China and exposes the unfairness and suffering much more common and universally felt by ordinary women than those described by Betty Friedan about thirty years later. *The Patriot* depicts the formation and progress of an upper-class Chinese young man in searching the way to serve his country in a chaotic period when the fight between the Communists and Nationalists was interwoven with the fight between Chinese and Japanese. The novel, compared with most other novels on the same subject, is less partisan or nationalistic in its attitude toward these fights and more artistic in terms of character portrayal and literary description.

Pearl Buck's books also serve very well as one of the keys to understanding some fundamental differences between China and the United States. *The Exile* illustrates the life of an ordinary American missionary wife in China so vividly and convincingly that it makes Chinese readers realize that the missionary movement is not all imperialists' cultural invasion. All the political propaganda and many years of socialist education simply went to pieces after people had read this little biography, whose artistry and sincerity are irresistible. It is a common reading experience that the fond feelings toward the United States were evoked from old readers who would recall the good deeds the missionaries had done for Chinese people in need, and young readers were surprised to learn but firmly believe so much that is opposite to what they had been told in class and in the textbooks.

Fighting Angel, on the other hand, suggests some reasons why the missionary movement failed, and these reasons have not been well studied by scholars. Either because the suggestions are too subtle, or because American readers including critics did not wish to admit the reasons, they have not discussed the suggestions as much as I have in the previous chapter. However, few who have read the biography can fail to see the truth that the missionaries went to China for the Chinese as much as for themselves, if not more so. This book describes the dogged faith of her father who was rather blind to the real needs of the people around him and therefore, could not serve God by serving people. The biography unfolds a complete picture of a near saint working in the wrong time and reveals much of the inner world of her father, a representative of American missionaries and probably one of the best, who is still a failure as a missionary, as a husband, and as a father, possibly without his own awareness of it all. His tragic life is shown as full of contradictions between noble qualities and impracticalities that suggest the insufficiency of high mind and good intentions alone, and thus the biography forms one of the few vivid epitomes of the missionary movement, which is the most important event in the East-West cultural intercourse.

In her minor novels, *The Pavilion of Women*, *Kinfolk*, and *Peony*, Pearl Buck dealt with some interesting problems of the conflicts and confluence in the East-West cultural intercourse. In *The Pavilion of Women*, she portrayed what an ideal missionary, or rather, an ideal cultural messenger of the West is like in China. He does not preach but teaches. He builds no churches but a nursery home for abandoned girls. He serves people wholeheartedly rather than serving the abstract idea of God. By describing Brother Andre's activities she also expressed her suggestion about what China truly needed: the knowledge of natural sciences and ability of independent thinking, which we still need now, especially the latter.

In *Kinfolk*, we find more characters giving what China really needs. The two big decisions these American Chinese have made in the novel are first to serve their motherland and then to leave the city where they have worked for some time and go to work in their ancestral village. The significance of the second decision has never been discussed but it is no less important than the first one. The suggestion, I believe, is that the country needs help much more than the city, and to change China, the intellectuals must be prepared to work with the peasants, who are the majority of the Chinese population. This sounds like Mao's decision on the intellectuals during the Cultural Revolution. The fundamental difference is that one is by free will and the other is by force. The living and working conditions in the country are much worse than those in the city, but if the peasants are not educated, nothing will ever change in China. This plain truth, however, has not been learned by Chinese intellecturals, whose endeavor to win Chinese people more freedom and democracy, for instance, was not understood and supported by the peasants and farmers. As James C. Thomson concluded, Pearl Buck was, after all, right about the problem of China, which is always "the centrality and human reality of the Chinese peasants" (15).

In *Peony*, the first and foremost novel that illustrates the assimilation of some Kaifen Jews into the Chinese culture, she suggested that the key to cultural confluence is tolerance. The lack of it in the missionary movement, in contrast, is another reason for its failure. This is a valuable lesson for the present and future cultural exchanges everywhere in the world. By reading this novel, we Chinese also realize, rather sadly, that our good tradition of religious tolerance has been lost since the Communists took office, who, like Christian missionaries, are intolerant of other beliefs. This truth, seen by both Chinese and American readers, should help us avoid and perhaps even get rid of political or religious fanaticism. In *Peony* as well as in *The Pavillion of Women*, we also see the raison d'etre of some traditional Chinese institutions including concubinage and arranged marriage. By no means was Pearl Buck advocating these old customs, but by describing the life of a big family in old China as it was, she helped not only American readers but also modern Chinese readers understand why the customs existed, see the harmony they enjoyed in a family-oriented society that believed in collectivism not individualism, and recognize their positive as well as their negative side. Her novels are valuable in this respect because almost no other writers of her magnitude have bothered to justify the institutions; almost all modern Chinese literature just exposes their evils and their negative side. So do most of the writings by the missionaries and Western observers who asserted the superiority of the Western civilization in order to impose Western culture and values onto the East.

We should also remember that Pearl Buck was the first person who translated *Shui Hu Chuan,* one of the four classical Chinese novels, into English (*All Men Are Brothers*). This achievement alone should suffice to put her in the forefront of the greatest contributors to the cultural exchange between the East and West, but it has been largely ignored since Mark Van Doren wrote a chapter, "A Far Eastern Homer," in *The Private Reader* [1942], commending this novel, her translation, and her choice of the seventy-chapter edition to translate. He compared the brilliance and grandeur of the Chinese masterpiece with those of the *Iliad* and the *Odyssey* and said they need to be "supplemented by further comparisons" with the *Song of Roland*, the Robin Hood cycle, and the works of Rabelais, Cervantes, Fielding, and Dumas (189). In 1933, every reviewer and scholar commended Pearl Buck's tremendous endeavor in translating the Chinese novel of seventy chapters into beautiful English. Tai Jen confirmed the evaluation of the editor of *Saturday Review of Literature* by saying, "In view of the exceeding difficulty of rendering the work into English, Mrs. Buck has done a beautiful job" (162). Nathaniel Peffer, in commenting on the novel's being "realistic without photography, exciting without halloos" and on its "sure imagery without artificed fancies," said that "its beauty comes through the veil of translation, even into a language which is as structurally different as English, in which even rough verbal equivalents are often lacking." He continued to say that because Pearl Buck "is herself an artist, she has not only informed it with beauty but has managed to catch the distinctive flavor of Chinese speech. ... In choice of words, in moulding of phrase, in the rhythm and structure of sentences there are the salty tang, the mellowness, the subtle simplicities of the Chinese style. This is in itself an amazing literary feat" (1933, 3).

All the criticism is on the novel itself, not on her translation. Mark Van Doren warned the reader of the bloodiness, the cruel killing of innocent people, the gargantuan drinking, and even cannibalism in the novel, as he said, "Everything is there, in fact, in ultimate degree" (192). The reviewer for the *Christian Science Monitor*, too, advised, "Fastidious readers would turn from much of it with horror" (6). The bare presentation, without any gloss or polish, of the righteous outlaws, their noble benevolence and atrocious violence alike, probably offended many Western readers. This is quite likely the reason why the novel has not won popularity and exerted little influence in the West. The main criticism of the reviewer for the *New York Times Book Review* is, "There is (with all deference to Mrs. Buck's prefatory remarks) little or no moral indignation in the book" (2). William Plomer also challenged the "meaning of humanity" in the novel, "in which violence and vengeance and cunning and incessant action soon cease to surprise. Cannibalism becomes a commonplace and blood runs like water" (968). The worries of the Chinese students of Columbia University about Pearl Buck's publishing the translation of the novel proved to be reasonable.

The West cannot accept the novel not because she did not translate it well but because it lacks the moral values required by the audience. Sidney Shapiro's better translation (1988) of a longer edition (100 chapters) has not won more popularity than hers. Of course, this is only one of many reasons that the novel is not so well received as she expected it to be, but it gives a clear feedback to Chinese intellectuals about the relationship between literature and humanities, which we have not yet taken seriously. It does not mean that her efforts are all for nothing. At least, her courage and skill in translating such a long and difficult novel into English for the first time must be acknowledged and may well be worth studying. If someday in the future, this Chinese classic masterpiece is well and widely studied in the West and serves as a good book for understanding the Chinese culture and people or if it exerts any influence on the Western literature, some debt to Pearl Buck's pioneer work should be acknowledged.

In this study, I have discussed mainly the historic, cultural, and cognitive values of Pearl Buck's literary works, for I believe that these values are greater than the aesthetic value of her books, which other critics, especially Paul A. Doyle and Dody W. Thompson, have discussed more thoroughly than I am able to. What I need to make more as a suggestion than an assertion is that it is just the historical, cultural, and cognitive values she pursued more deliberately after 1942 that caused her novels to go downhill. She was, after all, a daughter of missionary parents. She tried to do with her pen what her father had failed to do with the Bible, to bring happiness to the Chinese people and other Asian peoples including the Koreans and Indians, by eulogizing their heroic deeds and by making Americans understand Eastern cultures through her novels. Different from her efforts in founding and running the East and West Association from 1941 to 1951, the same wish and effort in literature brought an inevitable artistic sacrifice. If *Dragon Seed* is weakened by war propaganda, the sequel, *The Promise,* is dominated by it. They are a literary illustration of her war essays such as "Tinder for Tomorrow," "What Are We Fighting for in the Orient?" and "Freedom for All" rather than an artistic world in which characters are realized men and women like Wang Lung and O-lan. Lacking knowledge of real battles, Pearl Buck rendered her imagination of guerilla warfare into two not very probable descriptions of the Chinese resistance against the Japanese invasion. Having lived in the United States for eight years and possibly been affected by Hollywood's love recipe, she seemed to forget that romantic love was not very important among the Chinese peasants in the 1930s or 1940s and made a big fuss of the love affair between Lao San, who is renamed Sheng by his military superior in *The Promise*, and Mayli in the already busy fighting described by both novels. The message outweighs artistry so much in *The Promise* that the novel can, at best, serve as a significant historic footnote to the Chinese campaign in Burma but can hardly touch sophisticated readers as a literary work.

If *Pavilion of Women* and *Peony* are not masterpieces, they are, at least, good novels in terms of creating a believable artistic world. They are about traditional Chinese life in the country with which Pearl Buck was familiar. Although the messages are strong in both novels, they are expressed through the life experiences of the main characters rather than the authorial subjectivity, especially in *Peony*. However, in *Imperial Woman*, "my best Chinese novel," and in *The Living Reed*, "the best among my Asian books," as she told G. A. Cevasco (1981, 20), I find too much explanation of the Asian histories and cultures. Granted that these books are historical novels and their backgrounds need to be made clear, the authorial explanation even permeates the characters' lives and activities, as if they could not be self-explanatory or readers' I. Q. were too low to make the necessary connections. Moreover, the descriptions of Tzu Hsi's life and personality are neither historically accurate in many aspects nor artistically convincing. Yehonala's free and frequent contact with Jung Lu within the forbidden city is impossible. Their love affair and the suggestion that Emperor Tung Chih is their son have no historical evidence---not even rumors. Nor are they artistically necessary to complete any theme or character. I cannot give the same criticism to *The Living Reed*, the Korean historical novel, but even if everything were accurate, I see little artistic necessity for Pearl Buck to give those suggestions about the intimate relationship between Il-han and the Queen, which takes too much of part 1. Yul-chun's long journey in China and Liang's love with the dancer girl in part 3 are even less relevant to the central theme. Perhaps Pearl Buck was trying to suggest Korea's close ties with China and the two countries' mutually dependent relationship, but her effort to explain the history and culture only made the novel "choppy, episodic, largely unfocused" (P. Doyle 1980, 139). Judging from the errors and weaknesses of *Imperial Woman* that I can spot, I would rank *The Living Reed* higher, but Korean critics may have a different judgment. Why she favored these two novels is indeed inexplicable.

These two novels, especially the latter, certainly have their historic and social values. However, Pearl Buck's other novels on or partly related to China, including *Letter from Peking, Satan Never Sleeps, The Three Daughters of Madame Liang*, and *All under Heaven*, are disappointing and ill serve her Nobel prize reputation. In these novels, ideology overbalances artistry, romantic sentiments overbalances realism, and the desire to report current issues and situations overbalances the effort to present China's reality, which she no longer knew exactly because she no longer was there. Unfortunately, she was evaluated by later critics more for such declining and mediocre novels, which, among other factors discussed earlier, eventually caused critics to ignore her altogether. More unfortunately, the Chinese Communist authorities criticized her, banned her books, and denied her visa to visit China because they were offended by these novels and ignored her earlier works that had helped China so much. Nevertheless, we are remembering and studying her more completely now. Some of her literary works still enchant and educate us. Many of the issues that she dealt with, particularly those concerning the conflicts between the East and West, are still facing us. Her function as a cultural bridge across the Pacific is seen more clearly than before and recognized as more than just historic.

Having discussed some of the historic significance and the cognitive function of a few of Pearl Buck's books, we can see what a shame it is that she has been neglected in the United States for so long. However, that the neglect was beginning to come to an end was marked by her centennial symposium held in Randolph-Macon Woman's College in March 1992. Many scholars have urged more social and cultural as well as literary studies to be conducted on her books. Xiongya Gao, a Chinese student at Ball State University, completed a doctoral dissertation in 1993 on the images of Chinese women in Pearl Buck's novels. A collection of the papers presented at the symposium was published in 1994 under the title of *The Several Worlds of Pearl S. Buck*, including representatively: James C. Thomson, Jr.'s reconsideration of Pearl Buck's critique and suggestion in the American quest for China; John d'Entremont's study of her contribution to American women's movement; David D. Buck's (no relation to Pearl or her first husband) research on her liberal and humanistic message brought to her American readers from an outsider's point of view; Peter Conn's essays discussing her as an artist as well as a humanitarian; and Deborah C. Raessler's essay demonstrating the pioneering significance of Pearl Buck's writings on handicapped children, which drew wide attention to the social problem in this country. Peter Conn has also written a cultural biography of Pearl Buck, and it has been adapted into a play performed in San Francisco. Pearl Buck's novels and stories are again taught in American colleges and universities.

More and more scholars are beginning to see the value of her works about women from a woman's point of view and about American culture from a multicultural point of view. They are beginning to realize that it would be a great loss if writers like Pearl Buck, owing to the difficulty of their classification, continued to slip away from the critical attention. No matter where a writer lives, no matter what his or her subject matter is, no matter what blood he or she has, as long as his or her book has social, cultural, aesthetic, or historic value, the writer deserves serious study. We should not continue to allow the traditional classification by nationality to prevent us from such studies. The nationality of the writer does not have to be the same as the subject of his or her writing. The roots of American literature are not only in Europe. The great books about China and Chinese people do not have to be written only by the Chinese. For example, the French writer Andre Malraux's classic, *La Condition Humaine*, known in English as *Man's Fate*, is a better novel about the great Shanghai uprising of 1927 than any Chinese novel on the same subject. As the world is becoming increasingly smaller with more and more modern technologies of communication and transportation, more and more multicultural creation and criticism will appear. The United States of America as a country of most diverse races and cultures should take the lead in multicultural studies of its literature. Americans are peoples who emigrated from all over the world, and so American literature, more than any other literature, is about all races and cultures; it has inherited more cultural traditions than any other literature, and it should have contributed more than any other literature to the understanding and appreciation of all peoples and cultures. Therefore, the study of this unique quality of American literature must be emphasized. Attention must be paid to new subject matters as much as to new styles.

It is mainly in subject matter that Pearl Buck made her unique contribution, as Carl van Doren pointed out, "*The Good Earth* for the first time made the Chinese seem as familiar as neighbors. Pearl Buck had added to American fiction one of its larger provinces" (353). She enlarged the territory of American literature, not only in settings and subject matter, but also in understanding humanities as a whole and on equal terms. She was the first celebrated woman novelist in the English language who had had a child, as Nancy Sorel maintained in "A New Look at 'Noble Suffering,'" written about the experience, and "served as a bridge between the symbolic approach of male novelists and the intimate, immediate tone of women who more and more began to portray childbirth as they experienced it" (1). Such experience is now discussed as an academic topic in books like Robbie P. Kahn's *Bearing Meaning: The Language of Birth*. Pearl Buck was also the first influential writer who dealt with the problems of retarded children, called public attention to the problems, and began to make a difference. Most important, she made it possible for Western readers to learn about China as it was with "sanity, compassion and understanding" through her artistic literary works (Gray 33). Her books, especially *The Good Earth* and *The Mother,* have realized some Chinese men and women so fully, described the continuity of their experience so truthfully, and reflected their sentiments, hope, despair, ideals, and expectations in such common terms as to make "American readers aware," as J. Donald Adams commented, "in the lives of a completely alien people, of universal human bonds" (1944, 125). Her phenomenal success opened up the possibility of writing on non-European and non-American scenes in this country.

Pearl Buck preceded many American writers including Richard N. Wright, John R. Hersey, Saul Bellow, Vladimir Nabokov, Bernard Malamud, Isaac B. Singer, Cseslaw Milosz, James Baldwin, Joseph Brodsky, Alice Walker, and Toni Morrison, whose main subjects are either non-American or about American minorities including Jews and Blacks. Her master-pieces---*The Good Earth, The Mother, The Exile,* and *Fighting Angel*---compare very well with the representative works of these writers. Her stories and novels certainly have reached a higher artistic level and a larger readership than did those of Edith M. Eaton, Maxine H. Kingston, Amy Tan, and Cathy Song. There is no reason not to anthologize Pearl Buck other than that she had no Chinese blood.

Moreover, hers was beyond a usual aesthetic achievement. She single-handedly changed the distorted image of the Chinese people in the American mind through literature. Chinese people were no longer seen as cheap, dirty, ridiculous coolies or sneaky, vicious, insidious devils. The majority of Chinese people were seen for the first time in literature as honest, kindhearted, frugal-living, hardworking, gods-fearing peasants who are much the same as American farmers. The change came at the crucial moment when China's national survival was threatened by the Japanese aggression. The change stimulated Americans to support the Chinese people in their resistance against the Japanese invasion and occupation. The change also helped American Chinese win their equal rights and dignity as fellow citizens and as human beings and led to the repeal of the Chinese Exclusion Act. Besides, her books have illustrated different views on some cultural issues, especially on the evaluation of Christian missions in China, helping readers see the achievements as well as the errors of the movement through vividly portrayed characters such as her own mother and father. Her books have also introduced new ideas about the conflicts between the East and West by demonstrating the tolerant Chinese attitude toward cultural differences and by describing China's different marriage system and how it worked from the point of view of a woman who knew both Eastern and Western institutions well. Her ideas reached a large readership through the success and popularity of her books. How readers received them and responded to them and what impact they had on readers are among many questions that are worth further study.

Other questions may include: How much influence did her success have on other writers of non-American subjects, particularly on writers of Chinese and Chinese American subjects? Maxine Hong Kingston acknowledged some influence in the Pearl Buck centennial symposium, but was the subject matter the only influence on her and other Chinese American writers? Did Pearl Buck's style, her speech presentation of Chinese characters, for example, which shows their education levels not so much by grammar and syntax as by literary idioms and allusions, influence other writers? After all, her novels have been the most successful in dealing with Chinese subjects and have met no comparison in

American literature as far as understanding China is concerned. Some scholar said, "China changed, but Pearl Buck did not change with it" (qtd. in Thomson 15). How different is China now from what we read in her books? How much is it still fundamentally the same? How different are the three-quarters of China's population, the peasants and farmers, from what they were at her time? How different is their relationship with land and with each other now from then? How valuable is it still to learn about China by reading Pearl Buck? What in her suggestions about the issues of racial and sexual equality and cultural conflict and confluence is still valid or valuable to us? How much influence, if any, did she have on the mainstream of American literature? Has any Chinese literary theory or style used in the books she wrote and translated been adopted by other writers of this country? What did we Chinese learn about ourselves from her books? What more can we learn now that we are no longer haunted by rabid nationalism and radical ideologies as we were in those fifty years from the 1930 to 1980?

With these questions rather than answers to them I end this book in the hope that more students and scholars will read and study Pearl Buck, who, I believe, is an indispensable figure in the cultural exchange and studies across the Pacific.

NOTES

1. These "Rural Literature" writers' representative works are: Wang Renshu's (Ba Ren's) "The Tired," Peng Jiahuan's "The Cow of Uncle Chen Sih," Wang Sidian's "The Paralytic," Pan Hsun's "The Heart of the Country," Hsu Chinwen's "The Native Land," and Hsu Yunor's "A Worn-out Shoe." For detailed discussion of the Chinese "Rural Literature" in the mid-1920s, see Huang Hsujee's *A Concise History of the Contemporary Chinese Literature*, pages 90-95.

2. For details of the creation, revision, and reviews of the opera see section 2, chapter 16, volume 3 of *A History of Contemporary Chinese Literature* by Tang Tao and Yan Jiayan, pp. 259-269. The responses to the opera quoted later are also from this part of the book. The English translation is mine.

BIBLIOGRAPHY

PRIMARY SOURCES

Novels

All under Heaven. New York: John Day, 1973.
American Triptych. John Sedges [pseud]. New York: John Day, 1958. Includes: *The Townsman, The Long Love, Voices in the House*.
The Angry Wife. John Sedges [pseud]. New York: John Day, 1947.
Bondmaid. London: Methuen, 1949.
Bright Procession. John Sedges, pseud. New York: John Day, 1952.
China Flight. Philadelphia: Blakiston (Triangle Books), 1945.
China Gold. Serialized in *Collier's*, 7 Feb.-18 Apr. 1942.
China Sky. Philadelphia: Triangle Books, 1942.
Come, My Beloved. New York: John Day, 1953.
Command the Morning. New York: John Day, 1959.
Death in the Castle. New York: John Day, 1965.
Dragon Seed. New York: John Day, 1942.
East Wind, West Wind. New York: John Day, 1930.
The Goddess Abides. New York: John Day, 1972.
God's Men. New York: John Day, 1951.
The Good Earth. New York: John Day, 1931.
The Hidden Flower. New York: John Day, 1952.
A House Divided. New York: Reynal, 1935.
House of Earth: The Good Earth; Sons; A House Divided. New York: Reynal, 1935.
Imperial Woman. New York: John Day, 1956.
Kinfolk. New York: John Day, 1949.
Letter from Peking. New York: John Day, 1957.
The Living Reed. New York: John Day, 1963.
The Long Love. John Sedges [pseud]. New York: John Day, 1949.
Mandala. New York: John Day, 1970.

The Mother. New York: John Day, 1934.

The New Year. New York: John Day, 1968.

Now and Forever. Serialized in the *Woman's Home Companion,* Oct. 1936-Mar. 1937.

Other Gods. New York: John Day, 1940.

The Patriot. New York: John Day, 1939.

Pavilion of Women. New York: John Day, 1946.

Pearl Buck Reader. Pleasantville, N.Y.: Reader's Association, 1985. Selection of novels.

Peony. New York: John Day, 1948.

Portrait of a Marriage. New York: John Day, 1945.

The Promise. New York: John Day, 1943.

The Rainbow. New York: John Day, 1974.

Satan Never Sleeps, New York: Pocket Books, 1962. Initially a movie script written by PSB from an outline by Leo McCarey.

Sons. New York: John Day, 1932.

This Proud Heart. New York: Reynal, 1938.

The Three Daughters of Madame Liang. New York: John Day, 1969.

The Time Is Noon. New York: John Day, 1966, 1967.

The Townsman. John Sedges [pseud]. New York: John Day, 1945.

Voices in the House. New York: John Day, 1953.

Young Revolutionist. New York: Friendship Press, 1932.

Drama

"The Big Wave." Television drama from her book *The Big Wave* for the National Broadcasting Company. Performed on Alcoa Hour, 30 Sept. 1956; also performed by the Hillsboro Arts and Drama Organization during Chautauqua week on the grounds of the PSB Birthplace in Hillsboro, 13 July 1977.

"China Speaks to America." *Asia* July 1943: 418-22. Radio play.

"Chinese Incident." *Asia* May 1942: 303-306; also in *Scholastic,* 26 Oct. 1942: 17-19. Radio play.

"Christine," with Charles K. Peck, Jr. Broadway musical, produced 28 Apr. 1960. Based on Hilda Wernher's novel *My Indian Family.*

"A Desert Incident." Produced at the John Golden Theater in New York City, 24 Mar. 1959. Ran only seven performances. Previously titled "The White Bird" and "Three against Time."

"The Empress." Play in three acts. Perkasie, Pa., 1937. It was not produced but typewritten copy in the New York Public Library and later developed into novel *Imperial Woman.*

"The Enemy." Starring Shirley Yamaguchu. Television play.

"The First Wife." Produced by the Chinese Theater, 27 Nov. 1945. Critical note in George Jean Nathan's *Theater Book of the Year, 1945-46.* New York: Knopf, 1946. 203.

"Flight into China." Play in three acts, produced at the Paper Mill Playhouse, Milburn, N. J., 11 Sept. 1939. Typewritten copy in the New York Public Library. Expanded into novel *Peony.*

"The No. 1 Christmas Tree in All the World." 1970.

"Satan Never Sleeps." Movie script written by PSB from an outline by Leo McCarey;

later published as a paperback novel.

"Sun Yat-sen." One-act play. *Asia* Apr. 1944: 170-74.

"Will This Earth Hold?" Radio play. *Asia* Nov. 1944: 506-10; also in *Radio Drama in Action*. Erik Barnow, ed., New York: 1945, 7-30.

Juvenile Literature

The Beech Tree. New York: John Day, 1954.

The Beech Tree & Johnny Jack and His Beginnings. New York: Dell, 1967.

The Big Flight. New York: John Day, 1964.

The Big Wave. New York: John Day, 1948.

The Chinese Children Next Door. New York: John Day, 1942.

The Chinese Story Teller. New York: John Day, 1971.

The Christmas Ghost. New York: John Day, 1960.

The Christmas Miniature. New York: John Day, 1957.

The Dragon Fish. New York: John Day, 1944.

Fairy Tales of the Orient. Ed. and intro. by PSB. New York: Simon, 1965.

A Gift for the Children. New York: John Day, 1971.

Johnny Jack and His Beginnings. New York: John Day, 1954.

The Little Fox in the Middle. New York: Macmillan, 1966.

The Man Who Changed China: the Story of Sun Yat-sen. New York: Random House, 1953.

Matthew, Mark, Luke, and John. New York: John Day, 1966.

Mrs. Starling's Problem. New York: John Day, 1973.

One Bright Day. New York: John Day, 1950.

One Bright Day and Other Stories for Children. New York: John Day, 1950.

Stories for Little Children. New York: John Day, 1940. British title: *When Fun Begins.* London: Methuen, 1940.

The Water-Buffalo Children. New York: John Day, 1943.

Welcome Child. New York: John Day, 1963.

The Young Revolutionist. New York: Friendship Press, 1932.

Yu Lan, Flying Boy of China. New York: John Day, 1945.

Translation

All Men Are Brothers. Trans. from one of the greatest classic Chinese novels, *Shui Hu Chuan.* 2 vols. PSB chose an English title from the Confucian saying: "All men around the four seas are brothers." New York: John Day, 1933.

Short Story Collection

East and West. New York: John Day, 1975. 7 stories with background in Asia and America that span a period of 30 years.

Escape at Midnight and Other Stories. Hong Kong: Dragonfly Books, 1963. Story "The Silver Butterfly" by Curtis Publishing Co., 1960. Paperback. 10 short stories.

Far and Near. New York: John Day, 1947. 14 stories of China, Japan, and America.

The First Wife and Other Stories. New York: John Day, 1933. 14 short stories.

Fourteen Stories. New York: John Day, 1961. British title: *With a Delicate Air.*

The Good Deed and Other Stories of Asia, Past and Present. New York: John Day, 1969. 9 Stories of Asia; 1 of Chinatown, N.Y.

Hearts Come Home and Other Stories. New York: Pocket Books, 1962. 14 stories from 3 collections: *The First Wife and Other Stories, Today and Forever, and Far and Near.*

The Lovers and Other Stories. New York: John Day, 1977. 6 short stories and 1 novella.

Mrs. Stoner and the Sea and Other Works. New York: Ace Books Paperback, 1976. 9 short stories and 3 other writings.

My Mother's House. Richwood, W.Va.: Appalachian Press, 1965. Ltd. edition of 500 copies autographed by PSB to be sold for $100 each for the sole purpose of purchasing her birthplace in Hillsboro, W.Va. First chapter "My Mother's House" is special contribution to book by PSB; 3 chapters are rpts. of articles about PSB and her birthplace.

Once upon a Christmas. New York: John Day, 1972. 14 stories and articles.

Pearl S. Buck's Book of Christmas. New York: Simon & Schuster, 1974. Produced by Lyle Kenyon Engel. Collection of 39 favorite Christmas stories by some of the world's greatest writers, selected by PSB, plus "Biographical Notes" on 33 authors represented. No writing of PSB included.

Secrets of the Heart. New York: John Day, 1976. 4 short stories and 1 novella.

Stories of China. New York: John Day, 1964. This book is identical in contents to *Twenty-Seven Stories.*

Today and Forever. New York: John Day, 1941. Serialized in *Woman's Home Companion* Oct. 1936-Mar. 1937. 13 short stories written in the 1930s.

Twenty-Seven Stories. Garden City, N.Y.: The Sun Dial Press, 1943. Combines 2 books: *The First Wife and Other Stories and Today and Forever.* This book is identical in content to *Stories of China.*

The Woman Who Was Changed and Other Stories. New York: Thomas Y. Cromwell, 1979. 5 short stories and 1 novella.

Biographies and Autobiographies

A Bridge for Passing. New York: John Day, 1962.

The Exile. New York: Reynal & Hitchcock, 1936. A much-condensed version serialized in the *Woman's Home Companion,* 1935-36.

Fighting Angel: Portrait of a Soul. New York: Reynal, 1936. Excerpt in Prochnow, H.V., ed. *Great Stories from Great Loves.* New York: Harper, 1944.

My Chinese Childhood. Newton, Iowa: Tamazunchale, 1982. 250 copies of this book have been printed from *My Several Worlds.*

My Several Worlds: a Personal Record. New York: John Day, 1954.

The Spirit and the Flesh. New York: John Day, 1944. Contains *Fighting Angel* and *Exile,* biographies of the author's father and mother, respectively.

Miscellany

American Argument: With Eslanda Goods Robeson. New York: John Day, 1949.

American Unity and Asia. New York: John Day, 1942. British title: *Asia and Democracy.* London: Macmillan, 1943.

Can the Church Lead? New York: 1946. Typewritten copy in the New York Public Library.

A Certain Star. New York: Hearst, 1957.

Children for Adoption. New York: Random House, 1964.
  Children Who Never Grew. New York: John Day, 1950.

China as I See It. New York: John Day, 1970.

China in Black and White. New York: John Day, 1945. An Asian Press Book, illus. with 82 Chinese woodcuts and commentary each by PSB. Copy in West Virginia University Library.]

China Past and Present. New York: John Day, 1972.

The Chinese Novel. Nobel lecture delivered before the Swedish Academy at Stockholm, 12 Dec. 1938. New York: John Day, 1939.

A Community Success Story: the Founding of the Pearl Buck Center. New York: John Day, 1972. Discussion with Elizabeth Waechter, Director.

Delights of Learning. Pittsburgh: U Pittsburgh P, 1960. Address delivered on the occasion of the University of Pittsburgh Honors Convocation, April 6, 1960.

East and West and the Novel: Sources of the early Chinese Novel. Peiping (Beijing): North China Union Language School cooperating with the California College in China, 1932. 2 addresses before the convocation of the North China Union Language School, Feb. 1932. Copy in U of Va. Library, Charlottesville. 40p.

Essay on Myself. PSB and *A Study of Pear S. Buck.* Lason Lindsey. New York: John Day, 1966. 2 essays are combined in this pamphlet.

For Spacious Skies: Journal in Dialogue. PSB and Theodore F. Harris. New York: John Day, 1966.

Freedom for All. New York: The Post War World Council, 1942. A reprint from the *New York Times* 15 Nov. 1941.

Freedom for India Now! New York: The Post War World Council, 1941.

Friend to Friend: a Candid Exchange Between Pearl Buck and P. Romulo. New York: John Day, 1958.

The Gifts They Bring: Our Debt to the Mentally Retarded. New York: John Day, 1965.

How it Happens. New York: John Day, 1947. Talk about the German people 1914-1933, with Erna von Pustau.

Illustrated Story Bible. New York: New American Library, 1980.

Insecurity Breeds Hatred. Labor Reports, 1945.

Is There a Case for Foreign Missions? New York: John Day, 1932. No. 18 in the "John Day Pamphlets."

The Joy of Children. New York: John Day, 1964.

The Kennedy Women: A Personal Appraisal. New York: Cowles Book, 1970.

Letters from Pearl S. Buck to Mr. Farrar, congratulating him for publishing Sally Salminen's *Katrina,* Farrar and Rinehart, 1937. Dated 23 Sept. 1937. Appeared as a broadside in the *New York Times Book Review* 17 Oct. 1937.

Like and Unlike in East and West. Dallas, Texas: Institute of Public Affairs, 1935. Mimeographed abstract.

My Chinese Childhood. Newton, Iowa: Tamazunchale Press, 1982.

New Evidence of the Militarization of America. Washington, D.C.: National Council Against Conscription, 1949. A report issued by Pearl Buck and others.

The Novel in the Making. New York: John Day, 1940.

Of Men and Women. New York: John Day, 1941.

On Discovering America. New York: Survey Associates, 1937.

Pearl Buck's Oriental Cookbook. PSB and L. K. Engel. New York: Simon & Schuster, 1972.

Pearl Buck Speaks for Democracy. Foreword by Mrs. Franklin D. Roosevelt. New York: Common Council for American Unity, 1942.

Pearl S. Buck's America. PSB and L. K. Engel. New York: Bartholomew House, 1971.

Pearl S. Buck: The Complete Woman. Kansas City: Hallmark, 1971. Selections from writings of Pearl S. Buck, ed. by C. Merton Babcock.

People. [East and West Association] New York. V1-4, no.8, Apr. 1945-Jan. 1950. This periodical was edited by Pearl Buck and Richard J. Walsh.

People of Japan. New York: Simon & Schuster, 1966.

Story Bible: Volume I the Old Testament. PSB and L. K. Engel. New York: Bartholomew House, 1971.

Story Bible: Volume II the New Testament. PSB and L.K. Engel. New York: Bartholomew House, 1971.

Story Bible. PSB and L. K. Engel. New York: Bartholomew House, hardcover, 1971. 2 vols. in 1.

Story of Dragon Seed. New York: John Day, 1944.

Talk about Russia with Masha Scott. New York: John Day, 1945.

Tell the People. New York: John Day, 1945. Talks with James Yen about the mass education movement.

Through China's Gateway: A Series of Six Sound Film-Strips by Pearl Buck. Presented by the East and West Association. New York: 1947. 5 pamphlets, which may be found in the New York Public Library.

Tinder for Tomorrow. New York: The Post War World Council, 1941.

To My Daughters, with Love. New York: John Day, 1967. 20 commencement addresses and other writings.

What America Means to me. New York: John Day, 1943.

What the Peoples of Asia Want. Chicago: Council on Foreign Relations, 1951. Typewritten copy in the New York Public Library.

Words of Love. New York: John Day, 1974. Illus. by Jeanyee Wong. Pearl Buck's only book of poetry selected from her "Treasure Book," (i.e., Diary). 17 poems in calligraphic writing and 22 illustrations with descriptions of Chinese art.

Articles in Books and Periodicals

"Advice to Unborn Novelists." Ed. W. H. and K. C. Cordell. *American Points of View.* 1935. New York: Doubleday, 1936. 390-401; also in *Saturday Review of Literature* 2 Mar. 1935, 513-14+.

"Alice Nash." *Training School Bulletin* Feb. 1950: 150-51.

"America's Gunpowder Women." *Harper's Magazine* July 1939: 126-35; *Reader's Digest* Aug. 1939: 10-15.

"America's Medieval Women." Ed. S. F. Anderson et al. *Our Changing World.* New York: Harper, 1939. 324-39: *Essay Annual* 1939. 63-75; *Harper's Magazine* Aug. 1938: 225-32."American Imperialism in the Making." *Asia* Aug. 1945: 365-68.

"Americans in Distress." *United Nations World* Apr. 1947: 26-29.

"American Looks at America." *Opportunity* Dec. 1937: 359-61.

"Appeal to California." *Asia* Jan. 1944: 21-23.

"Arms for China's Democracy." *Asia* Sept. 1938: 534-35.

"Artist in a World of Science." *Saturday Review* 20 Sept. 1958: 15-16+.

"Asiatic Problems." *Vital Speeches* 1 Mar. 1942: 303-305.

"At Home in the World." Child Study Association of America, *Our Children Today*. New York: Viking Press, 1952. 334-43. Ed. S. M. Gruenberg *Family in a World at War*. New York: Harper, 1942. 130-42.

"At Home with Pearl Buck." *Ladies' Home Journal* July 1965: 36.

"Atmosphere of Education." *National Education Association Journal* Mar. 1924: 326-36.

"Beauty in China." *Forum* Mar. 1924: 326-36.

"Bomb, Did We Have to Drop It?" *Reader's Digest* Aug. 1959: 11-15; *American Weekly* 15 Mar. 1959: 10-11, 16.

"Books About Americans for People in Asia to Read." *Asia* Oct. 1942: 600-601.

"Breaking the Barriers of Race Prejudice." *Journal of Negro Education* Oct. 1942: 444-53.

"Can England Trust Us?" *New York Times Magazine* 18 Apr. 1943: 10.

"Can the Church be Religious?" *Christian Century* 22 Dec. 1943: 1499-501.

"Center of New Life." *American Journal of Nursing* May 1943: 493-95.

"Child from Nowhere." *Ladies' Home Journal* Dec. 1962: 46-47.

"Child Who Never Grew." *Ladies' Home Journal* May 1950: 35-35; *Reader's Digest* Sept. 1950: 18-25.

"Children America Forgot." *Reader's Digest* Sept. 1967: 108-10.

"Children Are What You Make Them." *Forum* Dec. 1936: 253-55.

"Children Waiting." *Woman's Home Companion* Sept. 1955: 32-33.

"Children's Crusade for Children." *Parents' Magazine* May 1940: 21.

"China against Japan." *Asia* Feb. 1936: 79-80.

"China and the Foreign Chinese." *Yale Review* Mar. 1932: 539-47.

"China and the West." *Annals of the American Academy* July 1933: 118-31.

"China Front and the Future of Asia: Controversial Viewpoints," PSB et al. *Amerasia* Jan. 1943: 459-70.

"China Lost and Found." *National PTA Magazine* Mar. 1972: 28-31.

"China, Still the Good Earth." *Saturday Review of Literature* 8 Oct. 1949: 8-10.

"China the Eternal." *Living Age* 7 Feb. 1925: 324-30. *China Weekly Review*, 11 Apr. 1925: 162-64; *International Review of Missions* Oct. 1924: 573-84.

"China to America." Arch Oboler. *Free World Theater*. New York: Random House, 1944. 140-50.

"Chinese Attitude toward Graft." *Harper's Magazine* Jan. 1935: 190-98.

"Chinese Literature in Today's World." Ed. H. F. MacNair. *China*. Berkeley: U of California P, 1946. 397-405.

"Chinese Student Mind." *Nation* 8 Oct. 1924: 358-61.

"Chinese War Lords." *Saturday Evening Post* 22 Apr. 1933: 3-5.

"Chinese Women." *Pacific Affairs* Oct. 1931: 905-909.

"Come in, Mary." *Reader's Digest* Nov. 1965: 229-30+.

"Coming of Jesus." *Ladies' Home Journal* Dec. 1971: 83+. Excerpt from *The Story Bible*

"Communism in China." *Nation* 25 July 1928: 97-98.

"Conclusion: East and West." Ed. A. E. Christy. *Asia Legacy and American Life*. New York: John Day, 1945. 231-35.

"Conflict and Cooperation across the Pacific Today." *Opportunity* Sept. 1935: 264-66.

"Creative Spirit in Modern China." *Asia* Sept.-Oct. 1934: 526-29, 601-605.

"Darkest Hour in China's History." *New York Times Magazine* 17 Dec. 1944: 9.

"Does World Government Mean More Government?" *United Nations World* Feb. 1947: 22-25. n. p.

"Don't Throw Away the Best Part." *Collier's* 1 Aug. 1942: 11.

"Do You Want Your Children to be Tolerant?" *Better Homes and Gardens* Feb. 1947: 33.

"Dream for Danby." *Yankee Magazine* July 1971. n. p.

"Early Chinese Novel." *Saturday Review of Literature*. 6 June 1931: 873-74.

"East and West." *American Mercury* May 1945: 526-29.

"Easter 1933." *Cosmopolitan* May 1933: 16-17.

"Education for Victory." *Nebraska Education Journal* May 1944: 153; *Texas Outlooks* Nov. 1944: 29.

"Elementary Teacher is a Champion for the Less Fortunate Child." *Instructor* Jan. 1952: 11.

"Elements of Democracy in the Chinese Traditional Culture." Jamaica, N.Y.: Center of Asian Studies, St. John's University, 1969. St. John's paper in Asian Studies, No. 5.

"Emotional Chinese." *Trans-Pacific* 30 Oct. 1926: 3.

"Emotional Nature of the Chinese." *Nation* 22 Sept. 1926: 269-70.

"Exile's Gift." *Saturday Review of Literature* 19 Oct. 1940: 9.

"Fiction and the Front Page." *Yale Review* Mar. 1936: 477-87.

"Fifty Years in the Training School is an Honorable Record." *Training-School Bulletin* Dec. 1948: 143-46.

"Films for Neighbors." Ed. C. Starr. *Ideas on Film*. New York: Funk and Wagnalls, 1951. 82-6; *Saturday Review of Literature*. 14 Jan. 1950: 38.

"Food for China." *Survey Graphic* July 1947: 377-79.

"For a People's Peace." *Progressive Education* Nov. 1942: 367.

"Foreigners under Fire." *Asia* Nov. 1937: 806-07; Mar. 1938: 208.

"Free China Gets to Work." *Asia* Apr. 1939: 199-202.

"Freedom, East and West." *Common Sense* Sept. 1942: 291-94.

"Freedom for All." *Asia* May 1942: 324-26.

"Freedom to be Free." *New York Times Magazine* 28 Feb. 1943: 14.

"Friendly Homes of Bucks County." *American Home* Oct. 1961: 38-43+.

"Friends and Enemies of China." *Asia* Apr. 1936: 279-80.

"Future of the White Man in the Far East." *Foreign Affairs* Oct. 1940: 22-23.

"Giants Are Gone." *Asia* Nov. 1936: 710-14. Autobiography.

"God Becomes a Convenience." *Forum* Sept. 1936: 99-105.

"Good People of Japan." *United Nations World* Feb. 1949: 14-16.

"Heart of Democracy." *Vital Speeches* 15 April 1942: 395-97. Abridged version entitled "Freedom for All."

"He Who Lives, Wins." *Asia* Nov. 1939: 635-36.

"Higher Nationalism." *World Tomorrow* 7 Dec. 1933: 658-59.

"Historic Basis of Friendship." *Current* June 1971: 3-5.

"How I Feel about America." *Pittsburgh Press* 7 June 1970. n. p.

"I Am the Better Woman for Having My Two Black Children." *Today's Health* Jan. 1972: 20-23+.

"In China, Too." *Atlantic* Jan. 1923: 68-72.

"In Search of a New Book." *Wilson Bulletin* May 1935: 469-70.

"In Search of Readers." Ed. H. R. Hull. *Writer's Book*. New York: Harper, 1950. 2-5.

"In Search of Teachers." *Schoolman's Week Proctor*. Pennsylvania U. P. 1956: 17-27.

"Interview with My Adopted Daughter." *Reader's Digest* June 1946: 4-8.

"Introduction." Lin, Yu-t'ang. *My Country and My People*. New York: Reynal and Hitchcock, 1935. vii-xii.

"Introduction." Lin, Adet and Lin, Anor. *Our Family*. New York: John Day, 1939. 256.

"Introduction to the United States." *Saturday Review of Literature* 27 May 1939: 12-13.

"Is There a Case for Foreign Missions?" *Harper's Magazine* Jan. 1933: 143-55.

"It Takes Courage." *National Education Association Journal* Apr. 1948: 246.

"Japan Loses the War." *Reader's Digest* Aug. 1938: 38-40.

"Japanese Children." *Catholic World* Jan. 1953: 5.

"Joy of Children." *Reader's Digest* July 1965: 145-53. Excerpts from *Joy of Children*

"Laymen's Mission Report." *Christian Century* 23 Nov. 1932: 1434-37.

"Legend of Tchi-Nie: Adaptation." *McCall's* May 1964: 114-15+.

"Let Them Have Reality." *Child Study* May 1949: 74.

"Letters to the Editor." *Christian Observer* 5 Apr. 1899: letter written by six-year-old PSB. Copy in *Pearl S. Buck: a Biography* by T. F Harris, 86. PSB as a child also had several stories and writings published in English newspaper, *Shanghai Mercury*, under the pen name "Novice."

"Letter to Germany." *Common Ground* Winter 1946: 3-9.

"Like and Unlike in East and West;" *Vital Speeches* 12 Aug. 1935: 718-20.

"Listen to the People, United Nations!" *United Nations World* Oct. 1947: 27-31.

"Literature and Life." Ed. A. L. Bader and C. F. Wells. *Essay for Our Time*. New York: Harper, 1947. 201-10. Ed. I. E. Taylor and J. S. Redding. *Reading for Writing*. New York: Ronald, 1952. 98-108; *National Education Association Journal* Sept. 1938: 171-76; *Saturday Review of Literature* 13 Aug. 1938: 3-4.

"Make it Freedom's War." *New Republic* 21 Dec. 1942: 824-25. Speech at Nobel prize winners dinner, Dec. 10; abridged.

"Man Who Showed China the Vision." *New York Times Magazine* 12 Mar. 1944: 9.

"Manners and Civilization." Ed. T. H. Johnson. *Men of Tomorrow*. New York: Putnam, 1942. 231-47.

"Message to Randolph-Macon." *Randolph-Macon Woman's College Alumnae Bulletin* 1943. 13-16.

"Mind of the Militarist." *Asia* Jan. 1938: 9-10.

"Missionaries of Empire." Ed. J. Barnes. *Empire in the East*. New York: Doubleday, 1934. 241-66.

"Most Unforgettable Character I've Met." *Reader's Digest* Oct. 1946: 69-73.

"Mr. Clinton Stops Starvation." *United Nations World* Dec. 1949: 25-28.

"Must We Have Orphanages?" *Reader's Digest* Nov. 1955: 57-60.

"My Debt to Dickens." *English Review* Apr. 1936: 408-12; *Saturday Review of Literature* 4 Apr. 1936: 11; *Essay Annual*, 1937: 114-19.

"My World." *Ladies' Home Journal* Nov. 1964: 36+; Jan. 1965: 18+; Mar. 1965: 36.

"New Education for a New Day." *Progressive Education* May 1944: 219; *Texas Outlook* Mar. 1944: 25; *Virginia Journal of Education* Jan. 1944: 181.

"New Modes of Chinese Marriage." *Asia* Aug. 1927: 650-53.

"New Nationalism." *International Digest* Sept. 1931: 50-52.

"New Patriotism." *China Weekly Review* 20 June 1931, 104-105.

"New Tools for Schools." *Far Eastern Survey* 11 Jan. 1943: 10-11.

"New Traveler in China." *Asia* Oct. 1946: 473-76.

"Nineteen Stockings by the Chimney Piece." *Reader's Digest* Dec. 1963: 49-52.

"No Union without China!" *Asia* Sept. 1941: 524.

"Note on the Price of Rice and Power." *United Nations World* Sept. 1948: 17.

"Old Chinese Nurse." *Fortnightly* June 1932: 757-70.

"Old Trick of the West." *Asia* Aug. 1939: 456.

"On Discovering America." *Survey Graphic* June 1937: 312-25; *Scholastic* 8 Jan. 1938, 23E-24E; *Reader's Digest* July 1937: 9-11.

"On Writing of Novels." *Randolph-Macon Woman's College Alumnae Bulletin* June 1933: 3-10.

"Open Letter to the Chinese People." *Asia* Feb. 1938: 126-28.

"Our Dangerous Myths about China." *New York Times Magazine* 23 Oct., 1949: 9; *Reader's Digest.* Jan. 1950: 69-72.

"Our Last Chance in China." *Common Sense* Aug. 1944: 265-68.

"Pearl Buck." Ed. Clifton Fadiman. *I Believe.* New York: Simon, 1939. 33-42.

"Pearl Buck Speaks for Democracy." *Common Council for American Unity.* New York City, 1942. Forword by Mrs. Eleanor D. Roosevelt.

"Pearl Buck Talks of Her Life in China." *China Weekly* Nov. 1932: 145-46.

"Pearl S. Buck's Cookbook," PSB and L. K. Engel. *Ladies' Home Journal* Apr. 1973: 104-05+. Excerpt.

"Pearl S. Buck's Message to New York Chapter." *Randolph-Macon Woman's College Alumnae Bulletin* 1935. 16-17.

"People, East and West." *Asia* June 1943: 328-29.

"People in Pain." *Reader's Digest* Nov. 1941: 159-60.

"People Will Be Free." *United Nations World* Dec. 1948: 6-7.

"Pill and the Teenage Girl." *Reader's Digest* Apr. 1968: 111-14.

"Plain People of China." *Asia* July 1941: 352-60.

"Portrait of My Father." *American Mercury* Nov. 1936: 359-72. Excerpt from *Fighting Angel.*

"Postwar China and the United States." *Asia* Nov. 1943: 613-15.

"President Truman's Point 4." *Fortnightly* Feb. 1950: 69-75.

"Protestant among the Presbyterians." *America* 29 Apr., 1933: 77.

"Protesting an Unfavorable Review of Lillian Smith's 'Killers of the Dream.'" *New York Times* 4 Dec. 1949: 2.

"Psychological Setting." *Institute of Public Affairs*, Dallas, Texas: 1935. Mimeographed.

"Pursuit of Happiness." *Seventeen* Dec. 1963: 112+.

"Quarter Century: Its Human Tragedies." *Look* 26 Sept. 1961: 94-96+.

"Questions Indians Ask Me." *Asia* May 1946: 201-203.

"Race Barrier That Must Be Destroyed." *New York Times Magazine* 31 May 1942: 3-4.

"Reading and the American Public." Address, July 1966. *ALA Bulletin.* Oct. 1966: 931-36.

"Real Triangle of Life." *Child Study* Apr. 1941: 67-80.

"Recognition and the Writer." *Saturday Review of Literature* 25 May, 1940: 13-14.

"River." *Christian Century* 30 Dec. 1931: 1651-52.

"Room in the Inn." *Ladies Home Journal* Dec. 1950: 34-35.

"Rose Kennedy." *Good Housekeeping* June 1970: 68-71+. Excerpt from *The Kennedy Woman.*

"Rulers of China." *Asia* Feb. 1935: 71-75.

"Save the Children for What?" *Journal of Educational Sociology* Dec. 1943: 195-99.

"Saving the Good Earth." *Ave Maria* 26 Apr. 1947: 515.

"Security in a Cage." *Survey Graphic* March 1938: 167-69.

"Sexual Revolution." *Ladies' Home Journal* Sept. 1964. [Excerpt from *Children for Adoption*]

"Should Gandhi's Assassin Be Killed?" *United Nations World* Mar. 1948: 64.

"Soldier of Japan." *New Republic* 7 June 1939: 134.

"Solitary." *Commentary* Apr. 1946: 7-11.

"Soul of China." *Living Age* 1 Apr. 1930: 168-76.

"Soul of the East." *Good Housekeeping* Dec. 1932: 20-21.

"Spirit behind the Weapon." *Survey Graphic* Nov. 1942: 539-42.

"Spiritual Revulsion." *Sign* June 1942: 670.

"Take Time to Read Good Books." *Library Journal* 15 Apr. 1937: 332.

"Talks with Marsha." *Asia* May-Nov. 1945: 221-25, 273-77, 334-38, 401-405, 449-53, 497-501, 546-49.

"Teachers for Fascism's Heirs." *Common Sense* Feb. 1944: 45-48.

"Tell the People." *Asia* Jan. 1945: 49-71.

"Thanks to Japan." *Asia* May 1938: 279-81.

"They Who Are Not Yet Born." *Good Housekeeping* Dec. 1940: 28-29.

"Tinder for Tomorrow." *Asia* Mar. 1942: 153-55.

"Total Victory." *New Republic* 1 June 1942: 761-62.

"Touch of Life." *Atlantic Monthly* Nov. 1954: 45-48. Excerpt from *My Several Worlds*.

"Tribute to Dr. Machen." *New Republic* 20 Jan. 1937: 355.

"Understanding the Chinese." *Rotarian* Jan. 1944: 14-16.

"Wanted: Real Woman." *Good Housekeeping* Apr. 1962: 67. Essay, slightly revised, pub. as "Changing Relationships between Men and Women." Ed. Beverly B. Cassara. *American Women: the Changing Image*. Boston: 1962: 3-10.

"Warning about China." *Life* 10 May 1943: 53-54.

"Warning to Free Nations." *Asia* Mar. 1941: 161.

"We Can Free the Children." *Woman's Home Companion* June 1956: 38-39+.

"We Must Quit Playing Santa Claus." *New York Times Magazine* 10 Jan. 1943: 9.

"We Need, Most of All, the World View." *New York Times Magazine* 28 Apr. 1946: 11.

"We Need the World View." American Association of School Administrators. *Official Report* 1948: 154-65; *Texas Outlook* Aug. 1948: 4-8.

"Welcome House." *Reader's Digest*. July 1958: 46-50.

"Western Weapons in the Hands of the Reckless East." *Asia* Oct. 1937: 672-73; *Reader's Digest* Nov. 1937: 6-7.

"What America Means to Me." *Common Ground* Summer 1943: 3-10; *Coronet*, Apr. 1950: 115. An address delivered at a United States treasury bond rally in Allentown, Pa., 24 Feb. 1943.

"What Asians Want." *Christian Century* 27 June 1951: 760-63.

"What Chinese Parents Can Teach Us." *Parents' Magazine* Nov. 1941: 18-19.

"What I Learned from Chinese Women." *Vogue* June 1972: 136-37+. Interview by D. McConathy, ed.

"What Is Loyalty?" *Parents Magazine* Feb. 1953: 27.

"What Religion Means to Me." Ed. W. H. Cordell. *Molders of American Thought, 1933-34*. Garden City, N.Y.: Doubleday, 1934. 199-209. *Forum* Oct. 1933: 195-200.

"What We Are Fighting for in the Orient." *Christian Science Monitor Magazine* 25 Apr.

1942: 1-2.

"When a Daughter Marries." *Good Housekeeping* Sept. 1949: 38.

"Where Are the Young Rebels?" Ed. J. D. McCallum et al. *College Omnibus, 1936.* New York: Harcourt, 1936. 252-61; *Harper's Magazine* Sept. 1935: 429-27.

"Where Shall They Go for Glory?" *Good Housekeeping* June 1941: 48.

"Why ... Should I Care?" *Saturday Review of Literature* 20 Aug. 1932: 49-50.

"Will a Miracle Child Be Born This Year?" *Ladies' Home Journal.* Dec. 1970: 3+.

"Wise Chinese." *Fortnightly* Jan. 1935: 24-35.

"Woman Nobody Knows." *Pictorial Review* Jan. 1932: 21.

"Woman of the World." *United Nations World* Mar. 1947: 24-28.

"Woman's Role in the World." *Independent Woman* Sept. 1941: 259.

"Women and War." *Ladies' Home Journal* May 1940: 18.

"Words of Love." *Good Housekeeping* July 1974: 82-83. (Poems)

"World and the Victor." *Asia* July 1938: 393-94.

"World of Tomorrow." *Asia* Nov. 1941: 620.

"World Understanding through Reading." *American Library Association Bulletin* 1 Sept. 1948: 341-48.

"Writing of *East Wind: West Wind.*" Comp. Elmer Adler. *Breaking into Print.* New York: Simon & Schuster, 1937. 29-34; also in *Colophon* New York: Dec. 1932: 1-4.

"Yen of China." *United Nations World* Feb. 1948: 48-53.

"Young Chinese Discovers China." *English Review* Dec. 1935: 726-30.

"Your Boy and U.M.T." *Christian Century* 19 Dec. 1951: 1475-76.

SECONDARY SOURCES

Abeel, David. *Journal of a Residence in China, and the Neighboring Countries.* New York: Praeger, 1836.

Adams, J. Donald. Rev. of *The Mother,* by Pearl Buck. *New York Times* 14 Jan. 1934: sec. 5, pp. 1, 18.

---. Rev. of *Sons,* by Pearl Buck. *New York Times Book Review.* 25 Sept. 1932: 1.

---. "Speaking of Books." *New York Times Book Review.* 22 Sept. 1963: 2.

---. *The Shape of Books to Come.* New York: Viking, 1944.

Albert, R. F. Rev. of *Young Revolutionist,* by Pearl Buck. *Christian Century* 6 Apr. 1932 49: 450.

Allen, Marian. "Ah Foo, the Fortune Teller." *Overland Monthly.* 2nd. ser. 65 Mar. 1915: 249.

"American Academy Awards Howells Medal to Pearl S. Buck." *Publishers' Weekly* 23 Nov. 1935: 1896.

Anderson, Carl L. *The Swedish Acceptance of American Literature.* Philadelphia: U of Pennsylvania P, 1957. 113-14, 149, 153.

Anthony, S. B. "Woman's Next Step." *New York Times Magazine* 12 Jan. 1941: 11.

Armstrong, Anne. Rev. of *Sons,* by Pearl Buck. *Saturday Review* 5 Nov. 1932 154: 481.

"At Home with Pearl Buck." *Ladies' Home Journal* July 1965: 36.

Atkinson, Brooks. Rev. of play, "A Desert Incident," by Pearl Buck. *New York Times Book Review* 25 Mar. 1959: 40.

Ayscough, Florence. Rev. of *The Good Earth,* by Pearl Buck. *Saturday Review of Literature 7,* 21 Mar. 1931: 676.

---. Review of *The Mother*, by Pearl Buck. *Saturday Review of Literature 10*, 13 Jan. 1934: 401.

Bacon, Francis. *Of the Proficience and Advancement of Learning Human and Divine. The Works of Francis Bacon*. 10 vols. London: Baynes, 1824.

Baldwin, E. V. Rev of *Dragon Seed*, by Pearl Buck. *Library Journal 67*, 15 Jan. 1942: 86.

Barnes, Anne. "They Have Their Exits." Rev. of *The Rainbow*, by Pearl Buck. *Times [London] Literary Supplement* 5 Nov. 1976: 1405.

Barnett, Suzanne W. and John K. Fairbank. Ed. *Christianity in China*. Cambridge: Harvard UP, 1985.

Bartlett, R. M. "East and West---One World: Pearl S. Buck." *They Work for Tomorrow*. New York: Association Press and Fleming H. Revell, 1943. 32-40.

Basalla, George. Rev. of *Command the Morning*, by Pearl Buck. *Library Journal 84*, 1 May 1959: 1531.

Batelle, Adah F. "The Sacking of Grubbville." *Overland Monthly* 2nd ser. 20 Dec. 1892: 573.

Bazelon, D. T. Rev. of *How It Happens*, by Pearl Buck. *Nation 164*, 15 Feb. 1947: 190.

Beach, Joseph Warren. *The Twentieth Century Novel*. New York: 1932, 233. Discusses *The Good Earth*.

Becker, May Lamberton. *Golden Tales of the Far West*. New York: Dodd, 1935.

Bell, Mary. "Sing Kee's Chinese Lily." *Overland Monthly*. 2nd. ser. 30 Dec. 1897: 531.

Bellman, Samuel I. "Popular Writers in the Modern Age: Constance Rourke, Pearl Buck, Marjorie Kinnan Rawlings, and Margaret Mitchell." Ed. M. Duke et al. *American Women Writers: Bibliographical Essays*. Westport: Greenwood, 1983. 353-78.

Benet, Stephen V. and Rosemary. "Two-World Success Story: Pearl Buck." *New York Herald Tribune* 18 Jan. 1942. sec. 9, p. 5.

Bentley, Phyllis. "The Art of Pearl S. Buck." *English Journal* 24 Dec. 1935: 791-800.

Bevans, Charles, I. Ed. *Treaties and Other International Agreements of the United States of America, 1776-1949*. Washington, D.C.: U.S. G.P.O., 1971. vi.

Bierce, Ambrose. "The Haunted Valley." *Overland Monthly* 8 July 1871: 88.

Biggers, Earl Derr. *Behind that Curtain*. 1928. New York: Bantam, 1974.

---. *The Black Camel*. 1929. New York: Bantam, 1975.

---. *Charlie Chan Carries on*. 1930. New York: Bantam, 1975.

---. *The Chinese Parrot*. 1929. New York: Bantam, 1975.

---. *The House without a Key*. New York: Collier, 1925.

---. *Keeper of the Keys*. 1932. New York: Bantam, 1975.

"Biographical Sketch." *Scholastic* 4 Feb. 1939: 12.

"Biographical Sketch." *Wilson Bulletin* Sept. 1931: 12.

Birmingham, F. A. "Pearl Buck and the Good Earth of Vermont." *Saturday Evening Post* Spring 1972: 70-73+.

Bitker, M. M. "Window on Several Worlds." *Saturday Review* Oct. 1961: 41.

Block, Irwin. *The Life of Pearl Buck*. New York: Crowell, 1973.

Boatwright, Taliaferro. Rev. of *Command the Morning*, by Pearl Buck. *New York Herald Tribune Book Review* 3 May 1959: 4.

Bock, Esther B. "Ah Choo." *Overland Monthly* 2nd. ser. 76, Sept. 1920: 49.

Bogardus, E. S. "Culture Distance in *A House Divided*." *Sociology and Social Research* May 1936: 473-77.

Boswell, James. *Life of Johnson*. Ed. R. W. Chapman. London: Oxford UP, 1980.

Boutwell, George S. and Rossiter Raymond to James G. Blair, 16 Mar. 1871. "Mining Statistics West of the Rocky Mountains." U. S. Congress, *Executive Documents 10*, 42nd Cong., 1st sess. (Washington, D. C., 1871), serial 1470.

Bowman, J. R. *The Pacific Tourist*. New York: Praeger, 1882.

Breed, Eleanor. Rev. of *Come, My Beloved*, by Pearl Buck. *San Francisco Chronicle* 25 Aug. 1953: 15.

Brenkman, John. *Culture and Domination*. Ithaca: Cornell UP, 1987.

Brenni, Vito J. "Pearl Buck: A Selected Bibliography." *Bulletin of Bibliography and Magazine Notes,* 22 (May-Aug. 1957): 65-69; 23 (Sept.-Dec. 1957): 94-96.

Brickell, Herschel. Rev. of *Fighting Angel*, by Pearl Buck. *Review of Reviews 94*, Dec. 1936: 12.

---. Rev. of *The Mother*, by Pearl Buck. *New York Evening Post* 20 Jan. 1934: 7.

Bristo, Horace. Rev. of *The People of Japan*, by Pearl Buck. *Saturday Review 49*, 5 Nov. 1966: 44.

Brooks, Van Wyck. *The Writer in America*. New York: Avon Books,1953. 187. Discusses *The Good Earth*.

Brown, C. M. Rev. of *Peony*, by Pearl Buck. *Saturday Review of Literature 31*, 29 May 1948: 23.

Browne, Thomas. "Of Language, and Particularly of the Saxon Tongue," *The Prose of Sir Thomas Browne*. Ed. Norman Endicott. Garden City, N. Y.: Anchor Books, 1967.

Bruere, M. B. "The Woman Nobody Knows." *Pictorial Review* Jan. 1932: 21+.

Buck, David D. "Pearl S. Buck in Search of America." *The Several Worlds of Pearl Buck*. Ed. Elizabeth J. Lipscomb, Frances E. Webb, and Peter Conn. London: Greenwood, 1994. 29-43.

Bullock, F. H. Rev. of *Come, My Beloved*, by Pearl Buck. *New York Herald Tribune Book Review*. 9 Aug. 1953: 3.

---. Rev. of *God's Men*, by Pearl Buck. *New York Herald Tribune Book Review* 8 Apr. 1951: 3.

---. Rev. of *Letter from Peking*, by Pearl Buck. *New York Herald Tribune Book Review* 7 July 1957: 1.

---. Rev. of *My Several Worlds*, by Pearl Buck. *New York Herald Tribune Book Review* 7 Nov. 1954: 1.

---. Rev. of *Of Men and Women*, by Pearl Buck. *New York Herald Tribune Book Review* 11 May 1941: 24.

---. Rev. of *Other Gods*, by Pearl Buck. *Books* 25 Feb. 1940: 4.

---. Rev. of *The Townsman*, by John Sedges. *Weekly Book Review* 3 June 1945: 6.

Burdick, Eugene. Rev. of *The Living Reed*, by Pearl Buck. *Book Week 1*, 15 Sept. 1963: 5.

Burdick, H. F. Rev. of *Letter from Peking*, by Pearl Buck. *Library Journal 82*, July 1957: 1775.

Burt, Struthers. Rev. of *The Promise*, by Pearl Buck. *Saturday Review of Literature 26* Dec. 1943: 6.

Burton, K. "Spiritual Revolution." *Sign* June 1942: 670.

Burton, W. "Celestial Mooncalf." *China Weekly Review* 29 June 1935: 172.

Butcher, Fanny. Rev. of *Come, My Beloved*, by Pearl Buck. *Chicago Sunday Tribune* 9 Aug. 1953: 3.

---. Rev. of *Command the Morning*, by Pearl Buck. *Chicago Sunday Tribune* 3 May 1959: 1.

---. Rev. of *Letter from Peking*, by Pearl Buck. *Chicago Sunday Tribune* 7 July 1957: 1.

---. Rev. of *The Mother*, by Pearl Buck. *Chicago Daily Tribune* 13 Jan. 1934: 15.

---. Rev. of *My Several Worlds*, by Pearl Buck. *Chicago Daily Tribune* 7 Nov. 1954: 1.

---. Rev. of *Sons*, by Pearl Buck. *Chicago Daily Tribune* 24 Sept. 1932: 14.

Callahan, W. M. Rev. of *Dragon Seed*, by Pearl Buck. *Commonweal 35*, 20 Feb. 1940: 439.

Campbell, Shirley Young. "Pearl Buck Shorts." Charleston, W. Va.: *Gazette-Mail* 25 Sept. 1977: 23m. Review of *The Lovers and Other Stories*.

Canby, Henry S. "The Good Earth, Pearl Buck, and the Nobel Prize." *Saturday Review of Literature* 19 Nov. 1938: 8.

Canham, E. D. Rev. of *My Several Worlds*, by Pearl Buck. *Christian Science Monitor* 4 Nov. 1954: 5.

Cargill. Oscar. "Pearl Buck as a Naturalist." *Intellectual America.* New York: MacMillan, 1941. 146-54.

Carpenter, Charles. "The Birthplace of Pearl Buck." *West Virginia Review* Jan. 1937: 144+.

Carson, E. H. A. "Pearl Buck's Chinese." *Canadian Bookman 21*, June-July 1939: 55-59.

Catel, Jean. "Pearl Buck." *Etudes Anglaises* Jan.-Feb. 1939: 98-99; also in "Pearl Buck, prix Nobel de Literature 1938." *Mercure de France* 1 Jan. 1939: 236-41; *Illustration* 31 Dec. 1938: 593.

Cevasco, G. A. "Pearl Buck and the Chinese Novel." *Asian Studies* 5 Dec. 1967: 437-50. On *The Good Earth*.

---. "Pearl Buck's Best Books." *Notes on Modern American Literature* Summer 1981: 5 (3), item 19.

---. Rev. of *The Image of the Chinese Family in Pearl Buck's Novels*, by Doan-Cao-Ly. *Chinese Culture*. 6 Oct. 1965: 107-109.

Chamberlain, John. Rev. of *A House Divided*, by Pearl Buck. *Current History 41*, Feb. 1935: v.

Chambers, Robert W. "The Maker of Moons." *Hauntings and Horrors: Ten Grisly Tales*. Ed. Alden H. Norton. New York: Berkeley, 1969.

Chauhan, Pradyumna S. "Pearl S. Buck's *The Good Earth*: The Novel as Epic." *The Several Worlds of Pearl_S. Buck*. Ed. Elizabeth J. Lipscomb, Frances E. Webb, and Peter Conn London: Greenwood, 1994. 119-125.

Chen, Jack. *The Chinese of America*. San Francisco: Harper, 1980.

Cheng, Yinzhen. Ed. *Nobel Prize Literature: 23 (1938)*. Taibei, Far Perspective Press, 1981.

Chi, Ch'ao-ting. Rev. of *Sons*, by Pearl Buck. *New Republic 72*, 26 Oct. 1932: 299.

"Child Study Award Given for *Big Wave*." *Publishers' Weekly* 26 Mar. 1949: 1441.

Chin, Frank. "Interview: Roland Winters." *Amerasian Journal* 2 Fall 1973: 1.

Christy, Arthur. *The Orient in American Transcendentalism*. New York: Columbia U P, 1932.

"The Church and China." *Methodist Quarterly Review XXXII*, 1850. 593.

Cohen, Warren I. *America's Response to China: An Interpretative History of Sino-American Relations*. New York: Wiley, 1971.

Confucius et al. *The Four Books*. Trans. James Legg. New York: Paragon, 1966.

Conley, Phil, and William T. Doherty. "Winner of the Nobel Prize." *West Virginia History*. Charleston, W.Va.: Education Foundation, Inc., 1974: 43-44. Textbook.

Conn, Peter. "Pearl S. Buck and American Literary Culture." *The Several Worlds of Pearl*

S. Buck. Ed. Elizabeth J. Lipscomb, Frances E. Webb, and Peter Conn. London: Greenwood, 1994. 111-117.

---. "Rediscovering Pearl S. Buck." *The Several Worlds of Pearl S. Buck.* Ed. Elizabeth J. Lipscomb, Frances E. Webb, and Peter Conn. London: Greenwood, 1994. 1-5.

---. "Welcome House: A Forty-Year History." *The Several Worlds of Pearl Buck.* Ed. Elizabeth J. Lipscomb, Frances E. Webb, and Peter Conn. London: Greenwood, 1994. 77-79.

Coolidge, Mary R. *Chinese Immigration.* New York: Holt, 1909.

Cooper, A. C. and C. A. Palmer "Pearl S. Buck: East Meets West." *Twenty Modern Americans.* New York: Harcourt, 1942. 291-307.

Cournos, John and John S. Norton. "Pearl Buck." *Famous Modern American Novelists.* New York: Dodd, 1952. 85-91.

Cowie, Alexander. *The Rise of the American Novel.* New York: 1948, 748. On *The Good Earth.*

Cowley, Malcolm. Rev. of *A House Divided,* by Pearl Buck. *New Republic 81,* 23 Jan. 1935: 309.

---. "Wang Lung's Children." Rev. of *The Patriot,* by Pearl Buck. *New Republic 99,* 10 May 1939: 24+.

Crane, William W. "The Year 1899." *Overland Monthly* 2nd ser. 21 June. 1893: 579-89.

Crichton K. "Preacher's Daughter." *Collier's* 7 Feb. 1942: 20+[Interview].

"Crumbling Foundation." *Time* 25 July 1969: 60.

Cwiklik, Robert. *Pearl S. Buck.* New York: Kipling, 1988.

---. *Pearl S. Buck: China's Witness.* New York: Kipling, 1989.

Dagi, Teo Forcht. "Medical Ethics and the Problem of Role Ambiguity in Mikhail Bulgakov's 'The Murderer' and Pearl S. Buck's 'The Enemy'". *Literature and Medicine.* 1988 v7. 107-22.

Dailey, Jeanette. "Sweet Burning Incense." *Overland Monthly* 2nd. ser. 77 Jan.-Feb. 1921: 9-14.

Dangerfield, George. Rev. of *The Patriot,* by Pearl Buck. *Saturday Review of Literature 19,* 4 Mar. 1939: 5.

Danton, George H. *The Culture Contacts of the United States and China.* New York: Columbia UP, 1931.

Davis, Hassoldt. Rev. of *The Patriot,* by Pearl Buck. *Nation 148,* 4 Mar. 1939: 269.

Dawson, Emma F. "The Dramatic in My Destiny." *Californian 1,* Jan. 1880: 5.

Dawson, Raymond. *The Chinese Chameleon: An Analysis of European Conceptions of Chinese Civilization.* London: Oxford UP, 1967.

Day, John. "The Story of *The Good Earth.*" Postscript in Pearl Buck's *The Good Earth,* 1931. New York: John Day, 1977. 309-16.

De Bra, Lemuel. *Ways that Are Wary.* New York: Burt, 1925.

De Riencourt, Amaury. *The Soul of China.* New York: Coward-McCann, 1958.

"Death and Tributes." *New York Times* 7 Mar. 1973: 1:5, 40:3, 42:2. *The Times,* 7 Mar. 1973: 1:5.

Defoe, Daniel. *The Works of Daniel Defoe.* 8 vols., 16 pts. Philadelphia: Morris, 1903.

Delano, Amasa. *A Narrative of Voyages and Travels.* 1817. New York: Praeger, 1970.

Dennett, Tyler. *Americans in Eastern Asia.* New York: Macmillan, 1922.

D'Entremont, John. "Pearl S. Buck and American Women's History." *The Several Worlds of Pearl Buck.* Ed. Elizabeth J. Lipscomb, Frances E. Webb, and Peter Conn. London: Greenwood, 1994. 45-53.

"Desert Incident." *New Yorker* 4 Apr. 1959; also in *Saturday Review* 11 Apr. 1959: 35; *Theater Arts* June 1959: 11.

Deshpande, H.V. "Antipathies and Sympathies': A Study of Religious Encounter in Pearl S. Buck's *Peony, The Hidden Flower and Mandala. American Studies* Mar. 1988: 87-100.

Dicker, Herman. *Wanderers and Settlers in the Far East: A Century of Jewish Life in China and Japan.* New York: Twayne, 1962.

Dickstein, Lore. "Posthumous Stories." *New York Times Book Review* 11 Mar. 1979: 20+.

Doan-Cao-Ly. *The Image of the Chinese Family in Pearl Buck's Novels.* Saigon: Duc-Sinh, 1964. [Doctoral diss., St. John's U., Brooklyn, N. Y. Analytic study of Chinese families in six books: *Dragon Seed*, 109-22; *East Wind: West Wind*, 31-66; *House of Earth*, 67-94; *The Mother*, 128-31; *The Patriot*, 95-108; *Pavilion of Women*, 131-40.]

Dobree, Bonamy. Rev. of *The Good Earth*, by Pearl Buck. *The Spectator 146*, 2 May 1931: 710.

Doi, Makiko. Rev. of *The People of Japan*, by Pearl Buck. *Library Journal 91*, Aug. 1966: 3724.

Doolittle, Erasmus. "Recollections of China." *Sketches by a Traveller*, by Silas Holbrook. Boston: Carter and Hendee, 1830.

Doolittle, Justus. *Social Life of the Chinese.* New York: Harper, 1865.

Dooner, Pierton W. *Last Days of the Republic.* San Francisco: Alta, 1880.

Doyle, C. W. *The Shadow of Quong Lung.* Philadelphia: Lippincott, 1900.

Doyle, Paul A. Preface in *Pearl S. Buck.* Twayne's United States Authors Series. New York: Twayne, 1965.

---. "Pearl Buck's Short Stories: A Survey." *English Journal* 1966: 62-68.

---. *Pearl S. Buck.* New York: Twayne, 1980. Revised Edition.

Duchene, Anne. Rev. of *Imperial Woman*, by Pearl Buck. *Manchester Guardian* 11 May 1965: 6.

Duffus, R. L. Rev. of *American Argument*, by Pearl Buck. *New York Times* 23 Jan. 1949: 21.

Dulles, F. R. Rev. of *Talk about Russia*, by Pearl Buck. *New York Times* 6 Jan. 1946: 22.

Durdin, Peggy. Rev. of *The Living Reed*, by Pearl Buck. *New York Times Book Review* 22 Sept. 1963: 40.

"Earth to Earth." *Time* 19 Mar. 1973: 81.

Eaton, Edith M. (Sui Sin Far) "A Chinese Ishmael." *Overland Monthly* 2nd. ser. 34 July 1899: 43.

Edgar, Betsy Jordan. "Our House: The Birthplace of Pearl S. Buck." Parsons, W.Va.: McClain Print, 1965.

Eddy, Sherwood. Rev. of *The Exile*, by Pearl Buck. *Saturday Review of Literature 13*, 8 Feb. 1936: 5.

Emerson, Ralph W. *The Journal & Miscellaneous Notebooks.* Ed. William Gillman et al. Cambridge: Belknap Press of Harvard UP, 1961.

Esherick, Joseph W. *Lost Chance in China: The World War II Despatches of John S. Service.* New York: Random House, 1974.

Espey, J. J. Rev. of *God's Men*, by Pearl Buck. *New York Times* 8 Apr. 1951: 4.

---. Rev. of *Imperial Woman*, by Pearl Buck. *New York Times* 1 Apr. 1956: 5.

---. Rev. of *Pavilion of Women*, by Pearl Buck. *Weekly Book Review* 24 Nov. 1946: 6.

Evans, Ernestine. Rev. of *Talks about Russia*, by Pearl Buck. *Weekly Book Review* 30 Dec. 1945: 2.

Fadiman, Clifton. Rev. of *Dragon Seed*, by Pearl Buck. *New Yorker* 24 Jan. (1942) 17:64.

---. Rev. of *Of Men and Women*, by Pearl Buck. *New Yorker* 10 May. (1940) 17: 87.

---. Rev. of *Other Gods*, by Pearl Buck. *New Yorker* 24 Feb. (1940) 16: 76.

---. Rev. of *The Patriot*, by Pearl Buck. *New Yorker* 4 Mar. (1939) 15: 74.

---. Rev. of *The Promise*, by Pearl Buck. *New Yorker* 30 Oct. (1943) 19: 89.

Fairbank, John K. *China: A New History*. Cambridge: Harvard UP, 1992.

---. *Chinese-American Interactions*. New Brunswick, N. J.: Rutgers UP, 1975.

---. Ed. and Intro. *The Missionary Enterprise in China and America*. Cambridge: Harvard UP, 1974.

---. *The United States and China*. 1948. Cambridge: Harvard UP, 1979.

Fanning, Edmund. *Voyages and Discoveries in the South Seas*. 1924. Upper Saddle River, N. J.: Gregg Press, 1970.

Feikema, Feike. Rev. of *Kinfolk*, by Pearl Buck. *Chicago Sun* 24 Apr. 1949: 8X.

Feld, Rose. Rev. of *The Promise*, by Pearl Buck. *Weekly Book Review* 31 Oct. 1943: 5.

Finn, James. *The Jews in China*. London: Wertheim, 1843. Reprinted by Cheng Wen, Taipei, 1971.

Finnie, G. F. Rev. of *Fighting Angel*, by Pearl Buck. *Crozer Quarterly*. Apr. (1937) 14:183.

Fitzgerald, Charles P. "Opposing Cultural Traditions, Barriers to Communication." *Christian Missions in China: Evangelists of What?* Ed. and Intro. Jessie G. Lutz. Boston: Heath, 1965.

Flanagan, J. T. Rev. of *The Townsman*, by John Sedges. *Book Week* 3 Jan. 1945: 1.

Fleming, P. F. Rev. of *Pearl S. Buck: A Biography*, by T. F. Harris. *Catholic World* Dec. 1969: 138-39.

Foell, E. W. Rev. of *Command the Morning*, by Pearl Buck. *Christian Science Monitor* 7 May 1959: 11.

Fokkema, D W and Elrud Kunne-Ibsch. *Theories of Literature in the Twentieth Century*. New York: St. Martin, 1977.

Forbes, H. R. Rev. of *God's Men*, by Pearl Buck. *Library Journal 76*, 15 Mar. 1951: 513.

---. Rev. of *Hidden Flower*, by Pearl Buck. *Library Journal 77*, 15 May. 1952: 894.

---. Rev. of *Kinfolk*, by Pearl Buck. *Library Journal 74*, 1 Apr. 1949: 546.

---. Rev. of *Peony*, by Pearl Buck. *Library Journal 73*, 15 Apr. 1948:651.

Forsythe, Sidney A. *An American Missionary Community in China*. Cambridge: Harvard UP, 1985.

Frank, Grace. Rev. of *Portrait of a Marriage*, by Pearl Buck. *Saturday Review of Literature 29*, 19 Jan. 1945: 37.

Fukuyama, Francis. *The End of History and the Last Man*. New York: Avon, 1992.

Fuller, Edmund. Rev. Of *Voices in the House*, by John Sedges. *Chicago Sunday Tribune* 29 Mar. 1953: 5.

---. Rev. Of *Letter from Peking*, by John Sedges. *Saturday Review 40*, 13 July 1957: 15.

Galik, Marian. *Milestones in Sino-Western Literary Confrontation 1898-1979*. Wiesbaden: Otto Harrassowitz, 1986.

Gannett, Lewis. Rev. of *A House Divided*, by Pearl Buck. *New York Herald Tribune* 21

Jan. 1935: 11.

---. "Books and Things." Rev. of *The Chinese Novel*, by Pearl Buck. *New York Herald Tribune* 5 Aug. 1939: 9.

Garrison, W. E. Rev. of *A House Divided*, by Pearl Buck. *Christian Century 52*, 13 Mar. 1935: 336.

Gay R. M. Rev. of *Sons*, by Pearl Buck. *Atlantic Bookshelf* Nov. 1932.

Gayn, Mark. Rev. of *Tell the People*, by Pearl Buck. *New York Times Book Review* 25 Mar. 1945: 20.

Gilbert, Rodney. Rev. of *Imperial Woman*, by Pearl Buck. *New York Herald Tribune Book Review* 1 Apr. 1956: 1.

Giles, Herbert A. *A Chinese Biographical Dictionary*. London-Shanghai: Kelly & Walsh, 1898; reprinted in Peiping, 1939.

Girson, Rochelle. "Welcome House Project, Bucks County, Pa." *Saturday Review* 26 July 1952: 21.

Goodrich, Samuel G. *A System of Universal Geography*. Boston: Collins, 1833.

---. *The Tales of Peter Parley about Asia*. Philadelphia: Butler, 1859.

Grant, Gordon. "The Provocation of Ah Sing." *Overland Monthly*. 2nd. ser. 79 (Jan. 1922): 25.

Gray, James. "Gods by Adoption." *On Second Thoughts*. Minneapolis: U of Minnesota P, 1946. 10-35.

Greenfeld, Josh. Rev. of *The People of Japan*, by Pearl Buck. *Book Week* 9 Oct. 1966: 8.

Grose, G. R. Rev. of *The Mother*, by Pearl Buck. *Christian Century 51*, 4 Apr. 1934: 465.

Gutzlaff, Charles. *Chinese Repository I*. Canton: Bridgeman, 1832. 126.

Hackett, Alice Payne and James Henry Burke. *80 Years of Best Sellers*. New York: Bowker, 1977.

Hackett, Francis. "A Sketch: Pearl Buck." *Herald Tribune*, "Book Week" 15 Sept. 1963. Remarks on *The Townsman*.

Hallstrom, Per. "The Nobel Prize Presentation Speech" *Nobel Prize Literature 23, 1938*. Ed. Cheng Yinzhen. Taibei: Far Perspective Press, 1981. 3-11.

Hanson, James. "The Winning of Josephine Chang." *Overland Monthly* 2nd. ser. 75 June 1920: 493.

Harker, Charles R. "The Revenge of a Heathen." *Overland Monthly* 2nd. ser. 15 Apr. 1890: 386.

Harris, Theodore F. *Pearl S. Buck: A Biography*. New York: John Day, 1969.

---. *Pearl S. Buck, Vol. 2: Her Philosophy in Her Letters*. New York: John Day, 1971.

Harwood, H. C. Rev. of *The Good Earth*, by Pearl Buck. *Saturday Review 151*, 16 May 1931: 722.

Hatcher, Harlan. *Creating the Modern American Novel*. New York: Farrar, 1935.

Havermale, Hazel. "The Canton Shawl." *Overland Monthly* 2nd. ser. 64 (Sept. 1914): 269.

Hayford, Charles W. "The Good Earth, Revolution, and the American Raj in China." *The Several Worlds of Pearl S. Buck*. Ed. Elizabeth J. Lipscomb, Frances E. Webb, and Peter Conn. London: Greenwood, 1994. 19-27.

Hedden, W. T. Rev. of *American Argument*, by Pearl Buck. *Saturday Review of Literature 32*, 5 Feb. 1949: 13.

Hemmings, F. W. J. *The Age of Realism*. Harmondsworth: Penguin, 1974.

Henchoz, Ami. "A Permanent Element in Pearl Buck's Novels." *English Studies* 25 Aug.

1943: 97-103.

Hendricks, Walter. Rev. of *The Promise,* by Pearl Buck. *Book Week* 31 Oct. 1943: 1.

Hoban, Jr. James L. "Scripting *The Good Earth*: Versions of the Novel for the Screen." *The Several Worlds of Pearl S. Buck.* Ed. Elizabeth J. Lipscomb, Frances E. Webb, and Peter Conn. London: Greenwood, 1994. 127-144.

Holub, Robert C. *Reception Theory: A Critical Introduction.* New York: Methuen, 1984.

---. *Crossing Borders: Reception Theory, Post-structuralism, Deconstruction.* Madison: U of Wisconsin P, 1992.

Hormel, O. D. Rev. *American Argument,* by Pearl Buck. *Christian Science Monitor* 17 Mar. 1949: 18.

Howells, William. *Criticism and Fiction.* New York: Harper, 1891.

Hoylman, Alta. "Pearl Buck's Own Good Earth." *Modern Maturity* Feb.-Mar. 1978: 50-51.

Hoyt, C. A. Rev. of *Death in the Castle,* by Pearl Buck. *Saturday Review 48,* 24 Apr. 1965: 54.

Hsia, C. T. *A History of Modern Chinese Fiction, 1917-1957.* New York and London, 1961. Remarks on *Imperial Woman* by Pearl Buck.

Hsu, Francis L. K. *Americans and Chinese: Two Ways of Life.* New York: Schuman, 1953.

Hsu, Pei-tsu. "The Love of Land in Pearl Buck's *The Good Earth* and Willa Cather's *O Pioneers!*" *Fu Jen Studies 12,* 1979: 71-82.

Huang, Hsiujee. *A Concise History of Comtemporary Chinese Literature.* Beijing: The Chinese Youth Press, 1984.

Hughes, Riley. Rev. of *Hidden Flower,* by Pearl Buck. *Catholic World 175,* July 1952: 316.

---. Rev. of *Imperial Woman,* by Pearl Buck. *Catholic World 183,* Apr. 1956: 69.

---. Rev. of *Command the Morning,* by Pearl Buck. *Catholic World 189,* July 1959: 326.

Hunter, William C. *The "Fan Kwae" at Canton before Treaty Days, 1825-1844.* London: 1882.

Hutchinson, Paul. Rev. of *The Good Earth,* by Pearl Buck. *Christian Century 48,* 20 May 1931: 683.

---. Rev. of *Sons,* by Pearl Buck. *Christian Century 49,* 5 Oct. 1932: 1206.

Inazawa, Hideo. *America Joryu Sakka Ron: Cather, Buck, McCuller no Sekai.* Tokyo: Shimbisha, 1977.

Ince, E.C. "Where the Twain Meet." *Christian Science Monitor Magazine.* 5 Feb. 1944: 4. Interview.

Irvin, Block. *The Lives of Pearl Buck: A Tale of China and America.* New York: Cromwell, 1973.

Irwin, Richard G. *The Evolution of a Chinese Novel: Shui Hu Chuan.* Cambridge: Harvard UP, 1953.

Isaacs, Harold. *Scratches on Our Minds: American Images of China and India.* New York: John Day, 1958.

Jacobs, Hayes. "Pearl S. Buck." *Writer's Yearbook* 1963: 40.

Janeway, Elizabeth. "The Optimistic World of Miss Buck." Rev. of *Hidden Flower,* by Pearl Buck. *New York Times Book Review.* 25 May 1952: Sect. 7, 4.

---. Rev. of *My Several Worlds,* by Pearl Buck. *New York Times Book Review.* 7 Nov. 1954: 4.

Jen, Tai. "A Chinese Classic." Rev. of *All Men Are Brothers,* trans. by Pearl Buck. *Saturday Review of Literature 10,* 7 Oct. 1933: 162.

---. Rev. of *Sons*, by Pearl Buck. *Satruday Review of Literature 9*, 24 Sept. 1932: 123.

Jenkins, Lawrence W. Ed. *Bryant Parrott Tilden of Salem, at a Chinese Dinner Party, Canton, 1819*. Princeton: Princeton UP, 1944.

Johnson, M., *Comp.* "American First Editions." *Publishers Weekly* 20 Jan. 1934: 125-273.

Johnston, Esther. Rev. of *Other Gods*, by Pearl Buck. *Library Journal 65*, 1 Mar. 1940: 209.

Jones, Claire. *The Chinese in America*. Minneapolis: Lerner, 1972.

Jones, Dorothy B. *The Portrayal of China and India on the American Screen 1896-1955*. Cambridge: Harvard UP, 1955.

Jones, H. M. Rev. of *Dragon Seed*, by Pearl Buck. *Saturday Review of Literature 25*, 17 Jan. 1942: 5.

Kabbani, Rana. *Europe's Myths of Orient*. Bloomington: Indiana UP, 1986.

Kang, Younghill. Rev. of *The Good Earth*, by Pearl Buck. *New Republic* 1 July 1931: 185. Controversial article; editorial comment: 186.

Kiang, Kang-hu. "A Chinese Scholar's View of Mrs. Buck's Novel." Rev. of *The Good Earth*, by Pearl Buck. *New York Times Book Review* 15 Jan. 1933: 2, 16. Attacks PSB for giving false view of Chinese life. PSB's reply in the same issue, entitled: "Mrs. Buck Replies to Her Chinese Critics," p. 14; also in *My Several Worlds*, 281-82, and as introduction in First Modern Library Edition of *The Good Earth*.

Kim, Elaine H. Headnote of "Younghill Kang,*" The Heath Anthology of American Literature*. Ed. Paul Lauter. 1990. Lexington: Heath, 1994, 2nd ed. vol. II. 1948-1949.

King, B. M. "One Reason Why There Is a Layman's Mission Inquiry: *The Good Earth*." *Christian Century* 16 Nov. 1932: 1412.

King, Nancy. "From Literature to Drama to Life". Ed. N. McSaslin et al. *Children and Drama*. Lanham: U. P. of America, 1986. 164-77.

King, Nicholas. Rev. of *Friend to Friend*, by Pearl Buck and Romulo C. Pena. *New York Herald Tribune Book Review* 15 Feb. 1958: 11.

Kirkland, Winifred M. and Frances Kirkland, "Pearl Buck." In their *Girls Who Become Writers*. New York: Harper, 1933.

Klausler, A. P. Rev. of *Command the Morning*, by Pearl Buck. *Christian Century 76*, 26 Aug. 1959: 972.

Kublin, Hyman. Ed. and Intro. *Jews in Old China: Some Western Views*. New York: Paragon, 1971.

---. Ed. and Intro. *Studies of the Chinese Jews*. New York: Paragon, 1971.

Kunitz, Stanley J., ed., *Twentieth Century Authors*. New York: Wilson: 1955.

La Farge, Ann. *Pearl Buck*. New York: Chelsea House: 1988.

Langlois, Walter, G. "The Dream of the Red Chamber, The Good Earth, and Man's Fate: Chronicles of Social Change in China." *Literature East and West* 11 Mar. 1967: 1-10.

Las Vergnas, Raymond. "Vent de Chine." *Hommes et Mondes* Aug. 1949: 678-82.

Lask, Thomas. "A Missionary Heritage." *New York Times Book Review* 7 Mar. 1937: 40.

Latourette, Kenneth S. *A History of Christian Mission in China*. New York: Macmillan, 1932.

---. Rev. of *Fighting Angel*, by Pearl Buck. *Saturday Review of Literature 15*, 5 Dec. 1936: 10.

Lawrence, Margaret. "Priestesses." *School of Femininity*. New York: Stoles, 1936. 311-

38.

LeBar, Barbara. "The Subject Is Marriage." *Journal of Evolutionary Psychology* Aug. 1988: 264-69.

Lee, Henry. "Pearl S. Buck---Spiritual Descendant of Tom Paine." *Saturday Review of Literature* 5 Dec. 1945: 16-18. Account of her wartime activities.

Legge, James. Trans. *The Four Books: Confucian Analects, the Great Learning, the Doctrine of the Mean, and the Works of Mencius,* by Confucius et al. New York: Paragon, 1966.

Leisy, Ernest E. *The American Historical Novel.* Norman: U of Oklahoma P, 1950. 205.

Lemon, R. "Biographical Sketch of Pearl Buck." *Saturday Review.* 31 Mar. 1956: 12.

Leslie, Donald D. *The Survival of the Chinese Jews: The Jewish Community in Kaifeng.* Leiden: Brill, 1972.

Lewis, Ethel C. "China to Hillsboro." *West Virginia Review* Apr. 1943.

Lin, Taiyi. *Lin Yutang: A Biography.* Beijing: Chinese Drama Press, 1994.

Lin, Yutang. *The Importance of Living.* New York: Reynal, 1937.

---. *Moment in Peking.* New York: John Day, 1939.

---. *My Country and My People.* New York: Reynal, 1935.

---. *The Wisdom of Confucious.* New York: Random, 1938.

Lindsay, Jason. *A Study of Pearl S. Buck.* New York: John Day, 1966. Second part of a pamphlet subtitled *Essay on Myself,* by Pearl Buck.

Lindsay, Lucy F. "Sang." *Overland Monthly* 2nd. ser. 69 (Jan. 1917): 57.

Linn, Nick. "Miss Buck, the West Virginian." *Business Communication,* 1965. Interview by editor C. & P. Telephone Company publication.

Lipsky, Eleazar. Rev. of *Command the Morning,* by Pearl Buck. *Saturday Review 42,* 16 May 1959: 31.

Littell, Robert. Rev. of *Dragon Seed,* by Pearl Buck. *Yale Review 31,* Spring 1942: x.

Liu, Haiping. "Pearl S. Buck's Reception in China Reconsidered." *The Several Worlds of Pearl Buck,* ed. Elizabeth J. Lipscomb, Frances E. Webb, and Peter Conn. London: Greenwood, 1994. 55-67.

Liu, Zaifu and Gang Lin. "The Political Modes of Writing in Modern Chinese Novels: Comments on *The Spring Silkworms* and *The Sun Shines upon the Sanggan River.*" *Twenty-first Century 11,* June 1992: 92-101.

London, Jack. "White and Yellow." "Yellow Handkerchief." *Tales of the Fish Patrol.* New York: Macmillan, 1905.

---. "The Unparalleled Invasion." *Curious Fragments: Jack London's Tales of Fantasy Fiction.* Ed. Dale L. Walker. Port Washington, N. Y.: Kennikat, 1975. 109-20.

Lorelle. "The Battle of Wabash." *Californian 2,* Oct. 1880: 364-76.

Lutz, Jessie G. Ed. and Intro. *Christian Missions in China: Evangelists of What?* Boston: Heath, 1965.

Lux, Louise. Rev. of *Kinfolk,* by Pearl Buck. *New York Times Book Review* 24 Apr. 1949: 30.

Lynch, W. S. Rev. of *The Townsman,* by John Sedges. *Saturday Review of Literature 28,* 16 Jan. 1945: 30.

MacAfee, Helen. Rev. of *The Good Earth,* by Pearl Buck. *Yale Review 20,* Summer 1931: vi.

---. Rev. of *A House Divided,* by Pearl Buck. *Yale Review 24,* Spring 19354: viii.

Maclay, R. S. *Life among the Chinese.* 1861. New York: Praeger, 1972.

MacMillan, Mary. "Born Between East and West." Rev. of *For Spacious Skies,* by Pearl

Buck. *Saturday Review 49*, 23 July 1966: 51.

Mao, Tse-tung. *Quotations from Chairman Mao Tse-tung*. Ed. Stuart R. Schram. New York: Praeger, 1967.

---. "Talks at the Yenan Forum on Art and Literature." *Selected Works of Mao Tse-tung.* vol. 4 1941-1945. 63-93. New York: International Publishers, 1956.

Marconi, Barbara. Rev. of *The New Year*, by Pearl Buck. *Library Journal 93*, 1 Mar. 1968: 1017.

Marshall, Margaret. Rev. of *Of Men and Women*, by Pearl Buck. *Nation 152*, 14 Jan. 1941: 698.

Mathews, Frances Aymar. *The Flame Dancer*. New York: Dillingham, 1908.

Matthews, T. S. Rev. of *The Good Earth*, by Pearl Buck. *New Republic 75*, 19 July 1933: 268.

McGrory, Mary. Rev. of *Pavilion of Women*, by Pearl Buck. *New York Times Book Review* 24 Nov. 1946: 6

Meade, Edwin R. *The Chinese Question. New York Times* 7 Sept. 1877.

Medhurst, William. *China: Its State and Prospects*. London: Snow, 1838.

Merton, J. K. Rev. of *This Proud Heart*, by Pearl Buck. *Commonwealth 27*, 11 Mar. 1938: 556.

Mezey, P. M. Rev. of *American Argument*, by Pearl Buck. *San Francisco Chronicle* 20 Feb. 1949: 19.

Miller, Stuart Creighton. "Ends and Means: Missionary Justification of Force in Nineteenth Century China." *The Missionary Enterprise in China and America*. Ed. John K. Fairbank. Cambridge: Harvard UP, 1974. 249-82.

---. *The Unwelcome Immigrant*. Los Angeles: U of California P., 1969.

Milner, Florence. Rev. of *This Proud Heart*, by Pearl Buck. *Boston Transcript* 12 Feb. 1938: 1.

Mok, P. K. Rev. of *Young Revolutionist*, by Pearl Buck. *Books* 1 May 1932: 2.

Mohler, E. Y. Rev. of *The Townsman*, by Pearl Buck. *Springfield Republican* 3 Jan. 1945: 4d.

Moore, Charles A. Ed. *The Chinese Mind: Essentials of Chinese Philosophy and Culture.* Honolulu: U of Hawaii P, 1967.

More, Phil. "Chung's Baby." *Overland Monthly,* 2nd. ser. 31 (Mar. 1898): 233.

"Mrs. Buck Lauds Chinese, Faces Missionaries' Charges." *Newsweek* 22 Apr. 1933: 26.

"Mrs. Buck under Fire as a Heretic." *Literary Digest* 6 May 1933: 15.

"Mrs. Buck's Resignation." *Literary Digest* 13 May 1933: 17.

Muehl, J. F. Rev. of *Come, My Beloved*, by Pearl Buck. *Saturday Review 36*, 15 Aug. 1953: 10.

Muir, Jane. *Famous Modern American Women Writers*. New York: Dodd, 1959.

Munn, L. S. Rev. of *Portrait of a Marriage*, by Pearl Buck. *Springfield Republican* 9 Dec. 1945: 4d.

Munro, Donald J. *The Concept of Man in Early China*. Stanford: Stanford UP, 1969.

Nabokov, Vladimir. "Good Readers and Good Writers." *The Norton Reader: An Anthology of Expository Prose*. Ninth Edition. Ed. Linda H. Peterson. New York: Norton, 1996.

Nakamura, Hajime. *The Ways of Thinking of Eastern Peoples*. 1960. New York: Greenwood, 1988.

Nathan, George Jean. *Theatre Book of the Year 1945-46*. New York: Knopf, 1946. 203. Review of the play "The First Wife."

New York Times Book Review. 2 May 1933, and several other issues in 1933 were news stories on controversy over views in "Is There a Case for Foreign Missions?"; 9 Apr. 1933, remarks on missionary influence; 29 Oct. 1932, articles on possible warlord model for character Wang the Tiger.

Ng, Poon Chew. "The Treatment of Exempt Chinese." *Chung Sai Yat Pao.* San Francisco: 1908.

Nicholl, L. T. Rev. of *Fighting Angel,* by Pearl Buck. *Books* 29 Nov. 1936: 3.

"Nobel Prize for Literature." *Time* 24 Nov. 1938: 67.

"Nobel Prize for Pearl Buck." *Literary Journal* 1 Dec. 1938: 928.

"Nobel Prize Winners." *New York Times.* 11 Nov. 1938; rpt. in *Randolph-Macon Woman's College Alumnae Bulletin* Feb. 1939: 2-3. Editorial.

Norr, William. *Stories of Chinatown: Sketches in the Chinese Colony of Mott, Pell and Doyers Street.* New York: Norr, 1892.

Norris, Frank. "After Strange Gods." *Overland Monthly,* 2nd. ser. 24 (Oct. 1894): 375.

---. "Thoroughbred." *Overland Monthly,* 2nd. ser. 25 (Feb. 1895): 196.

North, Sterling. Rev. of *Talk about Russia,* by Pearl Buck. *Book Week* 9 Dec. 1945: 2.

"Notes on Current Books." Rev. of *East and West,* by Pearl Buck. *Virginia Quarterly Review* Spring 1976: 59-60.

"O Pu Sing Sin; Awarded the Annual Nobel Prize in Letters." *Newsweek* 21 Nov. 1938: 33-34.

Obituary. *Christianity Today.* 30 Mar. 1973: 29; *Good Housekeeping* June 1973: 32; *Publishers Weekly* 12 March 1973: 35.

Obituary. *New York Times* 7 Mar. 1973: 1+, 42; 10 Mar. 1973: 34.

O'Brien, Kate. Rev. of *Dragon Seed,* by Pearl Buck. *The Spectator 168,* 1 May. 1942: 428.

---. Rev. of *Other Gods,* by Pearl Buck. *The Spectator 164,* 15 Mar. 1940: 390.

Olechno, Gillian. Rev. *To My Daughters, with Love,* by Pearl Buck. *Library Journal 92,* Aug. 1967: 2796.

Opfell, Olga S. *The Lady Laureates: Women Who Have Won the Nobel Prize.* London: Scarecrow, 1978.

Overton. Jeanne K. "Pearl Buck: Bibliography and Criticism." Typescript photocopy. Boston: Simmons College, 1942.

Owen, Lattimore. Rev. of *Tell the People,* by Pearl Buck. *Weekly Book Review 8,* Apr. 1945: 5.

Owen, Margaret. Rev. of *The Promise,* by Pearl Buck. *Library Journal 68,* 15 Oct. 1943: 845.

Owens, Olga. Rev. of *Other Gods,* by Pearl Buck. *Boston Transcript* 24 Feb. 1940: 1.

Palmer, C. B. Rev. of *The Promise,* by Pearl Buck. *News York Times Book Review* 31 Oct. 1943: 6.

Parton, Margaret. "Call to China." Rev. of *My Several Worlds,* by Pearl Buck. *Saturday Review 37,* 6 Nov. 1954: 17.

Patrick N. "China As Viewed through the Eyes of Pearl Buck." *Scholastic* 18 Jan. 1936: 14.

"Pearl Buck and the Presbyterian Fundamentalists." *China Weekly Review* 22 Apr. 1933: 282-83.

Pearl Buck Center. "Buck, Pearl S., 1892-1973." New York: John Day, 1972.

"Pearl Buck Delighted by Project." *Morgantown Post* 6 Mar. 1970: 5A. Interview concerning project by WV Federation of Women's Clubs to purchase and restore

PSB's birthplace.

"Pearl Buck Finds That East and West Do Meet." *New York Times* 20 Nov. 1938: sec. 7, 4, 19.

"Pearl Buck, Grand Prix Nobel de Literature." *Illustration* 31 Dec. 1938: 593.

"Pearl Buck, Heretic." *Nation* 17 Mar. 1933: 546.

"Pearl Buck Joins John Day Staff." *Publishers' Weekly* 11 Aug. 1934: 419.

"Pearl Buck Wins Coveted Pulitzer Novel Prize." *China Weekly Review* 11 Jan. 1932: 41.

"Pearl Buck Wins Nobel Literature Prize; Third American to Get the Swedish Award." *New York Times.* 11 Nov. 1938. 1, 5.

"Pearl Buck's Presence Lingers on at Her Farm." *Philadelphia Inquirer* 16 Feb. 1975.

"Pearl Buck's Wish Comes True 1 Year after Death." Charleston Sunday *Gazette-Mail* 5 May 1974: 1G. Illus. Dedication of the Pearl S. Buck Birthplace Museum, Hillsboro, W.Va.

"Pearl S. Buck." *Wilson Bulletin* Sept. 1931: 12.

"Pearl (Sydenstricker) Buck." *Current Biography Yearbook 1956.* New York: H. W. Wilson, 1956. 82.

"Pearl S. Buck: A Native West Virginian." *West Virginia Review* Apr. 1933: 203.

"Pearl S. Buck Estate, Dedicated as National Historical Site." *New Herald* Perkasie, Pa. 25 June 1975.

"Pearl S. Buck Receives Amethyst Cross of Malta Award." *Training School Bulletin,* Vineland, N. J. Feb. 1956: 259.

Pearsall, R. P. "The Revelation." *Overland Monthly* 2nd ser. 58 (Dec. 1911): 485-94.

Peffer, Nathaniel. "A Splendid Pageant of the Chinese People." Rev. of *All Men Are Brothers,* trans. by Pearl Buck. *New York Herald Tribune Books* 15 Oct. 1933: 3.

---. Rev. of *East Wind: West Wind,* by Pearl Buck. *New York Herald Tribune Books* 18 May 1930: 6.

---. Rev. of *The Good Earth,* by Pearl Buck. *New York Herald Tribune Books 1* March 1931: 1.

---. Rev. on *Sons,* by Pearl Buck. *New York Herald Tribune Books* 25 Sept. 1932: I.

The People of China. Philadelphia: American Sunday School Union, 1844.

Perry, H. A. Rev. of *The Exile,* by Pearl Buck. *Boston Transcript* 8 Feb. 1936: 3.

Peterson, Virgilia. Rev. of *Letter from Peking,* by Pearl Buck. *New York Times Book Review* 7 July 1957: 4.

Petrie, Dennis W. Rev. of *Pearl Buck: A Woman in Conflict,* by Nora Starling. *Modern American Studies 31,* Winter 1985: 727-730.

Pinchot, Mary. Rev. of *Pavilion of Women,* by Pearl Buck. *Atlantic Monthly 179,* Jan. 1947: 111.

Plomer, William. "A Chinese Pageant." Rev. of *All Men Are Brothers,* trans. by Pearl Buck. *The Spectator 151,* 29 Dec. 1933: 968.

Pollak, Michael. *Mandarins, Jews, and Missionaries: The Jewish Experience in the Chinese Empire.* Philadelphia: The Jewish Publication Society of America, 1980.

Poore, Charles. "Books of the Times." *New York Times Book Review* 24 Apr. 1949: 23.

Prager, Arthur. Rev. of *The Three Daughters of Madame Liang,* by Pearl Buck. *Saturday Review 52,* 12 July 1969: 37.

"Presbyterians and Mrs. Buck." *Christian Century* 26 Apr. 1933: 547-48.

Prichard, Amy. "Lessons in Aging." *NRTA Journal* Sept.-Oct. 1976: 9.

Pritchett, V. S. *Scientific American* July 1959: 159-60+. Review of *Command the*

Morning.

"Publishers Promote Books of Nobel Winner." *Publishers' Weekly* 19 Nov. 1938: 1831-32.

Quinn, Arthur H. *American Fiction: An Historical and Critical Survey.* New York: D. Appleton Century, 1936.

Rabb, Jane M. "Who Is Afraid of Pearl S. Buck?" *The Several Worlds of Pearl S. Buck.* Ed. Elizabeth J. Lipscomb, Frances E. Webb, and Peter Conn. London: Greenwood, 1994. 103-110.

Raessler, Deborah Clement. "Pearl S. Buck's Writings on Handicapped Children." *The Several Worlds of Pearl S. Buck.* Ed. Elizabeth J. Lipscomb, Frances E. Webb, and Peter Conn. London: Greenwood, 1994. 81-99.

"Rainbow." *Times Literary Suplement* 5 Nov. 1976: 1405a.

Rainey, H. P. Rev. of *Tell the People*, by Pearl Buck. *Saturday Review of Literature 28*, 14 Apr. 1945: 25.

Randolph, Jennings. U. S. Senator, W.Va. *Congressional Record.* Proceedings and Debate of the 93rd Congress, First Session, Vol. 119, No. 35, Washington, D. C., Tuesday, 6 Mar. 1973. Tribute on the day of her death.

Rawski, Evelyn S. "Elementary Education in the Mission Enterprise," *Christianity in China.* Ed. Suzanne W. Barnett and John K. Fairbank. Cambridge: Harvard UP, 1985. 135-151.

Read, M. D. Rev. of *Hidden Flower*, by Pearl Buck. *Library Journal 77*, 15 Sept. 1952: 1525.

Reichwein, Adolf. *China and Europe: Intellectual and Artistic Contacts in the Eighteenth Century.* Trans. J. C. Powell. New York: Knopf, 1925.

Reid, Forrest. Rev. of *The Patriot,* by Pearl Buck. *Spectator 162* , 21 Apr. 1939: 684.

Reinhold, H. A. Rev. of *How It Happens*, by Pearl Buck. *Commonwealth 45*, 7 Mar. 1947: 525.

Rennert, Maggie. Rev. *Death in the Castle,* by Pearl Buck. *Book Week* 4 July 1965: 11.

Reshaw, C., Jr. "Visit with Pearl Buck." *National Wildlife* Dec. 1971: 28-42.

Rev. of *All Men Are Brothers*, trans. by Pearl Buck. "A Rich Panorama of Chinese Life." *New York Times Book Review* 5 Nov. 1933: 2.

Rev. of *All Men Are Brothers*, trans. by Pearl Buck. *Christian Science Monitor* 7 Oct. 1933: 6.

Rev. of *Come, My Beloved*, by Pearl Buck. *New Yorker 29*, 15 Aug. 1953: 80.

Rev. of *Command the Morning*, by Pearl Buck. *Booklist 55*, 15 Mar. 1959: 382.

Rev. of *Command the Morning*, by Pearl Buck. *Kirkus 27*, 1 Mar. 1959: 183.

Rev. of *Command the Morning*, by Pearl Buck. *Times [London] Literary Supplement* 11 Sept. 1959: 517.

Rev. of *Dragon Seed*, by Pearl Buck. *New Republic 106*, 9 Feb. 1942: 214.

Rev. of *Dragon Seed*, by Pearl Buck. *Springfield Republican* 25 Jan. 1942: 7e.

Rev. of *Dragon Seed*, by Pearl Buck. *Time 39*, 26 Jan. 1942: 80.

Rev. of *Dragon Seed*, by Pearl Buck. *Times [London] Literary Supplement* 18 Apr. 1942: 197.

Rev. of *East Wind: West Wind*, by Pearl Buck. *New York Times Book Review* 20 Apr. 1930: 8.

Rev. of *The Exile*, by Pearl Buck. *Christian Century 53*, 5 Feb. 1936: 237.

Rev. of *The Exile*, by Pearl Buck. *Times [London] Literary Supplement* 15 Feb. 1936: 135.

Rev. of *Fighting Angel,* by Pearl Buck. *Christian Century 54,* 7 Apr. 1937: 462.

Rev. of *Fighting Angel,* by Pearl Buck. *Christian Science Monitor* 1 Dec. 1936: 18.

Rev. of *Fighting Angel,* by Pearl Buck. *Springfield Republican* 13 Dec. 1936: 7e.

Rev. of *Friend to Friend,* by Pearl Buck and Romulo C. Pena. *Springfield Republican* 21 Dec. 1958: 7D.

Rev. of *The Good Earth,* by Pearl Buck. *New Statesman and Nation 1,* 16 May 1931: 430.

Rev. of *The Good Earth,* by Pearl Buck. *New York Times Book Review* 15 May 1931: 6.

Rev. of *The Good Earth,* by Pearl Buck. *Springfield Republican.* 15 May 1931: 7e.

Rev. of *A House Divided,* by Pearl Buck. *Atlantic Bookshelf 155,* Apr. 1935: 12.

Rev. of *A House Divided,* by Pearl Buck. *New York Times Book Review* 20 Jan. 1935: 3.

Rev. of *A House Divided,* by Pearl Buck. *Times [London] Literary Supplement* 24 Jan. 1935: 46.

Rev. of *How It Happens,* by Pearl Buck. *Christian Science Monitor* 1 Mar. 1947: 14.

Rev. of *How It Happens,* by Pearl Buck. *New Yorker 22,* 11 Jan. 1947: 85.

Rev. of *Imperial Woman,* by Pearl Buck. *Times [London] Literary Supplement* 1 Jan. 1956: 325.

Rev. of *The Kennedy Women,* by Pearl Buck. *Christian Century 87,* 3 Jan. 1970: 700.

Rev. of *Letter from Peking,* by Pearl Buck. *Kirkus 25,* 1 May 1957: 336.

Rev. of *Letter from Peking,* by Pearl Buck. *Times [London] Literary Supplement* 27 Sept. 1957: 582.

Rev. of *The Living Reed,* by Pearl Buck. *New Yorker 39,* 12 Oct. 1963: 213.

Rev. of *The Mother,* by Pearl Buck. *Springfield Republican* 18 Feb. 1934: 7e.

Rev. of *The Mother,* by Pearl Buck. *Times [London] Literary Supplement* 25 Jan. 1934: 58.

Rev. of *My Several Worlds,* by Pearl Buck. *Kirkus 22,* 1 Sept. 19542: 603.

Rev. of *My Several Worlds,* by Pearl Buck. *New Yorker 30,* 6 Nov. 1954: 186.

Rev. of *Of Men and Women,* by Pearl Buck. *New York Times Book Review* 22 Jan. 1941: 5.

Rev. of *Other Gods,* by Pearl Buck. *Christian Science Monitor* 11 Mar. 1940: 18.

Rev. of *Other Gods,* by Pearl Buck. *Springfield Republican* 25 Feb. 1940: 7e.

Rev. of *Other Gods,* by Pearl Buck. *Times [London] Literary Supplement* 9 Mar. 1940: 121.

Rev. of *The Patriot,* by Pearl Buck. *Catholic World 149,* Jan. 1939: 375.

Rev. of *The Patriot,* by Pearl Buck. *Springfield Republican* 12 Mar. 1939: 7e.

Rev. of *The Patriot,* by Pearl Buck. *Times [London] Literary Supplement* 8 Apr. 1939: 201.

Rev. of *Pavilion of Women,* by Pearl Buck. *Kirkus 14,* 1 Nov. 1946: 553.

Rev. of *Pavilion of Women,* by Pearl Buck. *New Yorker 22,* 23 Nov. 1946: 122.

Rev. of *Pavilion of Women,* by Pearl Buck. *Time 48,* 25 Nov. 1946: 110.

Rev. of *Peony,* by Pearl Buck. *Catholic World 167,* Aug. 1948: 477.

Rev. of *Peony,* by Pearl Buck. *Kirkus 16,* Mar. 1948: 147.

Rev. of *Peony,* by Pearl Buck. *New York Herald Tribune Weekly Book Review* 9 May 1948: 17.

Rev. of *Peony,* by Pearl Buck. *New Yorker 24,* 15 May 1948: 121.

Rev. of *Peony,* by Pearl Buck. *Springfield Republican* 30 May 1948: 10B.

Rev. of *Portrait of a Marriage*, by Pearl Buck. *New Yorker 21*, 1 Dec. 1945: 130.

Rev. of *The Promise*, by Pearl Buck. *Christian Science Monitor* 14 Nov. 1943: 14.

Rev. of *Sons*, by Pearl Buck. *Newstatesman and Nation*. 4, 3 Dec. 1932: 704.

Rev. of *Sons*, by Pearl Buck. *Times [London] Literary Supplement* 6 Oct. 1932: 708.

Rev. of *Talk about Russia*, by Pearl Buck. *Christian Science Monitor* 29 Nov. 1945: 16.

Rev. of *This Proud Heart*, by Pearl Buck. *Christian Science Monitor* 9 Feb. 1938: 16.

Rev. of *This Proud Heart*, by Pearl Buck. *Springfield Republican* 13 Feb. 1938: 7e.

Rev. of *This Proud Heart*, by Pearl Buck. *Time 31* 14 Feb. 1938: 66.

Rev. of *This Proud Heart*, by Pearl Buck. *Times [London] Literary Supplement* 5 Mar. 1938: 155.

Rev. of *The Three Daughters of Madame Liang*, by Pearl Buck. *Christian Science Monitor* 10 July 1969: 11.

Rev. of *The Townsman*, by John Sedges. *Commonwealth 42*, 8 Jan. 1945: 193.

Rev. of *The Townsman*, by John Sedges. *Kirkus 13*, 1 May 1945: 183.

Rev. of *To My Daughters, with Love*, by Pearl Buck. *New York Times Book Review* 17 Dec. 1968: 21.

Rev. of *Voices in the House*, by John Sedges. *Kirkus 21*, 1 Feb. 1953: 77.

Rev. of *Young Revolutionist*, by Pearl Buck. *Commonwealth 16*, 4 May 1932: 27.

Rev. of *Young Revolutionist*, by Pearl Buck. *New Statesman and Nation 3*, 19 Mar. 1932: 374.

Richards, G. R. B. Rev. on *A House Divided*, by Pearl Buck. *Boston Transcript* 19 Jan. 1935: 1.

---. Rev. of *The Mother*, by Pearl Buck. *Boston Transcript* 13 Jan. 1934: 1.

Richardson, Maurice. Rev. of *Command the Morning*, by Pearl Buck. *New Statesman 58*, 12 Sept. 1959: 328.

Riggan, William. "The Nobel Prize in Literature: History and Overview." *The Nobel Prize Winners: Literature*. vol. II (1927-1961). Ed. Frank N. Magill. Pasadena: Salem, 1987: 1-26.

Rizzon, Beverly. *Pearl S. Buck: The Final Chapter*. Palm Springs, Calif.: ETC Publications, 1989.

Roberts, Edith. Rev. of *Portrait of a Marriage*, by Pearl Buck. *Book Week* 9 Dec. 1945: 22.

Roberts, Edmund. *Embassy to the Eastern Courts*. 1837. Wilmington, Del.: Scholarly Resources Inc. 1972.

Rogers, N. G. Rev. of *Mandala*, by Pearl Buck. *New York Times Book Review* 25 Oct. 1970: 57.

Rohmer, Sax. *The Hand of Fu-Manch*. 1917. New York: Pyramid, 1962.

---. *The Insidious Doctor Fu-Manchu*. 1913. New York: Pyramid, 1961.

---. *The Return of Dr. Fu-Manchu*. 1916. New York: Pyramid, 1961.

Ross, James R. *Escape to Shanghai: A Jewish Community in China*. New York: Macmillan, 1994.

Ross, Mary. Rev. of *American Argument*, by Pearl Buck. *New York Herald Tribune Weekly Book Review* 6 Feb. 1949: 17.

---. Rev. of *The Exile*, by Pearl Buck. *New York Herald Tribune Weekly Book Review* 9 Feb. 1936: 3.

---. Rev. of *A Houses Divided*, by Pearl Buck. *New York Herald Tribune Weekly Book Review* 20 Jan. 1935: 3.

---. Rev. of *Kinfolk*, by Pearl Buck. *New York Herald Tribune Weekly Book Review* 24

Apr. 1949: 6.

---. Rev. of *The Mother*, by Pearl Buck. *New York Herald Tribune Weekly Book Review* 14 Jan. 1934: 3.

---. Rev. of *Peony*, by Pearl Buck. *New York Herald Tribune Weekly Book Review* 9 May 1948: 17.

---. Rev. of *Portrait of a Marriage,* by Pearl Buck. *New York Herald Tribune Weekly Book Review* 9 Dec. 1945: 6.

---. Rev. of *This Proud Heart*, by Pearl Buck. *New York Herald Tribune Weekly Book Review* 13 Feb. 1938: 4.

Rugoff, Milton. Rev. of *Dragon Seed*, by Pearl Buck. *Books* 25 Jan. 1942: 3.

Ruschenberger, W.S.W. *A Voyage round the World.* Philadelphia: Grigg & Elliot,1838.

Russell, Bertrand. *The Problem of China.* New York: Century, 1922.

Said, Edward W. *Orientalism.* New York: Vintage, 1979.

---. *Culture and Imperialism.* New York: Knopf, 1993.

Sayings of Lao Tsu. Trans. Lin Yutang and R. B. Blakney. Taipei: Confucius Publishing Co., 1970.

Schneider, Isidore. Rev. of *East Wind: West Wind*, by Pearl Buck. *New Republic 63*, 21 May 1930: 24.

---. Rev. of *The Mother,* by Pearl Buck. *New Republic 78,* 14 Mar. 1934: 136.

---. Rev. of *Sons* by Pearl Buck. *Nation 135,* 16 Nov. 1932: 481.

Schoyer, Preston. Rev. of *Imperial Woman*, by Pearl Buck. *Saturday Review 39,* 31 Mar. 1956: 12.

Scoggin, M. C. Rev. of *Peony,* by Pearl Buck. *Horne Books 24,* July 1948: 290.

Sears, G. Emmerson. "Baxter's Beat." *Overland Monthly*, 2nd. ser. 55 (Mar. 1910): 293.

Seaver, Edwin. Rev. of *East Wind: West Wind,* by Pearl Buck. *New York Evening Post.* 12 Apr. 1930: 10m.

Shapiro, Sidney. Ed. and Trans. *Jews in Old China: Studies by Chinese Scholars.* New York: Hippocrene, 1984.

Sherk, Warren. *Pearl S. Buck: Good Earth Mother.* Philomath, Oregon: Drift Creek Press, 1992.

Shimizu, Mamoru. "On Some Stylistic Features, Chiefly Biblical, of *The Good Earth.*" *Studies in English Literature.* (Tokyo), 1964: 117-34.

Shine, C. A. Rev. of *Mandala*, by Pearl Buck. *Library Journal 95,* 15 Oct. 1970: 3486.

Shuck, H. et al. "Pearl S. Buck." *Nobel: The Man and His Prizes.* Nobel Foundation, Norman: U of Oklahoma P. 1951, 127.

Shuler, Max. "We Dream Too Much;" interview. *Christian Science Monitor Magazine* 29 Jan. 1936: 5. Interview.

Shumaker, Edith. Rev. of *Death in the Castle,* by Pearl Buck. *Library Journal 90,* 15 Apr. 1965: 1929.

Sinha, Simita. "The Novels of Pearl S. Buck---A Study in Major Themes." Diss. Lucknow University, India: 1974.

Smith, Arthur H. *Chinese Characteristics.* 1894. London: Kennikat, 1970.

Smith, D. P. "Pearl S. Buck." *The Nobel Prize Winners: Literature.* Vol. II (1927-1961). Ed. Frank W. Magill. Pasadena: Sale, 1987. 459-66.

Smith, Huston. Rev. of *Friend to Friend*, by Pearl Buck & Romulo C. Pena. *Saturday Review 41,* 22 Nob. 1958: 15.

Smith, Tony. *The Pattern of Imperialism: The United States, Great Britain, and the Late Industrializing World Since 1815.* London: Cambridge UP, 1981.

Snow, Edgar. "Pearl Buck's Worlds." *Rev. of My Several Worlds*, by Pearl Buck. *Nation 179*, 13 Nov. 1954: 426.

Snow, Helen F. "Pearl Buck, 1892-1973: An Island in Time." *New Republic* 24 Mar. 1973: 28-29.

Sorel, Nancy. "A New Look at 'Nobel Suffering.'" *New York Times Book Review* 26 Jan. 1986. 91: 1+.

Spence, Jonathan. *To Change China.* Boston: Little Brown, 1969.

Spencer, Cornelia. *Pearl S. Buck: Revealing the Human Heart.* Chicago: Encyclopaedia Britannica Press, 1964.

---. *The Exile's Daughter: A Biography of Pearl S. Buck.* New York: Coward-McCann, 1944.

Spiller, Robert E. et al. Ed. *Literary History of the United States.* New York: Macmillan, 1948, vol. II.

"Spotlight." *Arts and Decoration.* June 1936: 27.

Starling, Nora. *Pearl Buck: A Woman in Conflict.* Piscataway, N. J.: New Century, 1983.

Steen, S. L. Rev. of *The Kenndy Women*, by Pearl Buck. *Library Journal 95* 15 May 1970: 1831.

Stewart, J. Livinstone. *Chinese Culture and Christianity.* New York: Revell, 1928.

Stoer, M. W. Rev. of *Hidden Flower*, by Pearl Buck. *Christian Science Monitor* 29 May 1952: 15.

Stone, Geoffrey. Rev. of *The Mother*, by Pearl Buck. *Commonwealth 19*, 9 Mar. 1934: 528.

Stone, Shepard. Rev. of *How It Happens*, by Pearl Buck. *New York Times Book Review* 10 Aug. 1947: 20.

"Story Bible Recalls China Missionary." *American Bible Society's Magazine* Nov. 1971.

Strong, L. A. G. Rev. of *Young Revolutionist*, by Pearl Buck. *The Spectator 148*, 12 Mar. 1932: 388.

Stuckey, W. J. "Pulitzer Prize Novels." *The Good Earth.* 90-93.

Sullivan, Richard. Rev. of *Command the Morning*, by Pearl Buck. *New York Times Book Review* 3 May 1959: 29.

Sum, Grace C. K. "East/West Ties: American Children and the Work of the Pearl S. Buck Foundation." *The Several Worlds of Pearl S. Buck.* Ed. Elizabeth J. Lipscomb, Frances E. Webb, and Peter Conn. London: Greenwood, 1994. 71-75.

Swift, Esther M. "The World of Pearl Buck: A Life and a Bibliography." "The Author" Series in *Book Lover's Answer;* rpt. in *West Virginia Hillbilly* Richwood, W. Va., 13 March 1965.

Tang, Hsiaobing. "The Dialectics of Violence: A Rereading of *The Storm.*" *Twenty-first Century 11*, June 1992: 80-91.

Tang, Tao and Jiayan Yan. *A History of Contemporary Chinese Literature.* Vol. 3 Beijing: The People's Literature Press, 1985.

Tefft, C. L. Rev. of *The New Year*, by Pearl Buck. *Library Journal 93*, 15 May 1968: 2132.

Terry, C. V. Rev. of *The Townsman*, by Pearl Buck. *New York Times Book Review* 10 Jan. 1945: 5.

Thompson, Dody W. "Pearl Buck." *American Winners of the Nobel Literary Prize.* Ed. Warren G. French and Walter E. Kidd Norman: U of Oklahoma P, 1968. 85-110.

Thomson, James C. Jr. "Pearl S. Buck and the American Quest for China." *The Several Worlds of Pearl S. Buck.* Ed. Elizabeth J. Lipscomb, Frances E. Webb, and Peter

Conn. Westport, Conn.: Greenwood, 1994. 7-15.

Tong, Jean. "The China of Pearl Buck." Master's thesis. U of Montreal, 1953.

Townsend, Ebenezer. "Diary," *Papers*. New Haven: Colony Historical Society, 1888.

Tsai, Shih-shan Henry. *The Chinese Experience in America*. Bloomington: Indiana UP, 1986.

Tweedy, M. J. Rev. of *Come, My Beloved,* by Pearl Buck. *New York Times Book Review* 9 Aug. 1953: 5.

Tynan, Kenneth. *Curtains*. New York: 1961, 316. Review of play "A Desert Incident."

U. S. Bureau of Census. *Historical Statistics of U. S. 1789-1945*. Washington, D. C. 1949: 35.

Van Alen, E. L. Rev. of *The Exile,* by Pearl Buck. *North America 241*, Jan. 1936: 370.

Van Doren, Carl. *The American Novel, 1789-1939*. 1940. New York: Macmillan, 1970. 349-66. Remarks on *The Good Earth*.

Van Doren, Mark. "A Far Eastern Homer." *Private Reader* New York: 1942: 189-92.

---. Rev. of *The Exile,* by Pearl Buck. *Nation 142*, 12 Feb. 1936: 195.

---. Rev. of *A House Divided*, by Pearl Buck. *Nation 140*, 6 Feb. 1935: 165.

---. Rev. of *The Mother,* by Pearl Buck. in *Nation 138*, 17 Jan. 1934: 78.

---. Rev. of *This Proud Heart*, by Pearl Buck. in *Nation 146*, 12 Feb. 1938: 187.

Van Gelder, Robert. "Pearl Buck Talks of Her Work and Her Discovery of America." *Writers and Writing*. New York: Scribner, 1946. 26-28.

Varg, Paul A. "The Missionary Response to the Nationalist Revolution." *The Missionary Enterprise in China and America*. Ed. John K. Fairbank. Cambridge: Harvard UP, 1974. 311-35.

Venne, Peter. "Pearl Buck's Literary Portrait of China and the Chinese." *Fu Jen Studies 1*, 1968: 71-86.

Vollmershausen, Joseph. "*Pavilion of Women*: A Psychoanalytic Interpretation." *AJP,* 1950: 53-60.

Voiles, Jane. Rev. of *Command the Morning*, by Pearl Buck. *San Francisco Chronicle* 24 May 1959: 24.

---. Rev. of *God's Men*, by Pearl Buck. *San Francisco Chronicle* 15 Apr. 1951: 18.

---. Rev. of *Imperial Woman*, by Pearl Buck. *San Francisco Chronicle* 1 Apr. 1956: 18.

---. Rev. of *Kinfolk*, by Pearl Buck. *San Francisco Chronicle* 15 May 1949: 14.

---. Rev. of *Letter from Peking*, by Pearl Buck. *San Francisco Chronicle* 7 July 1946: 4.

---. Rev. of *Pavilion of Women*, by Pearl Buck. *San Francisco Chronicle* 1 Dec. 1946: 5.

---. Rev. of *Peony*, by Pearl Buck. *San Francisco Chronicle* 10 May 1946: 18.

Wagner, M. H. Rev. of *The Time Is Noon*, by Pearl Buck. *America 116*, 25 Mar. 1967: 471.

Wallace, Margaret. Rev. of *This Proud Heart*, by Pearl Buck. *New York Times Book Review* 13 Feb. 1938: 6.

Wales, Nym. Rev. of *Of Men and Women*, by Pearl Buck. *New Republic 105*, 8 Sept. 1941: 316.

Waley, Arthur. "A Tale of Righteous Bandits." Rev. of *All Men Are Brothers*, trans. by Pearl Buck. *The New Republic 77*, 22 Nev. 1933: 51.

Walsh, Richard J. "Pearl S. Buck." Introduction to *The First Wife and Other Stories*, New York: John Day, 1933, 9-32.

---. *A Biographical Sketch of Pearl S. Buck*. New York: John Day, 1936.

Walton, E. H. Rev. of *A House Divided* , by Pearl Buck. *Forum 93*, Mar. 1935: x.

Walton, E. L. Rev. of *The Good Earth* , by Pearl Buck. *Nation 132*, 13 May 1931: 534.

Ward, Eunice. "Ah Gin." *Overland Monthly,* 2nd. ser. 49 (May 1907): 393.

Warfel, Harry R. "Pearl S. Buck." *American Novelists of Today.* New York: American Book, 1951. 58-60.

Wayman, D. G. "Books, *My Several Worlds.*" *America* 6 Nov. 1954: 159-60.

"We Visit Pearl Buck." *Saturday Evening Post* 14 May 1960: 136.

Webb, John. *An Historical Essay Endeavoring a Probability That the Language Of the Empire of China is the Primative Language.* London, Baynes, 1669.

Weeks, Edward. Rev. of *The Time Is Noon,* by Pearl Buck. *Atlantic Monthly 219,* May 1967: 126.

Welliver, Mary Lee. "Pearl S. Buck's Manuscripts: The Harvest of Half a Century." Master's thesis, West Virginia University, 1977. Includes an overview of Pearl Buck's writing, the history of the manuscripts collection owned by the Pearl S. Buck Birthplace Foundation and a catalog of 71 book manuscripts, 34 of these originals.

West Virginia Heritage Encyclopedia. Richwood, W.Va..: 1976. Jim Comstock, comp. 50 vols. Vol. 4, 677. Lists references on PSB as found in several volumes.

Westervelt, Virginia Veeder. *Pearl Buck: A Biographical Novel.* New York: Elsevier / Nelson Books, 1979.

White, Emma Edmunds. "Pearl S. Buck." *Randolph-Macon Woman's College Alumnae Bulletin, XXXII* Feb. 1939: 4-12; rpt. in *West Virginia Heritage Encyclopedia.* Jim Comstock, comp. vol. 4. Richwood, W.Va.., 40-51.

White, William Charles. *Chinese Jews: A Compilation of Matters Relating to the Jews of Kai-feng Fu.* 1942. Intro. Cecil Roth. 2nd. ed. Toronto: U of Toronto P, 1966.

Whitmore, Anne. Rev. of *American Argument,* by Pearl Buck. *Library Journal 74,* 1 Jan. 1949: 54.

Whitney, Atwell. *Almond-Eyed: The Great Agitator; a Story of the Day.* San Francisco: Bancroft, 1878.

Wiley, Hugh. *Jade: and Other Stories.* New York: Knopf, 1922.

---. *Manchu Blood.* 1927. Reprint ed. New York: Books for Libraries, 1971.

Williams, Samuel Wells. *The Middle Kingdom.* New York: 1848.

Williamson, Margaret. Rev. of *Dragon Seed,* by Pearl Buck. *Christian Science Monitor* 21 Feb. 1942: 11.

---. Rev. of *Pavilion of Women,* by Pearl Buck. *Christian Science Monitor.* 17 Dec. 1946: 14.

Winegarten, Renee. "The Nobel Prize for Literature." *The American Scholar* Winter 1994: 63-75.

Witham, W. Tasker. "Pearl Buck." *Panorama of American Literature.* New York: Stephen Day, 1947. 306-08.

Wohlgelernter, Maurice. *Frank O'Connor.* New York: Columbia UP, 1977.

Wolf, A. F. Rev. of *God's Men,* by Pearl Buck. *Saturday Review of Literature 34,* 7 Apr. 1951: 23.

---. Rev. of *Pavilion of Women,* by Pearl Buck. *Saturday Review of Literature 29,* 23 Nov. 1946: 11.

Woltor, Robert. *A Short and Truthful History of the Taking of California and Oregon by the Chinese in the Year A. D. 1899.* San Francisco: Bancroft, 1882.

"Women's Ability, Courage, Brains Hailed by Miss Buck." *Morgantown Post* 9 Mar. 1970: 5A.

Wood, W. W. *Sketches of China.* Philadelphia: Morris, 1830.

Woodress, James. "Pearl (Syndenstricker) Buck 1892-1973." *American Fiction 1900-1950.*

Detroit: Gale Research Co., 1974. 43-45.

Woods, Katherine. Rev. of *Dragon Seed*, by Pearl Buck. *New York Times Book Review* 25 Jan. 1942: 3.

---. Rev. of *The Exile*, by Pearl Buck. *New York Times Book Review* 9 Feb. 1936: 1.

---. Rev. of *Fighting Angel*, by Pearl Buck. *New York Times Book Review* 29 Nov. 1936: 1.

---. Rev. of *Other Gods*, by Pearl Buck. *New York Times Book Review* 25 Feb. 1940: 1.

---. Rev. of *The Patriot*, by Pearl Buck. *New York Times Book Review* 5 Mar. 1939: 2.

Woodward, Frances. Rev. of *This Proud Heart*, by Pearl Buck. *Saturday Review of Literature 17*, 12 Feb. 1938: 10.

Woolf, S. J. "Pearl Buck Talks of Her Life in China." *China Weekly Review* 24 Sept. 1932: 145-46.

Wu, Lifu. "Fu Di Shu Ping." Rev. of *The Good Earth*, trans. by Lifu Wu. Shanghai: Liming Press, 1932.

Wu, William F. *The Yellow Peril*. Hamden, Conn.: Archon, 1982.

Yao, Hsih-pei. "What Pearl Buck Said about Lu Xun," *Lun Xun Monthly 6*, 1990: 38-42.

Yaukey, Grace S. *The Exile's Daughter; a Biography of Pearl S. Buck*. New York: Coward-McCann, 1944.

Young, Marilyn B. *Rhetoric of Empire*. Cambridge: Harvard UP, 1968.

Young, Robert. *White Mythologies: Writing History and the West*. New York: Routledge, 1990.

Yu, Yuh-chao. "Chinese Influence on Pearl S. Buck." *Tamkang Review 11*, Fall 1980: 24-41.

Zhang, Longxi. "The Myth of the Other: China in the Eyes of the West." *Critical Inquiry 15*, Autumn 1988: 108-131.

Zinn, Lucille S. "The Works of Pearl S. Buck: A Bibliography." *Bulletin of Bibliography 36*, 1979: 194-208.

INDEX

About the Author

KANG LIAO has been Lecturer and Director of English at Beijing Normal University. He has also taught at West Virginia University, State University of New York at New Paltz, and the University of Aberdeen, U.K. His publications include over one hundred encyclopedia entries and co-translations of *Mao: A Biography*, *The Rise and Fall of Lin Piao*, and *Fast Reading: A Teaching Manual*.

ISBN 0-313-30146-8

90000>

9 780313 301469

HARDCOVER BAR CODE

EAN